FUNDAMENTALS
OF GARDENING

**The American Horticultural Society
Illustrated Encyclopedia of Gardening**

FUNDAMENTALS OF GARDENING

The American Horticultural Society
Mount Vernon, Virginia

For the American Horticultural Society

President
Dr. Gilbert S. Daniels

Technical Advisory Committee
Everett Conklin
Mary Stuart Maury
Dr. John A. Wott

Fundamentals of Gardening Staff for The Franklin Library/Ortho Books

Editorial Director
Min S. Yee

Supervisory Editor
Lewis P. Lewis

Editor
Ken Burke

Art Directors
John Williams
Barbara Ziller

Creative Director
Michael Mendelsohn

Assistant Creative Director
Clint Anglin

Contributing Writers
A. Cort Sinnes
James McNair
Walter Doty
Lance Walheim
Scott Millard

Production Director
Robert Laffler

Production Manager
Renee Guilmette

For Ortho Books

Publisher
Robert L. Iacopi

For The Franklin Library

Publisher
Joseph Sloves

The cover photograph shows a colorful border garden of annuals and perennials carefully planned so that there will be continuous bloom throughout the growing season. Smaller plants have been put at the front of the border, with taller flowers growing in graduated heights behind them. Photo by Hedrich-Blessing.

Contributing Photographers
Michael Landis
Clyde Childress
William Aplin
Fred Lyon
James McNair
Michael McKinley
Colin McRae
Tom Tracy
Duane Hatch
Raymond B. Korbobo
J. A. French
Kenneth Myers
Joseph Parker
William R. Reasons
Otho S. Wells
Tim Wolfe
Dr. John Courter
Professor Robert Fletcher
Dr. Charles M. Sacamano
Martha S. Baker
Carl A. Totemeir
    Old Westbury Gardens
John Blaustein
Wolf von dem Bussche
Kent Kurtz
Bill Cunningham
Craig Heckman
Paul Thomas

Illustrators
Ron Hildebrand
Edith Allgood
Ebet Dudley
Craig Berquist
Ron Gallmeier
Link Malquist
Lenny Meyer
Rik Olson

Library of Congress Catalog Card Number 81-67192

Printed in the United States of America

12 11 10 9 8 7 6 5 4 3

A Special Message from
The American Horticultural Society

No single, surefire set of rules for gardening exists—not just because soils and climates vary from one region to another, but also because of considerations that have to do with individual gardeners: how much space is available, how much time a person wants to devote to gardening, whether flowers or vegetables or a combination are desired. But this being said, we can add that there is a basic core of knowledge and of procedures that, properly applied by the aspiring gardener, can substitute for the instincts of the experienced gardener. These fundamentals of gardening are the subject of this volume. Its underlying theme is that given interest, enthusiasm, and information, anyone can grow a successful garden.

We begin with a brief look at the parts of a plant, and the ingredients that cause them to grow. Although it's true that plants tend to grow even with no human intervention, there are some things they can't do without. You'll learn how to provide the elements that add up to a proper environment for the plants you choose for your garden, no matter what region you live in. (And if you're accustomed to the climate and growing season of one part of the country, and find yourself moving to another, the information given here will give you a start in your new location.) Further, you'll pick up a working knowledge of the tools needed to tend your plants, and tips on caring for these tools.

A pest-free, disease-free plot of flowers, fruits, and vegetables is a dream many of us have, but few of us attain. But with good general maintenance and a working grasp of controls, whether of the tried-and-true type or newly discovered methods, we can come close to attaining this ideal. And although gardening can easily, and happily, become one's main occupation in life, the person with limited time will be guided by this book toward a choice of plants that can be cared for in a few hours a week.

This book is intended to be especially valuable to first-time gardeners, but its usefulness does not stop there. An understanding of the fundamentals it covers is important to seasoned gardeners as well. Even if you have gardened for years, a review of all the factors required for a plant to thrive will stand you in good stead. In addition, knowledge of ways to alter and feed and prepare soil, and of the care of common varieties will result in a better garden. Like accomplished cooks who consult recipes long after they have mastered basic kitchen techniques, veteran gardeners need clear sources of information that allow them to refresh or expand their skills. And so, whether you are planning your first garden, or have acquired the envied green thumb of the seasoned hand, we expect that you'll consult this volume of your encyclopedia time and again.

Gilbert S. Daniels
President

CONTENTS

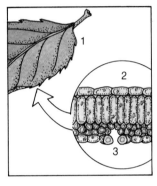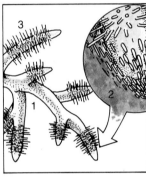

This chapter reviews, for the novice and the experienced gardener alike, the elements a plant needs to grow and to thrive, as well as the uses a plant makes of these basic ingredients. It also explains why you'll want to think of your garden as an environment—one you can alter to your benefit—and of your plants, even though you may have many varieties, as a unit.

Following the growing seasons is more than a matter of planting in spring and harvesting in fall. From region to region, from year to year, growing times vary. The climate of one side of a yard won't necessarily match that of the other side. And yet, as the tips in this chapter point out, there are ways to modify a garden's climate.

Planting and Transplanting   30

Methods of planting and protecting seeds outdoors are given as well as instructions for starting them indoors. Transplanting seedlings, shrubs, and trees each requires a different set of techniques, clearly spelled out in this chapter. Once you know the basics of direct seeding and transplanting, you can begin your garden.

General Maintenance   42

Weeds can spring up even in the best of gardens. A well-maintained garden is the result of regular attention—and good tools used properly. Choosing the right pruners, rakes, shears, gets you off to a good start, and keeping them clean and sharp assures their long usefulness. When, where, and how to prune is reviewed, as are a variety of weeding techniques.

Soil, Fertilizer, Mulch, and Water   50

An understanding of soil is important to gardening success. Several easily conducted tests will tell you whether your soil is clay, sandy, or loamy, acid or alkaline, and how much air and water it retains. Then, following the ways and means to alter and feed soil spelled out in this chapter, you can prepare the right type of soil for your needs.

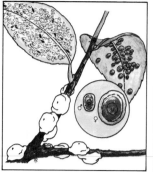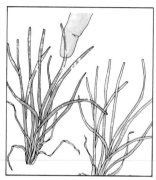

Gardeners welcome beneficial insects, but need controls to keep destructive ones at bay. Good general maintenance reduces the possibility of disease. Even birds and animals that we enjoy observing can become pests, unless plants are protected from them. Some plants are prone to diseases and attract destructive insects. Common problems and ways to avoid them are listed here.

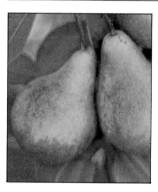

The abundant choice of plants available to gardeners assures that your needs and preferences can be satisfied. Characteristics and care of many of the plants you'll consider are given in this chapter, along with definitions of bulbs, shrubs, trees, vegetables, fruits, and berries. The lists of common plants that add beauty or practicality to a garden range from azaleas to zucchini.

You'll learn about types of lawns, how to care for a new lawn, and what a screwdriver has to do with keeping a lawn healthy. Some lawns need more care than others; some are better suited to your area than others. Ground covers require less maintenance, and can solve a number of landscape problems.

FUNDAMENTALS OF GARDENING

This unlikely but beautiful combination of
stock and cabbage highlights a vegetable
garden. Even the most practical garden
offers the gardener an opportunity for
imaginative experimental planting.

INTRODUCTION

*Gardeners are made, not born,
and anyone can become one. Start
slowly and learn as you go along.*

There is a world of difference between admiring a neighbor's garden set
lushly with flowers, vegetables, trees, shrubs, or any combination thereof,
and setting out to create a garden of your own. If you have been lucky
enough to grow up in a family of do-it-yourself gardeners, then you have at
least the feel, if not the precise knowledge, of how to make a garden. But if
you have never rubbed shoulders with other gardeners as they gardened,
much less set out your own plants, then you may find yourself staring
wistfully at showy flower beds, succulent melons, and shading trees, con-
vinced that such feats of horticultural magic are simply beyond the scope of
your far-from-green thumb.

To this we say: Don't give up before you start. What looks like green magic
can be done by anyone with the desire to learn. As with so many not-yet-
learned skills, successful gardening seems to require a vast amount of
knowledge at first; but if you take it slowly, getting the feel of each step
before going on to the next one, you will find yourself building up a
reservoir of gardening experience. There is nothing like actually getting
your hands full of sweet-smelling loamy soil, or watching the water droplets
glisten on your new lawn in the early morning, or burying your nose in your
newly bloomed, fragrant flowers to stir your heart and make you feel like
you've always been a gardener.

To make the learning process easier, we have broken down the information into chapters that first tell you what you need to *know* before you *do*,
and then what you need to *do* now that you *know*.

The first chapter, "Working with Your Climate," tells how the climate
affects your particular plot of ground, and what you can do to alter it in order
to broaden the range of what you can grow. (See pages 16–29.)

The second chapter, "Planting and Transplanting," discusses the differ-
ences among starting from seed, growing seedlings indoors, and buying
nursery transplants, and tells you how to plant them all. (See pages 30–41.)

"General Maintenance" tells you how to take care of the garden you've
gone to such lengths to make. (See pages 42–49.)

The next chapter, "Soil, Fertilizer, Mulch, and Water," explains that there's
more to soil than you might have thought, in terms of what it is, what it's
made of, whether your soil is clay, sand, or loam, whether it's acid or
alkaline, and how to improve it if it isn't the proper kind of soil for what you
want to grow. (See pages 50–61.) This chapter also discusses the feeding of
your plants—they need food regularly, although exact requirements vary
from plant to plant. (See pages 62–67.) The subject of the next section in this
chapter is mulches, both organic and synthetic. (See pages 67–71.) And the
section on "Watering" deals with a supposedly simple subject that needs
greater amplification; poor watering practices have ruined many an otherwise lovingly-tended garden. (See pages 70–73.)

"Treating for Pests and Diseases" gives some tips about how to recognize

and handle those insects, animals, and diseases that can invade the garden from time to time. (See pages 74–81.)

"Choosing Plants" is essentially an encyclopedia of vegetables, flowers, fruits, berries, shrubs, and trees. If offers an extensive (although by no means exhaustive) list of suggested varieties, where they are applicable. (See pages 82–129.)

"Lawns and Ground Covers" discusses cool-season and warm-season grasses, and ground covers, and how to plant and maintain them. (See pages 130–141.)

We suggest that you read through the entire book to get an overview before you go out and buy tools and start digging. After all, if you were cooking, you would read the recipe all the way through before you actually started to cook. However, although you may well someday be cooking your harvested vegetables, *Fundamentals of Gardening* differs from a cookbook: It has much in the way of suggestions and tried-and-true advice, but it has very few actual "recipes." There are too many variables to consider—your lifestyle, your available time, how much available gardening space you have, your soil and climatic conditions, and more—for us to provide a catch-all set of rules. However, whatever precise directions you find here are worth following. After all, it is the experienced cook who can get away with "a pinch of this and a pinch of that" and make the resulting dish come out delicious; the novice cook has to follow the recipe to the letter, measuring off level teaspoons of ingredients. Then later, as the magic of gardening becomes less mysterious, you can afford to bend the rules in the interest of experimentation and just general "green-thumb gardening."

A word of encouragement: Gardeners are made, not born. Your own interest and enthusiasm, coupled with the information you find in this book, will be enough to turn you into a seasoned gardener as your seasons in the garden come and go.

The Gardening Beginning

An understanding of a plant's anatomy and physiology isn't absolutely crucial in order to produce a rich, healthy crop; theoretical knowledge alone is no substitute for direct, hands-in-the-dirt experience. However, the more you know about your plants' functions and needs, the better you can serve those needs, and the healthier your plants will be.

How Plants Grow

In growing, a plant makes use of earth, water, air, and sun, taking in what it needs and giving off what it doesn't.

The Plant's Functions. *Roots.* These not only anchor the plant but also perform the following operations: collect water and nutrients; convey the water and nutrients to the leaves through the stem or trunk; store food; take in oxygen; and release carbon dioxide.

Stem or trunk. As mentioned, this conveys water and nutrients to the leaves, where food is manufactured. Then it distributes the food throughout the rest of the plant.

Leaves. These take in carbon dioxide; collect the energy of sunlight to produce food in a form usable by the plant (see "Photosynthesis"); and give off oxygen and water vapor.

Flowers. When present, flowers perpetuate the plant by attracting pollinating insects and forming seeds.

Photosynthesis. Plants make use of the sun's energy by means of the process called photosynthesis. The chlorophyll in the plant's green leaves absorbs and uses the sunlight to make food (carbohydrates) from carbon dioxide and water. Plants use these carbohydrates to grow.

Leaves

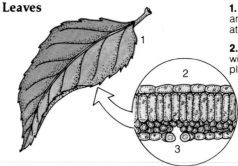

1. Leaves produce food for the plant and release water and oxygen into the atmosphere.

2. Chloroplasts are the chlorophyll bodies within cells in which photosynthesis takes place in order to manufacture carbohydrates (starches and sugars) for the plant. They give the leaf its green color.

3. Stomata are specialized "breathing" pores through which carbon dioxide enters and water and oxygen are released. They close when water is limited or under other stress.

Roots

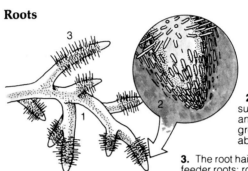

1. Feeder roots grow from the lateral roots and serve to transport water and nutrients absorbed by root hairs. They tend to be concentrated within the "dripline" (where the rain drips off the tree), but some may extend great distances.

2. Root caps produce a continuous supply of new cells that are sloughed off and serve to lubricate the advance of the growing root tip through the soil as it absorbs water and nutrients.

3. The root hairs are microscopic appendages to the feeder roots; root hairs absorb water and nutrients.

What Plants Need to Grow

Plants tend to grow despite the well-intentioned errors of beginning gardeners. But even the hardiest plants require certain basic ingredients—air; water; nutrients; light; heat; and a suitable environment.

Air in the soil. Plants require air in the soil more than almost anything else. The roots need to inhale oxygen and exhale carbon dioxide. Without sufficient air, the roots will suffocate and die.

In heavy soils, the pore space (space between soil particles) is very small. When watered, it fills up with the water, thus driving out the air. This makes the plant wilt, whereupon the alarmed novice gardener applies yet more water, effectively killing the plant with kindness.

However, it isn't only overwatering that will interrupt a plant's air supply. Sometimes a hard rain will cause the soil to crust over, which will cut off the air supply to the roots to some degree. Or repeated foot traffic will compact the top layer of the soil. Compacted soil will cause water to run off instead of to sink down into the soil, and also will choke off the roots' air supply.

Water. All plants need water *in balance*—that is, not too little and not too much. If a plant receives too much water, its roots may die (especially if soil drainage is inadequate). If a plant does not receive enough water, however, it will undergo what is called "water stress," and may die.

Unfortunately, because it is so easy to kill a plant with too much water, water has been called "the hazardous necessity." Since the plant's roots need moisture and air in order to grow, the medium in which the roots grow must allow air to circulate, so that the air can bring oxygen to the roots and take away the exhaled carbon dioxide. But when the air spaces are filled with water for too long, the supply of air is cut off; this retards root growth. The longer the air is cut off, the more the roots are damaged. The more the roots are damaged, the more the plant is damaged.

Nutrients. As with water, plants require nutrients in a continuous and uniform supply. In fact, plants need a small amount daily. Some slow-growing plants need only a very small amount; with these, you often can wait to apply the nutrients until the plant itself informs you of its needs (for example, a yellowing leaf tells you that nitrogen may be deficient). But it is not a good practice to depend on the plant to tell you when to add nutrients, especially with vegetables. Since vegetables are fast-growing, short-season plants, they require enough fertilizer in the soil to last them through their entire season. Insufficient nutrients may retard vegetable growth, thus reducing not only the yield but also, quite possibly, the quality of the produce.

Light. All plants need light. They use sunlight to make food (see "Photosynthesis"), and they use this food to grow. The very structure of a plant has to do with the nature and amount it receives. A lot of sunlight will cause a plant to grow short, sturdy stems. Insufficient light will result in long, thin stems. The plant's attempt to reach the brightest source of light may cause it to become misshapen. Houseplants that have been set and forgotten on windowsills are common victims; they may grow gangly and twisted trying to find some bright light to soak up.

Light affects the entire development of green plants, from seed germination through vegetative growth to flowering and fruiting.

Some plants are more light-sensitive than others. At one extreme is the flower that opens its petals to the sun during the day and closes them tightly at night. At the other extreme is the shade-tolerant plant, such as the fern that grows near a water source under a canopy of forest trees. And then there are all the middle-ground degrees of shade tolerance and intolerance.

How long the light is available to the plant also is a factor. Some plants grow vegetatively during the long days of summer, and flower in the fall, when days are shorter. For other plants, this cycle occurs in reverse. And yet other plants are not at all affected by day length.

Heat. The temperature range—roughly between 32° and 120° F.—in which plants can survive is relatively narrow. Although plants are not as cold-sensitive as humans are, extreme cold can freeze water from the cells of plants, causing the plants to die.

Heat tolerances vary among plants. Some plants are hardy enough to thrive in cold mountain weather; others require tropical climates. And different crops adapt differently to cold. For example, peas withstand cold better than melons; some varieties of apple, peach, and plum are hardier than others.

Plants are affected not only by the air temperature but also by the soil temperature. This is why mulches that keep the soil cool can keep plants going even during very hot weather (see "Mulching," pages 67–71).

Suitable environment. To grow and thrive, a plant needs all the elements mentioned thus far—air, water, nutrients, light, and heat. A plant that is well supplied with the right amounts of these elements will tend to be healthy and able to resist such threats as temperature extremes, weed competition, and pests and diseases.

If your environment does not initially seem suitable for plants, consider what changes can be made. Does the climate need to be altered in some way? (If so, see pages 24–25.) Is the soil sufficiently porous to allow water to drain through it, leaving sufficient air for the roots? (If not, see pages 56–61.) Is there an ancient tree on your property with foliage that keeps the sunlight from getting through to your other plantings? (If so, you might consider pruning the tree—see pages 46–47—or planting more shade-tolerant varieties.)

It helps to think of your garden as an environment rather than as a hodgepodge assortment of individual plantings. Even though you may end up with a wide variety of plants, they will all share the same air, soil, and, to a large degree, light. By considering them as a unit, you will be able to determine what your plant "family" needs, and how best to provide it.

Gardeners need to know how many clear, sunny days they can expect throughout the growing season. Cloud cover and fog can affect plant performance.

WORKING WITH YOUR CLIMATE

Climate can vary from yard to yard and year to year as well as from one section of the country to another.

The difference between a Midwestern winter and a Florida winter is apparent even to someone who hasn't lived through them; but did you know that right within your own neighborhood the climate can differ significantly enough from area to area to affect plant growth? To bring it all closer to home, your own garden provides a variety of climates. For example, since wind intensifies cold, on a clear winter day the north side of a house or barrier is colder than the south side.

If the climate in your garden doesn't suit the needs of your plants, you can vary it to some degree, by artificial means. The use of cold frames allows you to plant weeks earlier (especially if you heat with an electric cable). Raised beds will let you start working the soil early in spring, when ground-level beds are still recovering from winter. To protect a raised bed, you can build a simple frame, cover it with clear plastic, and you will then have a temporary greenhouse for the last frosty weeks of spring. (For more on climate alteration, see page 24.)

A little knowledge of what attracts heat and what dispels it can go a long way. Masonry, for example, soaks up heat and radiates it at night. Therefore, an espalier on the south side of a brick wall will leaf out, bloom, and bear fruit well before a freestanding tree of the same kind.

Winter Protection

It's not only from foot to foot that climates vary, but also from year to year. Just because a warm spell occurs one fall doesn't mean it won't be followed by a cold snap the next September.

Even in the coldest winter climates, you can reduce storm damage and protect your plantings from extremely low temperatures. For example, you can use snow as a mulch against the cold; it holds a good deal of air and insulates against below-freezing temperatures. Shake snow off evergreens whenever possible—it can damage the plant by building up until its weight snaps off branches or deforms the shape of shrubs.

Surprisingly, it's in winter that drought is a real danger—water is less available in frozen ground. To prevent wintertime drought, water and mulch thoroughly in the fall. This will keep the ground moist and the water in a liquid state. Good watering and mulching also will prevent much cold burn; mulching alone will keep roots from heaving out of the ground when it freezes, thaws, freezes, and so on.

Some plants will take a certain amount of cold very well unless prematurely defrosted by a warm spell. Hardy rhododendrons, many evergreens, and some deciduous varieties do better if protected from sun in cold weather to prevent unseasonable thawing. If planted in the open, they should be protected by a screen against winter wind and sun. For shallow roots, a thick mulch or snow cover is the answer.

Above: Shade cloth and other materials protect tender trees and plants from wind and sun.

Below: A portable hinged A-frame increases spring soil temperatures. The open ends permit air circulation.

Protection from Strong Winds

Wind is the major threat in winter, breaking snow-laden branches, drying exposed branches and foliage, and lowering the cold temperature even more. To protect against strong winds, a permanent windbreak of the hardiest plant material is the best solution. However, *some* of the wind must be able to blow straight through; it's the leeward turbulence thus created that holds the main force of the wind up *above* your garden.

Planting by the Season

The most important thing to recognize when you plant a vegetable garden is what "growing season" means. It's not strictly a matter of planting in spring and harvesting in fall.

The growing-season charts on pages 26–29 will help you get a fix on your climate and establish a pattern for planting schedules. The length of the growing season is only one clue to your climate in terms of vegetable production, however, and you will need to know how other weather elements affect your particular microclimate.

One of the cities on the charts will be similar to yours. Just how your garden will vary from the information on these charts depends on many climatic factors, including day length, the amount of shade or fog, the slope of your land, the elevation, and many others.

Two good examples of wide variations within regions are the Northeast and Atlantic coastal states and the South. The planting schedules shown for these areas in the illustrations on pages 20 and 21 should give you some idea of how to chart plantings in your climate. For more specific information on these and other regions, see the discussion, broken down by days of growing season, that accompanies the charts on pages 21–24.

Northeast and Atlantic coastal states. Depending on where in this area vegetable gardeners live, they will meet up with either of two kinds of growing weather. For example, near Washington or New York City, the summer may be hot and humid; but slightly to the north, the growing season may have many cool, overcast days. Hot-summer gardeners contend with leafy crops that bolt to seed before they can be picked; cool-summer gardeners have trouble with heat-loving crops that don't fruit, or refuse to ripen properly.

The growing season for vegetables depends on the three different usable parts of vegetables: leaf, root, and fruit (or seed). Each part likes a different combination of day-length and temperature. In Arlington, Virginia, for example, the hot weather and longer days of late spring may cause leafy vegetables to form seeds, in which case spring-planted lettuce will bolt immediately after the formation of the first large leaves. To avoid this situation, plant seedlings of lettuce, cabbage relatives, spinach, and so forth before the last frosts. The seedlings will stand quite a bit of cold (and even more if you build a plastic shelter over them on a frame) and will form their edible leaves before the intense hot weather comes. Then, in July, replant lettuce seeds and cabbage seedlings. Although they will quickly begin to form leaves, the first cool fall weather will keep them from going to seed, and they won't be bothered by the first frosts.

In cool-summer regions, however, although leafy crops may do well through the summer, fruiting crops that require high temperatures, such as tomatoes, eggplants, peppers, and melons, will do poorly. In Augusta, Maine, where there is insufficient heat, choose varieties that need the least heat: for example, early tomatoes and the smallest and earliest melons. Then supply extra heat by planting against walls, using foil reflectors, facing plantings full south, or building temporary greenhouses of clear plastic on simple frames to bake sugar into the melons.

Between the leafy plants and the fruiting plants are the root crops. These require a long time to form their roots. Very hot days during this period may send them into seed production and toughen or split the roots. The long growing-period of carrots and parsnips means that they must be planted right after frost to make a crop. For tender turnips and beets, start early in hot-summer areas, harvest young, and replant for a full crop. Even though the roots do well right through summer in cool areas, several plantings are still better than one. That way you get young, tender roots rather than old, woody ones.

Seed crops fall into two categories. Although beans and corn need heat, they grow quickly and can be sown several times, depending on how many days there are between the last spring frost and the first fall cold. In short-summer regions, use bush beans and early corn to speed things up. Further south, use pole beans and long-season corn for repeat sowings. Since green peas (the second category) need cool weather when they set their seed, cool summers work just right for them. In hot summers, plant seeds very early for the first (perhaps short) crop; then plant again in July for a fall picking. Shade the young, tender, growing plants from the worst heat.

Anywhere in the Atlantic states and New England, extend the growing season as much as you can. Keep the soil from being drenched in early spring. To avoid the long wait for the first plantings, in fall prepare a mound of soil with fertilizer and organic material; then cover the pile with a heavy plastic dropcloth. This will let the rain and snow run off, and you can use it for the earliest crops, such as lettuce, radishes, cabbage, and broccoli. With raised beds, protect the entire bed with plastic for the first seedlings. For the early crop, use seedlings rather than seed; seedlings will grow in whatever mild weather there is, and frost won't hurt the hardy plants.

Consider a cold frame to start seedlings, or even to grow the first crop of lettuce and radishes. If you don't have space for a cold frame, buy seedlings from your nursery. For tomatoes, peppers, eggplants, and melons, you almost *have* to plant seedlings to get a season that's long enough for fruit; however, in the longest-summer regions, melons may give you a crop from seed.

Above: Several varieties of lettuce are started with a shady north exposure, using aluminum foil to reflect and increase the amount of light.

Below: In a raised bed with a fiberglass coldframe on top, sweet potatoes thrived where they are not well adapted. At 10 p.m., temperatures were 2 to 5 degrees higher than the outside air. Ventilation was necessary in the daytime.

Early spring
Plant as soon as ground can be worked in
spring: broccoli plants, cabbage plants,
endive, kohlrabi, lettuce, onion sets, parsley,
peas, radishes, spinach, turnips.

Mid-spring
Plant these at the average time of last killing
frost: carrots, cauliflower plants, beets,
onion seeds, parsnips, Swiss chard. Plant
two weeks later: beans, corn, potatoes,
early tomato seeds.

Early summer
Plant when soil and weather are warm: lima
beans, cantaloupe, celery plants, crenshaw melons, cucumbers, eggplant plants,
pumpkins, pepper plants, potatoes for
winter, squash, tomato plants, watermelons.

Mid-summer—fall
Plant in late June or early July: beets,
broccoli, cabbage, cauliflower, kohlrabi,
lettuce, radishes, spinach, turnips.

To retain the heat in cool-summer regions, you can (to some extent) foil the clouds by making use of the sun's movement. In spring, the sun is still fairly low in the south; so to catch some of its heat, face plantings south and protect the other three sides. Plants that stand against or climb a south wall or fence get much more light and heat than those on flat ground. You can even trap heat by building mounds for planting, and then putting seedlings and seed on the south side of the mound.

In cool summers (or for spring and fall in hot-summer regions), you can get added heat by using reflectors—so much so, in fact, that you have to make sure your plants aren't getting cooked. Use a white, south-facing wall, or paint a piece of thin plywood or hardboard white and prop it on the north side, or the north, east, and west sides, of heat-loving plants (melons, for instance). For even more intense heat, glue aluminum foil onto a board. Foil reflectors may even bring out sugar in dwarf watermelons during cool summers, but be careful not to use them on sunny days or the leaves will burn.

Use a cold frame for an extra-late crop of salad greens and radishes (however, you'll need to grow them inside with a heating cable). Use the available sunlight in mid-fall to sprout the seed, and use the cable on cooler days. This procedure will give you some fresh greens during the first hard frosts, or even in the earliest snow.

Southern states. The southern climate is divided into two distinct climatic regions. For example, despite the relatively short distance between Huntsville, Alabama, and Mobile, Alabama, planting seasons differ appreciably: in Huntsville, cabbage seedlings are ready for planting in late July, but in Mobile they are planted at the beginning of winter.

The reason is that in inland locations such as Huntsville, winter is a dormant season in the garden. The climate is governed by the continental air mass. Along the Gulf in Mobile, however, summer is the hardest time; the moist heat encourages pests and disease. Through Columbia, Atlanta, and Tuscaloosa to Jackson and beyond is a mild intermediate band where winter is real but doesn't last as long, and where humid midsummer days are refreshed fairly often by a breeze.

The general rule for planting is "avoid the bad season," but obviously this means two different things. In mild-winter and hot-summer areas, put in tender crops in late winter and early spring so that you can harvest them before the heat, and put in hardy crops in fall so that they grow into or through winter.

In cold-winter areas, put in the first tender plants in April or May, and start the fall crops in July.

The need to plant both a summer garden and a winter garden will necessitate dividing your crops into two groups: cool-season and warm-season vegetables. The cool-season crops (cabbage and its relatives, peas, lettuce, spinach, and roots such as carrots, turnips, and radishes) will take a good deal of cold, but heat and long days may make them bolt to seed or get tough and hollow. In the very warmest climates, these will grow only in winter, so plant them in September and October, and again in January.

Warm-season crops such as melons, corn, tomatoes, beans, and squash can be planted from January in the Miami area to about March in Selma or Vicksburg. This means that you can harvest before the worst of the heat. A second planting of all but the melons and tomatoes can be made in August or September.

In intermediate regions where winter is mild but summer is severe, a little juggling will get you through. Set out the hardiest cool-season crops in late summer and again in February, and plant the tender crops such as melons in March and in July through August.

A long, cold winter offers less time for crops to mature, and therefore less opportunity for double planting. Plant mature, cool-season vegetables by July or early August; plant tender crops after the last frost in April. The longest growing season of this climate zone is in places like Nashville, Chattanooga, and Raleigh; the shortest in Richmond, Virginia, or Charleston, West Virginia.

Even here, however, you can make successive plantings of many quick crops. Keep planting lettuce, but for late plantings switch to more heat-tolerant kinds, and plant successive crops of radishes, bush beans, early-maturing sweet corn, and anything else that ripens quickly. Some of the root crops, such as beets and some turnips, can be planted in summer. Some rapid-growing heat lovers can be tricked into giving you two crops. *Before* weather permits, put out two or three bush-type summer squash seedlings; protect them with a plastic-covered frame for two or three weeks. When the seedlings are well-sprouted and real spring has arrived, put in seed for your second crop.

This procedure will also extend your fall and spring seasons by weeks. Place vining crops against south-facing walls or fences, and plant peppers or eggplant inside simple frames covered with plastic. At night, the walls will radiate enough daytime heat to ward off the earliest frost, and the plastic will hold in heat for bushy plants that are still maturing some fruit.

Vegetable Climates of the South

In the highest elevation and the shortest growing season in the South there may be as few as 160 growing days. But this is more than enough to grow corn and tomatoes as well as a wide variety of both early spring and fall vegetables. You can plant lettuce, endive, turnips, Chinese cabbage, and kale in midsummer for fall and early winter harvest.

In the long-season gardens of much of the South (220 to 250 days), the fall and winter garden can stretch the harvest season.

Growing season: 220 days or less. Inland areas have a fairly high number of clear days, while the coastal portions see less of the sun. The amount of rainfall varies greatly throughout the climate zone, with the western area receiving 20 or more inches annually while the eastern areas along the coast get twice that amount. The climate is versatile enough to allow spring and summer plantings of cool-season crops. The summer season is long enough and temperatures high enough to allow the commercial growing of to-matoes and cowpeas.

The 220-day growing season here is long enough to permit summer plantings of snap beans, carrots, sweet corn, and tomatoes, as well as fall plantings of the cool-season crops.

Plantings for fall and winter harvest should be in by early August.

Growing season: 220 to 250 days. There is considerable variation in climate from the south to the north portion of this zone. Cool-weather crops are planted in mid-February. Plantings of muskmelons and squash are delayed until mid-March. A succession of plantings is possible for bush, snap, and lima beans, both in spring from mid-March through May and again from July 1 through mid-August.

A long growing season of 250 days or more, under the influence of the South Atlantic and Gulf Coasts, gives the garden a definite spring and fall planting for the majority of crops. Broccoli, Brussels sprouts, Chinese cab-bage, and kale are planted in late summer—August and September. Warm-season crops, such as muskmelons, corn, and peppers, are planted early to avoid the hottest days and nights of summer.

Growing season: 250 to 365 days. A preference for late summer and fall plantings is found in the warmest portions of this climate zone. September is the best date for escarole, endive, lettuce, radishes, broccoli, and other cool-season crops. However, winter frost does occur, and snap beans, muskmelons, sweet corn, and peppers are not planted until the soil warms up in mid-February. Onion varieties planted in this zone are bred for

Tender vegetables	
Summer squash	August 10-20
Winter squash	July 15-25
Cucumbers	August 10-20
Beans (Bush lima)	August 10-20
Beans (Bush snap)	August 10-20
Beans (Pole)	July 15-25

Semi-hardy vegetables	
Irish potatoes	August 1-15
Carrots	August 1-15
Swiss chard	August 1-15
Beets	August 1-15
Lettuce	August 1-15
Turnips	August 1-15
Spinach	Sept. 10 - Oct. 10
Radishes	Sept. 10 - Oct. 10
Mustard	Sept. 10 - Oct. 10
Winter onions	Sept. 10 - Oct. 10

Beets, turnips, and other root crops do well in high-elevation areas with short growing seasons.

planting in September, to bulb in the short days of late winter and spring.

In the south portion of Florida, the normal planting season of northern states is reversed, starting with the cool-season vegetables in the early spring. "Early spring" is September for broccoli, cabbage, lettuce, English peas, and potatoes. October is "spring planting time" for beets, carrots, radishes, turnips, and spinach. Tomatoes are a winter and summer crop with a planting season from August to March. The starting dates for the warm-weather vegetables such as pole beans, sweet corn, peppers, cucumbers, and squash begin in January.

Vegetable Climates of the West

Season lengths in the West vary all the way from less than 100 days to virtually all year—360 days. But especially in the West, season length does not tell the whole story. For instance, note that Fresno and Seattle have about the same length of growing season. August temperatures in Fresno are above 90°, whereas in Seattle they barely reach 70°.

Growing season: 100 days or less. Just as in the South, this zone does have some high-elevation, short-season gardens. Carrots, beets, turnips, onion sets, and potatoes yield good crops if planted as soon as the ground can be worked. All cool-season leafy vegetables that can be harvested before they are mature can be grown successfully.

Spring weather may fluctuate from sub-freezing at night to the upper 60s or 70s by mid-afternoon. Many areas have only 60 frost-free days a year; some can expect frost every month.

In the 100-day areas, the last frost date in spring is often around May 30. July temperatures average 58° to 66° F.

In these high-elevation areas there's no chance for sweet corn. But winter squash, peppers, and the long-season leafy vegetables that can be harvested before they mature are okay. Most of the root crops (turnips, carrots, beets, etc.) are the best bet.

Growing season: 100 to 160 days. All the above-listed vegetables are easily grown with this season length. The early varieties of tomatoes, corn, and other warm-season vegetables can be added to the list.

This area includes those gardens east of the Cascades and at the lower elevations in the Rocky Mountains. July temperatures here of 66° to 72° are just right for the maximum growth of a wide variety of vegetables. Clear days, low humidities, and high light intensities promote rapid plant growth. From June through August the area receives more than 80 percent of possible sunshine. In the shortest growing season, the early maturing varieties of the warm-season crops should be selected.

Growing season: 160 to 200 days. Areas with season lengths within this range vary widely. There is sunny Pocatello, ID; high Denver, CO; and high desert Albuquerque, NM.

In areas such as the Columbia basin and the Lewiston and Boise valley areas of eastern Washington and Idaho, the growing season is about 190 days, and summer temperatures are warm. With the heat, high light intensities, and low humidities, the gardeners can successfully grow melons—even okra and peanuts.

In Utah, the St. George area enjoys a 200-day growing season, with July temperatures in the 80s.

In the high desert areas of New Mexico and Arizona, the frequency of summer temperatures in the 100° range is fairly high, and desert winds must be considered. Here, the end of the growing season is not abrupt, and a fall garden is usually the better bet.

Growing season: 200 to 250 days. The valleys north and south of San Francisco are a part of this category. Partially influenced by the ocean, summer temperatures here are consistently higher than neighboring coastal valleys. Warm-weather crops (corn, tomatoes, peppers, eggplant, etc.) thrive with this season. Normal winters are mild enough for a fall and winter garden of hardy crops.

Growing season: 250 to 300 days. The Portland area has a growing season of 260 days with the last frost of spring in early April and first frost of fall in late November. July temperatures average only 67°.

Around Tacoma and Seattle, the growing season is about 250 days. The last frost of spring is usually March 13 or 14, and the first frost of fall can be as late as November 18 to 24. But summer temperatures are low, with a July average of only 63°. From June through August, this area receives less than 60 percent of possible sunshine. It's a great climate for the cool-season vegetables, but only the early varieties of corn and tomatoes are sure to ripen. The length of the season partly offsets the coolness of the season.

In California, the cities of Fresno and Merced are within this season range. The long seasons, together with the high summer temperatures and 95 percent of the possible sunshine, make the ideal climate for the high-sugar melons such as crenshaw, honeydew, casaba, and Persian. Cool-weather crops in these areas are grown in the spring. Low temperatures and ground fog frequently discourage winter gardening.

Growing season: 300 days or more. The coastal areas of northern and southern California and the inland valleys of southern California are blessed with this long growing season.

Coastal areas are more or less under the direct influence of the ocean fogs. South of San Francisco is lettuce and artichoke country, with most of the cool-weather crops thrown in for good measure. Possible sunshine for the summer in San Francisco is 69 percent.

The flow of marine air is not uniform. The fog cover is broken by land forms, creating several consistently open areas where summer temperatures increase and warm-weather vegetables are grown.

The inland valleys of southern California make great vegetable-growing country. The area could be divided into as many as five separate zones, varying from one with marine influence to one with more nearly desert climate. Most of the areas enjoy more than 300 frost-free days.

Southern California coastal areas, from Santa Barbara to San Diego, have nearly all-year vegetable gardening. (The lima bean was once the indicator of this climate, being a vegetable that requires modest warmth and no hot, dry winds.) The pattern of marine air flow is not uniform. Summer warmth will vary due to local fog patterns.

Vegetable Climates of the Midwest, the North, and the Northeast

There may be a world of difference between Duluth MN and Berlin NH, but the problems of the short growing season are much the same.

The short-season gardeners have two things in their favor compared to gardeners in long-season areas. Their summer growing days are longer in length than those of their southern neighbors, and the growing season starts in high gear. All of the advance seeding indoors in peat pots and frost protection are a part of gardening in short-season areas.

Growing season: 150 days or less. Many vegetables fit this climate. Look for short-season varieties of long-season crops such as sweet corn, tomatoes, and melons. Consider hot-caps, clear plastic row covers, and black plastic mulch as extenders of the growing season. Lettuce, cabbage, and other cool-season crops do well through the summer here.

Gardeners where seasons are 120 days find themselves pressed in a fairly short time period between spring and fall frost. Cool-season crops do well through the summer. Potatoes and rutabagas are among the vegetables that

Tips for Climate Modification
To make it warmer:
Expose as much of the ground as possible to the sun.
Utilize paved areas, untilled ground, rock or masonry surfaces, and south slopes to radiate the sun's heat.
Make structural or plant "ceilings" to reflect outgoing radiation back at night.
Use plants and fences as windbreaks (see page 25).
Use mulches (see page 67).

To make it cooler:
Plant shade trees and vines.
Put up overhangs, awnings, or canopies to make it cooler in the day and warmer at night.
Plant ground covers (see page 138).
Prune lower growth on trees for increased air circulation.
Utilize the principle of evaporative cooling (from sprinklers and pools).

To make it less windy:
Use windbreaks (see page 25).
Make semi-enclosed outdoor living areas.

To make it more windy:
Prune low branches of trees.
Put in plants with an open or low growth.

To make it more humid:
Put in overhead planting.
Plant or make low windbreaks.
Plant ground covers (see page 138).
Use pools and sprinklers.

To make it drier:
Expose as much of the ground as possible to the sun.
Give the maximum ventilation.
Make sure the drainage system is efficient.
Use paved ground surfaces.

like it cool and thrive in this climate. Check the seed racks and catalogs for early, short-season varieties of the long-season crops, such as midget muskmelons that ripen in 60 days, and early 'Sunglow' corn that matures in 62 days.

To make the most of a growing season of about 150 days, give the warm-season crops a headstart by growing from seed indoors or by buying transplants to set out as soon as warm weather arrives. The early varieties of all long-season crops should be selected. Nights are cool enough to permit full-season crops.

Growing season: 150 to 170 days. In this zone, the additional growing days extend the season into October. However, the normal (if there is a normal) last frost date is in the first week in May. The best way to extend the harvest period is to start seeds in greenhouses, or indoors in peat pots, or let your nursery be your greenhouse. Take full advantage of the 160-day growing season by planting lettuce, endive, turnips, broccoli, Chinese cabbage, and kale in midsummer for fall and early winter harvest.

Growing season: 170 to 190 days. Here, vegetable gardeners look to October harvests and beyond. Carrots planted in mid-July will be large enough for storage in the ground (with mulch covering) as needed.

April 20 usually signals the last frost of spring where growing seasons are 180 days. Inland areas have a fairly high percentage of clear days whereas coastal portions see less sun. The amount of rainfall varies greatly throughout this climate zone. Parts of the western area receive only 20 inches of rain annually, while areas along the east coast receive twice that amount.

Growing season: 190 days or more. Here, vegetable gardeners extend the harvest season by a late planting of cool-weather crops for late fall and winter harvest. For example, in central Ohio these vegetables are planted as late as August 1: bush snap beans, beets, endive, kale, leaf lettuce, head lettuce, and radishes.

These are planted as late as August 15: mustard, collards, and turnips. The winter crop of spinach is seeded September 1.

The warmest areas in this climate zone are those along the southern borders of Missouri, Kentucky, and Virginia, where the growing season is about 200 days. This is, of course, long enough to permit summer plantings of snap beans, carrots, sweet corn, and tomatoes, as well as fall plantings of the cool-season crops.

Altering Your Climate

Although you can't turn an arctic tundra into a tropical rainforest, you can *improve* your climate. You can make it warmer or cooler, more or less windy, drier or more humid. The particular changes you will want to make depend on where you live and what you want to plant.

For example, along the damp, foggy coast of the Northwest, the summer sun is brought into homes and gardens as much as possible. In the hot-summer Midwest, however, the sun is screened out. And in chillier mountain regions, breezes that can circulate the sticky, humid air of the Gulf Coast and the eastern seaboard are not welcome.

Following are some general ways you can modify your climate. In areas where conditions vary widely from season to season, choose methods that will work in both summer and winter. Planting a deciduous tree, for example, will give you shade in summer and allow the sun to come through the leafless branches in winter.

Protection from the sun. You can use a single plant or a grouping of plants to block or filter the sun's rays. For complete shade, use plants with dense foliage or multiple layers. For a more filtered effect, use plants with open, loose foliage. A deciduous tree offers the best of both worlds—in hot

Left: A circular brick patio under a shade tree takes advantage of cool breezes created at the bases of large trees by ascending air.

Below: Deciduous trees screen the hot sun in summer. In winter bare branches allow maximum insulation. Partial foliage in transitional seasons filters the sun.

Center: A trellised shrub shades a window area from the summer sun.

summer, its leaves offer protection from the sun; in cold winter, the leaves fall off and allow the sun to shine through.

For shade plantings, choose trees that have high, arching contours but prune out branches that grow low (which would impede air circulation about the house).

Climbing and clinging vines also give summer shade and heat control, although to a lesser extent. When supported by trellises or covering outdoor areas, they make effective sun screens. When grown on masonry walls, they act as insulating blankets for both hot-summer sun and cold-winter winds.

"Plant awnings" can shade your windows in summer, when they are in full leaf, and give you full sun in winter (if you use a plant that sheds its leaves). Use a trellis or a wire netting close to the house above the window. Use an attractive vine with colorful flowers to add a splash of brilliance to the house, or even grapes (see pages 117–120), which are delicious when they ripen in the fall.

Protection from wind. You can soften the effect of strong prevailing winds by planting barriers of trees or shrubs. Species that grow quickly, such as cypress, poplars, and pines, are best; that way they won't take an inordinate amount of time to reach the desired height (at least one and a half times the height of your house). Plant the trees or shrubs at a distance from the house from four to six times their height. For example, to shield a 20-foot-high house, plant a hedge of tall evergreens 80 to 100 feet from the north side of the house. You can plant single, double, or triple rows (the latter two work even more effectively).

Because most of the cold-winter winds come from the north or west, plant the windbreaks on those sides of the house; if there is room, plant a row or two on the eastern side, as well. However, be sure to leave the south side open to the sun.

You can also use structures such as fences to obtain the same effect, although without quite the same esthetic advantages.

Warming up the soil. To increase soil temperature, you can use materials that have different absorbent properties.

Mulches—for example, marble chips, rocks, or bricks—often are used to conduct heat to the soil as well as to add visual interest to the bases of plants.

Loose organic mulches, on the other hand, such as grass clippings, leaves, or straw, insulate the ground by reducing the solar radiation that reaches the soil underneath and keep the soil cool.

Plastic film offers yet another solution. By raising soil temperatures, plastic film speeds up seed germination and produces yields that are higher in quantity and quality.

(See pages 67–71 for more on mulches.)

A mulch of pine bark chips provides the cool soil in which violets thrive. Other organic mulches will do the same thing.

Climates of the South

City	July % of Sunshine	Days of Growing Season	Inches of Rain	Days of Rain	Last Frost	First Frost	JAN.	FEB.	MARCH	APRIL	MAY	JUNE	JULY	AUG.	SEPT.	OCT.	NOV.	DEC.
Roanoke, VA	59	165	25″	66	4-14	10-26	45/25	47/27	54/32	65/40	74/50	81/58	85/63	84/62	77/55	67/43	55/34	47/27
Asheville, NC	59	195	26″	69	4-12	10-24	49/30	51/31	57/36	68/44	76/52	83/60	85/64	84/63	79/57	69/46	57/36	50/30
Lexington, KY	64	198	24″	66	4-13	10-28	43/25	45/27	55/34	66/43	75/53	84/62	87/66	86/64	81/58	69/47	54/36	45/27
Lubbock, TX	81	205	15″	40	4-1	11-9	53/26	57/29	65/34	74/44	82/54	91/64	92/66	92/66	84/58	75/47	62/33	55/27
Richmond, VA	65	218	29″	68	3-29	11-2	48/29	51/29	59/36	70/46	79/55	87/63	89/78	86/65	82/58	71/47	60/37	50/29
Louisville, KY	73	220	25″	68	4-1	11-7	44/26	46/28	56/35	67/45	77/54	85/63	89/67	88/65	82/58	71/47	55/36	46/28
Knoxville, TN	64	220	25″	73	3-31	11-6	50/33	53/33	60/39	70/48	79/56	86/65	88/68	87/67	84/61	73/49	59/38	50/33
Tulsa, OK	76	221	27″	56	3-25	11-1	46/26	52/30	60/36	70/47	78/58	87/67	93/71	93/70	86/62	75/51	59/36	49/30
Okla. City, OK	78	224	25″	56	3-28	11-7	46/27	51/30	60/37	70/48	77/58	86/67	92/70	93/70	85/62	73/51	59/37	49/30
Nashville, TN	69	224	24″	68	3-28	11-7	49/31	51/33	59/39	71/48	80/57	88/66	91/70	90/68	85/61	74/49	59/38	51/32
Texarkana, AR	77	233	28″	64	3-21	11-9	52/32	57/37	64/42	74/52	82/61	90/69	94/72	93/71	87/64	78/52	64/42	56/36
Ft. Smith, AR	74	234	29″	60	3-21	11-10	50/29	55/33	63/40	74/50	81/59	90/67	95/71	94/70	87/62	77/51	62/38	52/32
Raleigh, NC	62	237	30″	71	3-24	11-16	52/31	54/32	61/38	72/47	79/56	86/64	88/68	87/67	82/60	73/48	62/38	52/31
Memphis, TN	73	237	28″	62	3-20	11-12	51/33	59/35	61/42	72/52	81/60	89/69	97/72	92/70	86/63	76/52	62/40	53/35
Baltimore, MD	64	238	26″	68	3-28	11-19	44/25	45/26	54/32	66/43	76/53	83/61	87/66	85/65	79/58	68/46	56/34	46/26
El Paso, TX	78	238	6″	33	3-26	11-14	56/30	62/36	69/40	78/49	87/57	95/67	95/69	93/68	88/61	79/50	66/36	58/31
Birmingham, AL	62	241	33″	75	3-19	11-14	57/36	59/38	67/42	76/50	84/59	91/68	92/71	92/70	89/64	79/52	66/41	58/36
Little Rock, AR	71	241	31″	66	3-17	11-13	51/31	55/34	63/41	74/51	82/60	90/68	93/71	92/70	86/62	76/50	61/38	52/32
Atlanta, GA	62	242	29″	72	3-21	11-18	54/36	57/37	63/41	72/50	81/59	87/66	88/69	88/68	83/63	74/52	62/40	53/35
Norfolk, VA	66	242	34″	79	3-19	11-16	50/32	51/32	57/39	68/48	77/58	85/66	88/70	86/69	81/64	71/53	61/42	52/33
Dallas, TX	78	244	23″	51	3-18	11-17	56/36	59/39	67/45	75/55	83/63	91/72	94/75	95/75	88/67	79/57	66/44	58/38
Augusta, GA	62	249	34″	74	3-14	11-1	59/36	61/37	67/42	76/50	84/59	91/67	91/70	91/69	86/64	78/52	68/40	59/35
Columbia, SC	63	262	34″	74	3-14	11-21	58/36	60/36	66/42	76/51	85/60	91/68	92/71	91/70	86/65	77/52	67/41	58/34
Shreveport, LA	79	262	29″	67	3-8	11-15	57/38	60/41	67/47	75/55	83/63	91/71	93/73	94/73	88/67	79/55	66/45	59/40
Wilmington, NC	66	262	40″	79	3-8	11-24	58/37	59/38	65/43	74/51	81/60	87/68	89/71	88/71	84/66	76/55	67/44	59/37
Houston, TX	70	262	38″	80	3-14	11-21	64/44	66/46	72/51	78/59	86/66	91/72	92/74	93/74	89/69	82/60	71/51	65/46
Savannah, GA	61	275	41″	89	2-27	11-29	62/41	64/42	70/47	77/54	85/62	90/69	91/71	91/71	86/67	78/56	69/45	63/40
Montgomery, AL	66	279	38″	77	2-27	12-3	59/38	61/40	67/45	76/52	84/61	90/69	92/72	92/71	88/66	79/55	66/42	59/38
New Orleans, LA	58	292	47″	93	2-20	12-9	64/45	67/48	71/52	78/58	84/64	90/71	91/73	91/73	87/69	80/61	70/50	65/46
Charleston, SC	66	294	44″	94	2-19	12-10	61/38	63/40	68/45	77/53	84/62	89/69	89/72	89/72	85/66	77/55	68/44	61/39
Mobile, AL	61	298	58″	90	2-17	12-12	62/44	65/46	70/50	77/58	86/65	91/72	92/73	91/73	87/68	80/60	70/48	64/44
Jacksonville, FL	62	313	48″	103	2-16	12-16	67/45	69/47	73/51	80/57	86/65	91/71	92/73	91/73	88/71	80/62	72/51	67/46
Crps. Christi, TX	80	335	27″	73	1-26	12-27	67/47	70/51	74/56	80/63	86/69	90/74	93/75	94/74	90/71	84/64	74/54	69/49
Tampa, FL	61	349	51″	105	1-10	12-26	71/51	73/53	76/56	81/61	87/67	89/72	90/73	90/74	89/72	84/66	77/57	73/52
Miami, FL	65	365	60″	127	—	—	76/58	77/59	80/61	83/66	85/70	88/74	89/75	90/75	88/75	85/71	80/65	77/59

During Growing Season (spans July % of Sunshine, Days of Growing Season, Inches of Rain, Days of Rain, Last Frost, First Frost)

Average Maximum/Minimum Temperature (spans JAN.–DEC.)

Right margin annotations: 220 days or less; From 220 to 250 days; From 250 to 365 days

Climates of the West

City	July % of Sunshine	Days of Growing Season	Inches of Rain	Last Frost	First Frost	JAN.	FEB.	MARCH	APRIL	MAY	JUNE	JULY	AUG.	SEPT.	OCT.	NOV.	DEC.	
	During Growing Season					Average Maximum/Minimum Temperature												
Bend, OR	83	91	12"	6-8	9-7	42/17	53/23	50/23	65/28	58/32	78/43	80/43	84/48	69/36	63/31	48/24	43/26	160 days or less
Gt. Falls, MT	80	139	15"	5-9	9-25	29/12	36/17	40/21	54/32	65/41	72/49	84/55	82/53	70/48	59/37	43/26	35/18	
Cheyenne, WY	68	141	15"	5-14	10-2	38/15	41/17	43/20	55/30	65/40	74/48	84/54	82/53	73/43	62/34	47/23	40/18	
Reno, NV	92	155	7"	5-8	10-10	45/18	51/23	56/25	64/30	72/37	80/42	91/47	89/45	82/39	70/30	56/24	46/20	
Ogden, UT	81	155	16"	5-6	10-8	36/18	47/25	48/28	68/42	65/43	88/60	91/62	86/59	78/51	68/41	51/31	43/28	
Pocatello, ID	76	161	23"	4-28	10-6	32/18	46/29	45/30	64/36	62/38	81/48	82/49	86/51	66/43	59/35	42/28	37/26	From 160 to 200 days
Denver, CO	71	171	15"	4-26	10-14	44/14	52/24	54/26	63/39	75/46	76/57	88/61	83/57	81/49	69/37	51/20	49/21	
Centralia, WA	65	173	46"	4-27	10-17	44/31	54/37	52/35	64/39	63/42	74/50	76/50	82/56	68/49	61/42	53/39	46/36	
Pueblo, CO	78	174	12"	4-23	10-14	43/12	57/19	60/24	70/39	81/49	91/57	94/61	88/60	86/49	72/35	59/23	52/19	
Boise, ID	88	177	11"	4-23	10-17	36/21	44/27	52/30	61/36	71/44	78/51	90/58	88/57	78/48	65/39	49/31	39/25	
Santa Fe, NM	78	178	13"	4-24	10-19	36/15	46/22	49/25	61/36	71/43	85/54	85/57	84/58	78/49	69/70	55/30	47/17	
Yakima, WA	82	190	8"	4-15	10-22	36/19	46/25	55/29	64/35	73/43	79/49	88/53	86/51	78/44	65/35	48/28	39/23	
S.L. City, UT	84	192	15"	4-13	10-22	37/18	43/23	51/28	62/37	72/44	81/51	91/60	90/59	80/49	66/38	50/28	39/21	
Albuquerque, NM	76	198	8"	4-13	10-28	47/23	53/27	59/32	70/41	80/51	89/60	92/65	90/63	83/57	72/45	57/32	47/25	
Eugene, OR	60	205	43"	4-13	11-4	46/33	52/35	55/36	61/39	68/44	74/49	83/51	81/51	76/47	64/42	53/38	47/36	From 200 to 250 days
Santa Rosa, CA	65	207	30"	4-10	11-3	59/34	68/39	66/37	76/42	73/44	84/51	88/50	87/53	82/52	79/46	70/40	61/43	
Las Vegas, NV	87	239	4"	3-16	11-10	56/33	61/37	68/42	77/50	87/59	97/67	101/75	101/73	95/65	81/53	66/41	57/34	
Tucson, AZ	78	245	11"	3-19	11-19	63/38	67/40	71/44	81/50	90/57	98/66	98/74	95/72	93/67	84/56	72/45	65/39	
Fresno, CA	96	250	10"	3-14	11-19	55/36	61/39	67/41	74/46	83/52	90/57	98/63	96/61	91/56	80/49	66/41	55/37	
Eureka, CA	52	253	40"	3-10	11-18	53/41	54/42	54/42	55/44	57/48	60/51	60/52	61/53	62/51	60/48	58/45	58/43	
Seattle, WA	63	255	36"	3-14	11-24	45/35	50/37	53/38	59/42	66/47	70/52	76/56	74/55	69/52	62/46	51/40	47/37	From 250 to 300 days
Portland, OR	69	263	34"	3-6	11-24	54/39	59/37	55/37	68/39	65/45	79/52	84/53	89/59	73/52	65/46	54/37	52/40	
Riverside, CA	81	265	10"	3-6	11-26	65/42	76/44	67/42	78/48	72/51	88/57	96/60	92/63	87/57	84/53	79/45	69/47	
Marysville, CA	90	273	21"	2-21	11-21	51/35	66/40	66/41	80/50	74/50	94/61	95/60	94/61	86/57	80/51	67/42	58/43	
Red Bluff, CA	96	274	22"	3-6	12-5	54/37	59/40	64/42	72/47	81/54	89/62	98/67	96/64	91/60	78/52	64/43	55/38	
Bakersfield, CA	95	277	6"	2-21	11-25	52/37	63/41	69/44	75/50	84/56	91/62	99/69	96/67	91/62	80/53	68/44	57/38	
San Jose, CA	72	299	14"	2-10	1-6	57/38	65/44	63/42	73/47	68/48	79/56	82/56	80/58	79/55	74/51	66/45	60/46	
Phoenix, AZ	94	304	7"	2-5	12-6	65/38	69/41	74/45	84/52	93/60	101/68	105/77	102/76	98/69	88/57	75/45	66/38	300 days or more
Sacramento, CA	97	307	17"	2-6	12-10	53/37	59/40	64/42	71/45	79/50	86/55	93/57	91/57	88/53	77/49	64/42	58/38	
Pasadena, CA	87	313	19"	2-3	12-13	67/45	76/48	68/43	75/50	71/50	82/57	84/60	88/63	84/59	82/56	79/51	69/50	
Santa Barbara, CA	65	331	17"	1-22	12-19	66/42	71/44	66/44	70/49	69/52	71/55	75/57	77/61	76/58	74/55	76/47	68/51	
Palm Springs, CA	65	334	31"	1-18	12-18	70/42	83/47	77/44	91/55	87/56	106/69	110/75	106/75	100/67	93/61	82/48	72/47	
San Francisco, CA	66	356	21"	1-7	12-29	56/46	59/48	60/48	61/49	62/51	64/53	64/53	65/54	69/55	68/55	63/51	57/47	
Los Angeles, CA	82	359	14"	1-3	12-28	66/47	68/48	69/50	70/53	73/56	76/59	83/63	84/64	82/63	78/59	73/52	68/48	
San Diego, CA	67	365	9"	—	—	65/46	66/48	68/50	68/54	69/57	71/60	75/64	77/65	76/63	74/58	70/51	66/47	

Climates of the Midwest and North

City	July % of Sunshine	Days of Growing Season	Inches of Rain	Days of Rain	Last Frost	1st Frost	JAN.	FEB.	MARCH	APRIL	MAY	JUNE	JULY	AUG.	SEPT.	OCT.	NOV.	DEC.	
Duluth, MN	67	125	15"	47	5-22	9-24	18/−1	21/0	31/11	47/27	61/38	70/47	77/54	75/53	65/44	55/35	35/19	22/6	150 days or less
Bismarck, ND	75	136	10"	42	5-11	9-24	20/−2	23/2	37/17	55/32	67/42	76/52	85/59	83/55	72/45	59/33	38/18	26/5	
Huron, SD	77	149	12"	44	5-4	9-30	25/2	28/7	43/20	60/33	72/44	81/55	90/61	87/59	77/48	64/36	44/21	30/9	
Rapid City, SD	73	150	11"	44	5-7	10-4	31/9	36/12	43/20	57/32	67/43	76/52	86/59	85/57	74/47	62/36	47/24	37/14	
Sioux Falls, SD	75	152	16"	45	5-5	10-3	24/4	30/9	42/22	59/34	71/45	80/56	88/62	85/60	75/49	63/37	43/21	29/9	150 to 170 days
Marquette, MI	67	159	16"	60	5-13	10-19	26/13	27/13	33/20	47/32	59/41	70/51	76/58	74/57	66/50	55/41	39/28	29/19	
North Platte, NE	76	160	14"	45	4-30	10-7	37/11	42/16	50/23	62/35	72/46	82/56	89/62	88/60	78/49	67/36	51/23	40/15	
La Cross, WI	72	161	19"	54	5-1	10-8	25/6	29/10	41/22	57/36	70/48	79/58	85/63	82/61	73/52	61/40	43/26	29/12	
Green Bay, WI	64	161	16"	55	5-6	10-13	25/8	26/9	37/26	52/32	65/44	75/54	81/59	79/57	70/50	58/39	41/26	27/13	
Minneapolis/ St. Paul, MN	70	166	17"	55	4-30	10-13	22/2	26/5	37/18	56/33	69/45	78/55	84/61	81/59	72/48	61/37	41/22	27/9	
Sioux City, IA	71	169	18"	52	4-27	10-13	28/9	32/13	43/24	60/38	73/50	83/60	90/65	87/63	78/53	67/41	47/25	35/15	
Des Moines, IA	75	175	20"	55	4-24	10-16	29/11	32/15	43/25	59/38	71/50	81/61	87/65	85/63	77/54	66/43	47/28	34/17	
Fort Wayne, IN	71	179	20"	59	4-24	10-20	33/19	35/21	45/28	58/38	70/48	79/58	84/63	82/61	75/54	63/43	47/32	35/22	
Peoria, IL	69	181	21"	55	4-22	10-20	34/18	37/20	47/28	61/40	72/51	82/61	87/65	85/63	78/55	67/44	49/31	37/21	170 to 190 days
Detroit, MI	66	182	18"	58	4-21	10-20	34/19	35/19	44/26	58/37	70/47	80/57	85/61	84/60	76/52	65/43	49/32	37/23	
Springfield, IL	73	186	21"	59	4-20	10-23	36/20	41/22	50/30	65/42	76/52	85/62	90/66	87/63	80/55	69/49	52/32	40/24	
Pittsburgh, PA	63	187	20"	65	4-20	10-23	37/21	38/21	46/27	60/38	71/48	80/57	83/61	82/60	76/53	64/42	50/32	38/23	
Milwaukee, WI	70	188	18"	61	4-20	10-25	29/14	32/17	41/26	53/36	64/45	75/55	81/64	79/60	72/53	60/42	45/30	33/19	
Parkersburg, WV	63	159	21"	66	4-16	10-21	43/26	44/27	54/34	65/43	75/52	83/62	86/65	84/64	79/57	68/46	54/36	44/28	
Omaha, NE	81	189	23"	58	4-14	10-20	32/13	37/17	48/28	63/41	73/52	83/62	89/68	86/65	78/56	67/44	49/29	36/19	
Grand Rapids, MI	67	190	16"	52	4-23	10-30	31/17	32/16	42/24	57/35	69/45	79/56	85/60	83/58	74/50	63/39	46/28	34/20	
Chicago, IL	70	192	21"	61	4-19	10-28	33/19	35/21	44/29	57/40	69/51	80/61	84/67	82/66	75/57	63/47	47/33	36/22	190 days or more
Cincinnati, OH	76	192	21"	65	4-15	10-25	41/25	43/27	53/34	64/43	74/53	83/62	87/66	85/64	80/58	68/46	53/36	42/27	
Charleston, WV	63	193	22"	71	4-18	10-28	46/26	49/28	57/33	68/42	77/50	85/59	87/63	86/62	81/56	71/44	57/35	48/29	
Indianapolis, IN	74	193	22"	60	4-17	10-27	37/20	40/23	50/34	62/40	73/50	83/60	88/64	86/62	79/55	67/44	51/32	39/23	
Cleveland, OH	69	195	20"	68	4-21	11-2	36/21	34/21	45/28	57/37	70/48	80/53	85/63	83/61	76/55	64/44	49/34	38/24	
Columbus, OH	71	196	21"	64	4-17	10-30	39/22	40/23	50/30	61/39	73/49	82/52	86/63	84/60	78/55	66/43	51/33	39/24	
Lexington, KY	64	198	24"	66	4-13	10-28	43/25	45/27	55/34	66/43	75/53	84/62	87/66	86/64	81/58	69/47	54/36	45/27	
Topeka, KS	66	200	26"	57	4-9	10-26	39/19	44/23	54/31	66/43	75/52	85/63	91/68	89/66	81/57	71/45	54/31	43/22	
Springfield, MO	70	201	26"	59	4-12	10-30	43/24	47/27	55/33	66/45	75/54	85/63	90/67	90/66	83/58	72/47	56/34	46/27	
St. Louis, MO	71	206	23"	60	4-9	11-1	40/23	44/25	53/32	66/44	75/53	85/63	89/67	87/66	81/58	70/47	54/34	43/26	
Kansas City, MO	76	207	28"	61	4-6	10-30	40/23	45/27	43/34	66/46	75/56	85/66	92/71	90/69	83/60	72/47	55/35	44/28	
Wichita, KS	84	210	24"	56	4-5	11-1	41/23	48/26	56/34	67/45	75/54	86/65	92/69	92/68	83/60	71/49	55/35	45/26	
Evansville, In	77	216	24"	73	4-2	11-4	43/26	47/28	57/36	68/46	77/54	85/64	89/67	87/65	82/59	71/48	56/36	46/28	
Louisville, KY	73	220	25"	68	4-1	11-7	44/26	46/28	56/35	67/45	77/54	85/63	89/67	88/65	82/58	71/47	55/36	46/28	

Climates of the Northeast

City	During Growing Season						Average Maximum/Minimum Temperature												
	July % of Sunshine	Days of Growing Season	Inches of Rain	Days of Rain	Last Frost	1st Frost	JAN.	FEB.	MARCH	APRIL	MAY	JUNE	JULY	AUG.	SEPT.	OCT.	NOV.	DEC.	
Berlin, NH	46	109	12"	41	5-29	9-15	28/6	35/7	37/17	52/31	65/40	74/49	79/53	77/51	69/44	58/34	45/27	31/11	150 days or less
Greenville, ME	60	116	14"	43	5-27	9-20	24/4	29/7	35/14	49/28	63/38	72/48	78/52	75/50	66/43	54/34	41/25	27/10	
Caribou, ME	56	125	15"	54	5-19	9-21	20/1	22/3	32/14	45/28	60/39	69/49	75/54	73/52	64/43	52/34	37/23	24/7	
St. Johnsbury, VT	52	127	14"	46	5-22	9-23	29/7	34/11	40/19	56/32	69/42	78/51	82/55	80/53	72/47	60/36	46/28	32/13	
Pittsfield, MA	60	138	19"	49	5-12	9-27	31/13	32/13	40/22	53/33	66/43	75/51	79/56	78/55	70/47	60/37	46/29	34/17	
Canton, NY	59	140	15"	48	5-9	9-26	27/8	31/12	38/20	56/35	68/44	77/54	81/58	79/56	71/49	60/39	46/30	32/15	
Concord, NH	56	142	14"	48	5-11	9-30	32/9	33/10	43/21	56/30	69/41	78/50	83/55	80/53	72/45	62/34	48/26	34/14	
Burlington, VT	62	148	16"	58	5-8	10-3	28/8	28/8	39/20	53/32	67/43	78/53	82/58	80/56	71/48	59/38	44/28	31/14	
Worcester, MA	60	148	18"	50	5-7	10-2	31/17	33/17	41/25	54/36	66/44	74/55	79/61	77/59	70/52	60/41	47/31	34/20	
Altoona, PA	60	151	22"	62	5-6	10-4	35/20	39/22	45/26	62/39	71/46	78/55	83/59	81/58	75/51	64/41	50/31	38/22	
Watertown, NY	67	151	16"	50	5-7	10-4	28/10	31/14	38/23	55/36	65/46	75/56	80/61	79/59	71/51	60/41	47/32	33/17	150 to 170 days
Binghamton, NY	66	154	18"	56	5-4	10-6	30/17	31/17	39/24	53/34	65/45	73/54	78/58	76/57	69/50	59/41	45/31	33/21	
Bangor, ME	62	156	17"	47	5-1	10-4	28/12	32/14	38/22	52/34	64/44	72/52	78/58	77/56	68/49	57/39	46/31	32/17	
Williamsport, PA	60	164	19"	61	5-3	10-13	36/21	38/21	47/28	60/39	72/49	81/58	85/62	83/60	75/53	64/42	50/33	38/23	
Syracuse, NY	67	168	17"	60	4-30	10-15	32/16	32/17	40/25	55/37	68/47	78/57	82/62	81/60	72/52	61/42	47/33	35/21	
Portland, ME	65	169	16"	54	4-29	10-15	32/12	34/12	41/22	53/32	64/42	73/51	80/57	78/55	70/47	60/37	48/29	35/16	
Albany, NY	64	169	17"	58	4-27	10-13	31/14	33/15	42/24	57/36	70/46	79/56	84/60	81/58	73/50	62/40	48/31	35/18	
Bridgeport, CT	65	173	18"	49	4-26	10-16	37/22	37/21	45/29	55/37	67/48	76/58	82/64	80/63	74/56	64/45	52/35	40/25	170 to 190 days
Scranton, PA	63	174	19"	63	4-24	10-14	34/22	35/21	44/29	57/39	69/50	77/59	82/63	79/61	71/53	60/42	48/33	35/24	
Buffalo, NY	69	179	17"	60	4-30	10-25	31/18	31/17	39/24	53/34	66/44	75/54	80/59	79/58	72/51	60/41	47/32	34/21	
Hartford, CT	62	180	21"	59	4-22	10-19	36/18	38/18	47/27	60/36	72/47	81/57	86/62	83/60	76/52	65/41	51/31	39/20	
Wilmington, DE	65	191	23"	56	4-18	10-26	42/25	43/25	53/32	63/40	75/51	83/60	87/65	85/63	79/57	67/45	55/36	44/26	190 days or more
Winchester, VA	62	193	22"	63	4-17	10-27	43/26	47/28	52/32	68/44	76/52	83/60	88/65	86/63	80/56	69/46	56/36	45/28	
New Haven, CT	66	195	21"	54	4-15	10-27	37/21	37/21	46/28	55/37	66/47	75/56	80/62	79/61	73/54	63/43	52/34	40/24	
Providence, RI	63	197	21"	62	4-13	10-27	37/21	37/20	45/29	55/37	66/47	75/56	80/62	79/60	72/53	62/43	51/34	39/24	
Harrisburg, PA	68	204	21"	68	4-9	10-30	39/24	41/24	50/30	63/40	74/51	73/60	87/65	85/63	78/56	67/45	52/34	41/25	
Charlottesville, VA	62	209	28"	66	4-11	11-6	46/28	49/30	54/35	69/47	77/55	83/63	88/68	86/66	81/60	70/50	58/38	47/30	
Boston, MA	65	217	23"	73	4-5	11-8	37/23	37/23	45/31	56/40	68/50	76/60	82/65	80/63	73/57	63/47	52/38	40/26	
Trenton, NJ	67	218	25"	67	4-4	11-8	40/26	41/26	49/32	61/42	72/52	81/61	85/67	83/65	76/58	66/48	54/38	42/28	
Newark, NJ	65	219	24"	69	4-3	11-8	40/25	41/25	49/32	61/42	72/52	81/61	86/66	84/65	77/58	66/47	54/37	42/27	
New York City, NY	65	219	24"	69	4-7	11-12	40/27	40/26	48/33	60/43	71/53	80/62	85/68	83/67	77/60	66/50	54/40	42/30	
Washington, DC	63	225	26"	66	3-29	11-9	44/29	46/29	54/36	66/46	76/56	83/65	87/69	85/68	79/61	68/50	57/39	46/30	
Atlantic City, NJ	65	225	27"	65	3-31	11-11	43/27	43/26	50/32	60/42	71/51	79/61	84/66	82/65	76/58	67/48	56/38	45/28	
Philadelphia, PA	62	232	26"	70	3-30	11-17	40/24	42/25	50/32	63/41	73/52	82/60	86/65	84/63	77/56	67/44	54/35	42/25	
Baltimore, MD	64	238	26"	68	3-28	11-19	44/25	46/26	54/32	66/43	76/53	83/61	87/66	85/65	79/58	68/46	56/34	46/26	

PLANTING AND TRANSPLANTING

Indoors or outdoors, all plants require certain soil and climatic conditions for successful germination and healthy growth.

On first consideration, seeding would seem to be the simplest of procedures, requiring only an outstretched hand to scatter the seeds. But there's a bit more to it than that; even the most experienced gardeners have occasionally had seeds that failed to germinate.

For a first-time gardener, the biggest trap is overpreparing the seed bed. If the soil is raked until it is as fine as dust, the first rain or sprinkling will reward your efforts with a big mud pie; and when the soil then dries out, a tight crust of soil will imprison your seeds.

Heavy clay soil should really be modified (see pages 56–61), but you don't have to change the entire garden's-worth of soil—simply add organic material to each row to be planted.

Despite the predictions of early-spring thaws, don't rush the season. Wait until the *soil*, not just the weather, is warm. With some seeds—for example, corn and beans (especially limas)—the warmer the soil, the better their chances of successful germination.

How deep to plant a seed depends on your soil and the weather. Plant shallow in wet weather or in heavy soils; plant deeper in dry weather and in light, sandy soils. A somewhat more specific rule of thumb is to plant at a depth equal to four times the diameter of the seed.

Several crops, including parsnips, carrots, parsley, cress, and (to a lesser degree) lettuce, do best when planted ¼ inch or less deep. However, if you're doing a shallow planting for seeds with a long germination period, sprinkle them often to keep the soil's surface moist.

Direct Seeding

Seeds can be started indoors, or sowed directly outdoors. You can dig furrows for the seeds or scatter them over the soil in a swath pattern.

Row planting. To make straight rows, insert stakes at either end of the row-to-be and stretch a string between the stakes. Use a trowel to make shallow furrows, and a hoe for deeper ones.

Space small seeds evenly by tapping them directly from the packet or by rubbing a pinch of them between your fingers (as you might add "a pinch" of salt when cooking).

As an aid to even spacing of small seeds, mix them with white sand in a salt shaker, and shake the mix into the furrow. For yet more precise spacing, spread individual sheets of facial tissue in the seed furrow and place the seeds on these sheets. The seeds will show up against the white paper, allowing you to move them easily with a pencil or toothpick. And the tissue will rot away long before the seeds germinate. For the most meticulous spacing of all, use seed tape—it encloses exactly-spaced seeds in water-soluble plastic.

To maximize the use of your space when sowing carrot seed, sow randomly in a 6- to 12-inch-wide swath, then cover with ¼ inch of fine peat moss.

Direct Seeding Tips

Soil preparation, seasonal timing, and attention to the details of planting requirements will give seeds the best start toward becoming flourishing plants in your garden. The tips listed here will make planting easier for you.

Sowing small seeds
When the small size or color of seeds makes them difficult to see as you're sowing, lay sheets of tissue paper in the trench. The tissue will decompose quickly when covered and watered.

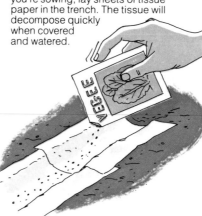

Spacing seeds
Space small seeds evenly by rubbing a pinch between fingers . . .

or tap them directly from the packet.

Trench greenhouse
To help start hard-to-germinate seeds such as tomatoes, peppers, and eggplant, plant seeds in a trench covered with clear plastic. Angle it so water drains off.

Seed tape is available for many plants—it is a water-soluble tape with seeds attached with the proper spacing.

Sowing carrots
To make the most of your space when sowing carrot seed, sow randomly in a swath 6 to 12 inches wide, and cover with ¼ inch of fine peat moss. Thin seedlings randomly and enjoy the sweet, tender miniature carrots as they grow.

To encourage the germination of warmth-loving seeds such as tomatoes, peppers, and eggplant, dig a "trench greenhouse"—that is, plant the seeds in a trench covered with clear plastic, angling the plastic to let water run off.

By whatever method the seeds are sown, use the flat back of a rake to firm the soil over a seed row.

Protecting your seeds. There are a variety of ways to protect your seeds from various kinds of damage. For example, you can cover the rows with burlap sacks and sprinkle them with water, as needed. The sacks will keep moisture in the soil. However, remember to remove them when the seedlings begin to emerge.

Or you can use a ⅛-inch-deep mulch of vermiculite, bark, or sawdust to prevent the soil from crusting and reduce the need for frequent sprinkling. If your area tends to be windy, contain the mulch in a slot to keep it from blowing away. Clear plastic makes a good mulch (see pages 70–71), but be sure to remove it as soon as the seedlings show.

If you sow seeds of carrots, beets, and leaf lettuce in 3- or 4-inch-wide bands rather than in a single line row, the first thinning will not be as critical, and carrot roots will have less of a tendency to tangle and malform. Although some thinning will be necessary, much of it will be in pulling baby carrots.

You can sow small seeds in groups of 2 to 6, with a few inches between groups. The seeds will help each other push the soil up if it threatens to crust over, which also helps ensure against seed failures.

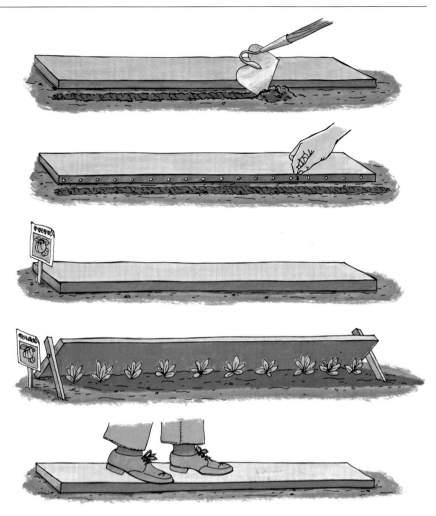

Using a planting board

You can use a 1- by 8-inch board in many ways in the garden. It can function as a straight edge to make furrows or to plant seed; if its edge is marked every inch or so with aluminum nails or brass tacks, it can be used to measure spacing between seeds (also transplants), and rows; it can hold in moisture and warmth until the seedlings emerge; propped up, it can protect new seedlings from hot sun or drying wind; and laid flat, it can be used for walking on, thus protecting soft soil.

Row planting

Stretch a string for straight rows. For deep planting furrows, use the corner of a hoe blade. For shallow furrows, use the handle. Firm the soil over a seed row with the flat back of a rake.

To keep new seedlings warm and moist, you can build a miniature greenhouse. Build a raised-bed box (see page 56), and make the seed bed 3 inches lower than the edge of the box. After planting, lay 2- by 2-inch stakes across the long end of the box and cover the entire area with clear plastic. Tack a 2 × 2 onto each end of the plastic to hold it down in the wind.

Thinning seedlings. The trick is to thin out seedling plants carefully, without disturbing the roots of those plants that should remain in the ground. The best way to avoid even touching the roots is to cut off the unwanted seedlings with scissors.

Seed-Starting Containers

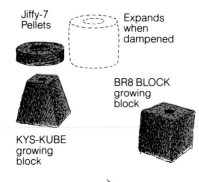

Jiffy-7 Pellets

Expands when dampened

BR8 BLOCK growing block

KYS-KUBE growing block

Sow seeds, two at a time, directly into plastic pots, KYS-KUBES, BR8 BLOCKS, or Jiffy-7 pellets. Water thoroughly and place on a tray in a plastic bag. They'll be ready to transplant when about 6 inches high.

Starting Seed Indoors

Growing seedlings indoors has its advantages: it gives the plant a headstart even though there is still frost outside and the ground is still wet; it lets you grow special varieties of vegetables, or get early color from annuals. No matter why you grow seedlings indoors, you must meet certain requirements in order to have trouble-free seedlings:

☐ A growing medium that is disease free;

☐ Sufficient warmth and moisture for the seed to germinate;

☐ Adequate light for stocky growth; and

☐ An adjustment period to get the indoor plants ready for outdoor conditions.

Garden centers sell a wide variety of germinating and growing materials to help you meet these requirements. Various seed-starter kits contain a growing medium, heating cables for bottom heat, and a plastic cover to create a small greenhouse. Or you can buy Kys Kubes, Jiffy-7s, peat pots and a synthetic soil mix, and heating cables, and arrange your own kit.

Start seeds in a medium that is free of disease-causing organisms. The synthetic soil mixes such as Jiffy Mix, Pro Mix, Redi Earth, and Super Soil provide excellent germinating and growing mediums—they are clean, sterile, and disease-free, and contain no weed seeds. Sow seeds right into the mix.

But first moisten the soil medium. Just place it in a plastic bag along with some water, and mix with your hand. Kys Kubes or Jiffy-7s must be completely saturated before they are used.

Sowing and germination. After filling flats with the mix, sow seed in rows spaced 2 inches apart. Cover seeds lightly and gently moisten with lukewarm (never cold) water. Place a sheet of glass on the flat or a plastic bag around it to maintain soil moisture until germination has occurred.

The *soil* must be at the correct temperature: 65° to 75° F. for most varieties (the air temperature should be between 70 and 75°). One way to achieve this

Starting Seeds Indoors

Here are some good ideas for starting seed and handling transplants.

Ventilation holes

Cottage cheese or margarine tubs make great seed-starting containers.

Wire wickets to hold plastic up

Seeds planted in a nursery flat. A large plastic bag around the flat seals in moisture and heat for quick germination.

The plastic bag works around a tray of pots, too.

Propagating mat or heating cables keep containers or flats at the proper temperature.

is from the bottom heat created by heating cables placed in the bottom of the flat. Again, use only warm water when watering.

Some types of seed germinate better if they experience a cold shock (to break dormancy) just before being sown. Put the following in the freezer compartment of the refrigerator for 48 hours prior to seeding: delphinium, snapdragon, primula, phlox, carnation, and aster. Immediately after the seeds have germinated, remove whatever cover you have used and place your seedlings in the light.

After the first two seedling leaves have appeared and the third leaf (or the first true leaf) appears, transplant the seedlings to a flat that can accommodate more space between plants, or into peat pots or individual containers. Small seedlings are preferable, at this stage—the large ones are more susceptible to transplanting shock. When transplanting, plant at about the same depth as they were in the seedling flat; firm the soil around the root.

Seed-starting methods. You can choose between two methods of starting seeds indoors. Since they are equally effective, select the one that appeals to you more.

One-step method. Sow seeds, two or more at a time, directly into plastic pots, peat pots, growing blocks, or Jiffy-7 pellets. Water thoroughly and place on a tray in a plastic bag. When the first true leaves appear, reduce the seedlings to one per pot by cutting off the extra plants with scissors. The seedlings will be ready to harden off before transplanting when they are about 6 inches high.

Two-step method. (1) Sow seeds in a tray of damp vermiculite. Set the seeds about ¼ inch deep. Cover, and water lightly. Then slip the tray into a plastic bag and keep it at about 75° F. Do not water until the seed has germinated. At that point, keep it only slightly damp. (2) Once the first true leaves have formed, transplant the seedlings to peat pots. Firm the soil around the roots and the stem. Then put the pots on a tray and place the tray inside a plastic bag until the seedlings are ready for hardening off.

Two-step Method

Step 1. Sow seeds in a small tray of vermiculite. Be sure medium is thoroughly damp before seeding. Set seeds about ¼ inch deep and about 2 inches apart. Cover seeds and water lightly. Slip tray into plastic bag and keep at about 75° F. No water is necessary until after germination and then only enough to keep vermiculite damp, not soaked.

Step 2. When the first true leaf is formed the seedlings are ready to go into 3- to 4-inch peat or plastic pots filled with soil mix (see text).

Pull seedling from vermiculite and set in small hole in soil mix so seed leaves (cotyledons) are about ½ inch from soil.

Press soil firmly around roots and stem.

Put pots on a tray and in a plastic bag until ready for hardening off. Wickets of coat hanger wire will keep plastic above plants.

How To Get Them Out

When many plants are grown together the roots intermingle. There is less damage if you pull instead of cut it out.

Turn six-pack over and push bottom of cell with your thumb. Hold soil ball with other hand.

Setting Out Transplants

When transplanting seedlings (whether home-grown or from nursery stock), keep these following points in mind: Use only healthy, compact plants; prepare and water the planting soil ahead of time; after planting, immediately protect the seedlings from heat, wind, and pests.

Choose nursery stock with compact foliage and good leaf color. Avoid leggy plants.

Home-grown seedlings should be "hardened off" for a week or two before being planted outdoors. This means placing them in protected, filtered sun in the morning and bringing them in at night.

When to transplant. Transplanting conditions are best soon after a rain, on a cloudy day, or in late afternoon. These conditions will enable the plants to get established with minimum stress. If you plant on a hot day, however, just set up a simple sunshade of lath or burlap for a day or two. If birds pose a problem, use bird netting, weighted down or buried at the edge.

How to plant transplants. Bury tomato and cabbage seedlings to the first set of leaves; they will root from the stem. Set other plants at the same depth as they were in their original container.

Before setting out the plants, dig and cultivate the soil, adding organic amendments and superphosphate or a complete fertilizer. Remove weeds —if left in the soil, they will interfere with root growth, harbor disease, and rob the soil of nitrogen.

For annuals, if you're using several colors or sizes of plants, smooth the soil surface and mark planting areas with string. Water deeply with a fine spray, and let the water soak in overnight.

If you plant from flats, *pull* the plants apart gently—cutting removes roots but pulling spreads them for quick rooting. Don't squeeze the soil or you will compact it and trap roots inside. Water and let drain any plants in packs or containers before you remove them, or the soil may crumble away. Snip off any long, coiled, bottom roots and carefully loosen side roots with a table fork to direct them outward. Then set the plants into their planting holes and firm the soil gently to remove air pockets. Mulch the ground around the plants; water again; then bait for slugs and snails, or surround the plants with stiff paper collars to ward off cutworms.

After transplanting. To protect your new transplant from sun and wind, prop up a tent of cardboard, a tilted board, or a pile of brush or prunings.

Transplanting

1. Ready the plant. If it's in a peat pot, tear the top edge off so it can't act as a wick and dry out the rootball.

2. If it's in a plastic, fiber, or clay pot, tip it out—don't pull it out by the stem.

3. After planting, firm the soil around the transplant. Then water lightly to settle the soil and remove any air pockets that may be left around the rootball.

4. To be sure the root area stays moist during the first few critical days, build a small temporary basin, a little larger than the root system.

Starting and Caring for Transplants

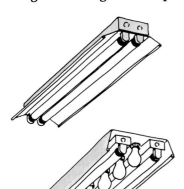

One way to grow a dozen or so tender plants indoors for setting out when the weather is right.

Gro-lamps are available in several sizes and models, or buy fluorescent tubes and make your own. The height of lights above the plants must be adjustable.

Trays protect furniture and make watering easy. All types of "soil" blocks and seed trays can be used.

To prevent fast drying-out of soil and to increase humidity, surround the growing areas with a tent of plastic film.

Good transplant   Leggy transplant

If you are planting tomatoes, both kinds of transplants should be planted deep. Roots will develop along the buried stems.

Cut-off milk cartons make excellent transplant containers; perforate around the bottom for drainage and easy removal when transplanting time comes.

Cut a plastic jug—plant in the bottom section. Use the top for protection when it's needed.

Taking Shrubs and Trees Home from the Nursery

When bringing home a large tree or shrub from the nursery, wrap it with a piece of cloth before letting it hang out of a car window or trunk. This will protect the plant from windburn as you speed down the highway. If possible, have a tree that's 8 feet tall or taller delivered, rather than trying to wedge it into your car.

At the nursery, do not have the can cut unless you intend to install your plant right away. A shrub or tree in a cut can is almost impossible to water properly. Be wary of shrubs and trees that seem much too large for their containers—their roots may have circled into knots. If so, these root-bound plants will never spread into your garden soil. If they live long enough to develop heavy top growth, the wind may knock them down. If you're after fast-growing plants, choose very young ones; 8-foot trees are tempting, but young ones will catch up in a season or two.

When planting time comes around, try simply lifting the plant out of the container. If it won't easily come out of a metal container, cut the can with tin snips or can cutters. Don't knock the can about trying to remove the plant.

Plastic containers and tapered cans usually do not have to be cut. Rather than yanking the plant, simply hold it in place at the top of the rootball and gently nudge the edge of the container. The plant should slip out easily (especially if it has already been watered).

Planting trees and shrubs. For shrubs and trees, dig a hole twice as wide and as deep as the rootball. Into the removed soil, blend an equal amount of organic material. Add superphosphate to the bottom soil. Then fill the hole with water, moisten the improved soil using starter solution, and let it drain overnight. If the water in the hole doesn't drain in a reasonable length of time, dig deeper, or else plant in raised beds (for *small* trees and shrubs).

The depth needs to be just right—not too deep, not too shallow. The planting hole should be just slightly deeper than the rootball; however, put back enough soil so that the plant sits no deeper than it was grown in at the nursery. For 1-gallon plants, dig the hole about 5 inches deeper than the rootball; for 5-gallon plants, about 9 inches deeper.

Planting bare-root trees. Make the planting hole at least 12 inches wider and 6 inches deeper than the spread and depth of the root system.

When digging the hole, set aside the top 6 inches of soil in one pile and most of the subsoil in another. Place the last few shovelfuls in another pile to build a dike around the watering basin later on.

Planting Hole

Width. Dig the hole twice the root-ball diameter or large enough to accommodate bare roots.

Depth. In clay soil, dig 1 to 2 inches deeper than the depth of the rootball or original soil line. In sandy soil or loam, the original soil level should be at or slightly higher than the garden soil.

Be sure bottom soil has settled, sides are straight up and down, roughened-up for easy root penetration, and the bottom is flat or slightly raised in the center (see text).

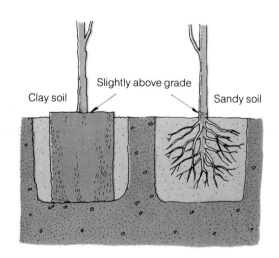

Clay soil

Slightly above grade

Sandy soil

Planting a Bare-Root Tree

Planting hole should be at least 12 inches wider and 6 inches deeper than the spread and depth of the root system.

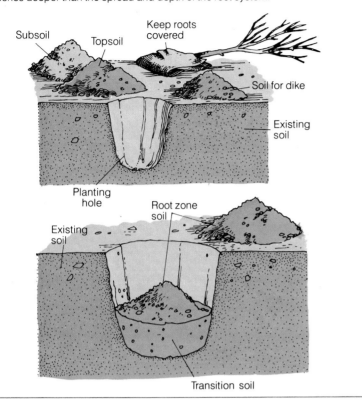

Subsoil — Topsoil — Keep roots covered — Soil for dike — Existing soil — Planting hole — Root zone soil — Existing soil — Transition soil

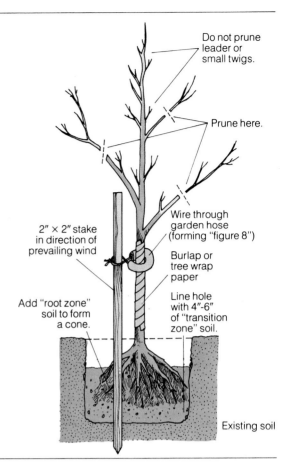

Do not prune leader or small twigs.

Prune here.

2" × 2" stake in direction of prevailing wind

Add "root zone" soil to form a cone.

Wire through garden hose (forming "figure 8")

Burlap or tree wrap paper

Line hole with 4"-6" of "transition zone" soil.

Existing soil

Using the top soil pile, mix up a "root zone" soil by mixing equal parts of organic matter and top soil. Also mix up a "transition soil," using 1 part organic matter to 4 parts soil from the second pile.

Loosen the soil in the bottom of the hole to encourage root penetration and better drainage.

Line the hole with 4 to 6 inches of "transition soil." Using the "root zone" soil, make a cone-shaped mound. Set the root crown at the same depth at which it originally grew (the soil-stained ring at the base of the trunk will give you this information). Work 2 or 3 shovelfuls of "root zone" soil under and around the roots to eliminate air pockets.

Before adding more soil, take a 2- by 2-inch stake about 6 to 8 feet long and drive it 6 inches from the trunk on the side toward the prevailing wind.

Fill the rest of the hole, and build a watering basin by placing a ridge or dike 4 to 5 inches high in a circle 2 to 3 feet away from the trunk.

Protection and pruning. To prevent sunscald, drying of bark, and borer damage, wrap the trunk with tree-wrapping paper, aluminum foil, or strips of burlap.

Prune to balance the top with the reduced root system. In general, cut back side branches about ⅓ their original length. Do not remove twigs and buds along the branches and upper parts of trunk in the first season of growth.

Staking. Newly planted trees and tall shrubs need to be staked for protection against wind damage. While this protection is essential, a tree that is *too* securely staked will not develop natural strength of its own. Therefore, always allow for some movement of the trunk in the wind. Eventually, the plant will be able to support itself, and the stake will no longer be necessary.

To secure the tree to the stake, thread a 12-gauge wire through a short length of garden hose and twist the wire loosely around the trunk. Tie the wire to the stake in the form of a figure eight.

Staking a Bare-Root Tree

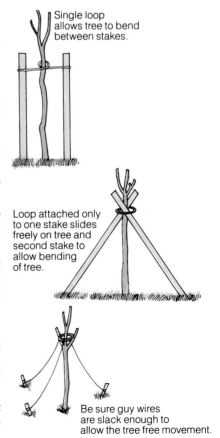

Single loop allows tree to bend between stakes.

Loop attached only to one stake slides freely on tree and second stake to allow bending of tree.

Be sure guy wires are slack enough to allow the tree free movement.

1. Bare-root rose ready for planting. Plant has been reduced to four healthy canes. Cut main roots to reveal white tissue (*not shown*). Resulting scarring will stimulate root growth. **2.** Place roots over a cone of soil and use a level pole to determine position of bud union. **3.** Fill hole with soil and tamp the soil around the roots with your feet. The bud union should be at the level previously determined. **4.** After soil is added and tamped, fill hole with water to settle soil around the roots. **5.** Loosely cover plant with soil to at least two-thirds of its height to protect from sun and wind.

Planting bare-root roses. Although roses can be bought balled-and-burlapped or as container plants, most gardeners buy bare-root plants. Plant these as soon as the weather permits, to give the roots a chance to start growing before the tops break into leaf.

Your bare-root roses may have dried out during the process of storage and shipping by the time you receive them. To plump them out again, bury the roots and tops in wet peat moss or sawdust for two to three days, or soak the plants (both roots and tops) in water overnight. Carry them to the planting area in a wheelbarrow or pail half-filled with water.

Prior to planting, examine roots carefully. Cut off any broken or injured roots. With a pair of pruning shears nip off ¼-inch tips on larger roots. This will promote quicker root formation.

Dig planting holes 1 foot deep, and wide enough to let the roots assume a natural position—usually, 14 to 16 inches. Into the soil that you've dug out, mix in about ⅓ peat moss or other organic matter. Using this soil, build a cone-shaped mound in the hole. This mound should support the roots and hold the plant high enough to keep the bud union at ground level. In areas where winter temperatures are below 10 degrees, the bud union should be 1 to 2 inches below ground level. Fill the hole ⅔ full of soil mixture and tamp to remove air pockets. Fill the remaining depression with water to ground level, and let it soak into the soil.

After the water soaks in, fill the hole with soil mixture, and firm gently. Use more soil mixture to form basins; these will keep water from running off. Spread a 2- to 3-inch layer of peat moss, ground bark, pine needles, sawdust, or other good mulch over the basin area or over the entire garden area. (Renew mulch yearly, as it breaks down quickly.)

Freezing temperatures or hot, drying winds will prevent buds from breaking. If your area is prone to such conditions, mound soil over the bushes, covering all the canes with 8 to 10 inches of soil. Or place a cylinder around the tops and fill with damp peat moss, ground bark, or similar material. Water slowly but thoroughly, and keep the soil moist until the cylinder is removed.

When new shoots form, remove soil or other material.

Watering roses. Two contradictory sayings describe how to water roses: "You can't give a rose too much water," and "Roses can't stand wet feet." But this contradiction is just an apparent one: roses thrive on water—indeed, they will suffer from water stress without it. However, the drainage must be good enough to allow air to remain in the soil. If water fills the soil without draining away, the air is driven out, and the roots drown. If soil in your area tends to be flooded for any period of time, or if the water table is high, consider growing roses in raised beds (see page 56).

Fertilization and insect/disease protection. You can choose from a wide variety of rose-care products, and these can be used in various combinations. Some gardeners like to feed with rose fertilizers and rely on spray-type fungicides to combat disease and insects.

Don't apply sprays to a dry plant—if the leaves lack water, the foliage may be damaged. (A plant that suffers from drought is more susceptible to spider

Planting from Containers

Nurseries sell plants in containers of various materials and shapes. Straight-sided cans should be cut at the nursery if you are going to plant the same day. If you are going to plant at a later date, don't have the can cut; a cut can is almost impossible to keep watered.

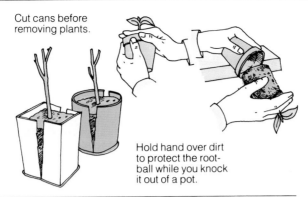

Cut cans before removing plants.

Hold hand over dirt to protect the root-ball while you knock it out of a pot.

After you take the plant out of the container check the roots. If roots circle the soil ball, spread out, or cut the larger roots in two or three places to reduce the possibility of girdling roots later on.

Roots that circle the soil ball within the can must be redirected before planting—pull the roots away from the ball so they extend outward . . .

or cut the larger roots in two or three places.

mite damage as well as damage from sprays.) Don't spray in the heat of midday—do it in early morning, after the dew has evaporated. If you spray with plain water at that time of day, the danger of mite damage and mildew infection will decrease. You won't have to spray for aphids, spider mites, white flies, leafhoppers and other sucking types, and leaf mining insects if you apply systemic rose care products every six weeks. This internal protection gives the plant the power to protect itself from its worst insect enemies, and this protection cannot be washed off by rain or water from sprinklers. Beneficial insects such as ladybugs and bees go unharmed. Systemic insect protection is available alone or combined with rose fertilizer.

Every successful program is based on a continuous supply of plant food and moisture, and protection against insects and disease of the region and the season. Choose the combination that fits your problem and your way of gardening. (For more information on insects and diseases, see pages 74–79.)

Planting from Containers

Plants in containers can be planted any time during the growing season.

Remove the plant from the container and check the roots. If they circle the soil ball, spread them out, or cut the larger roots in two or three places to reduce their chances of girdling later on.

For 1-gallon plants, dig a hole 12 × 12 inches; for 5-gallon plants, 20 × 20 inches. Backfill with soil mix to about 5 inches from soil level for 1-gallon size, 9 inches for 5-gallon size.

Water thoroughly to settle the soil. Remove the plant from the container and set it in the hole. Check to make sure the top of the rootball is at soil level. Fill in around plant with soil mix, packing it lightly as you fill. Build a basin two or three times as wide as the plant ball. Make it 2 or 3 inches deep for shrubs, 4 to 5 inches deep for trees. Spread a 2-inch layer of mulch in the basin.

To make sure that the ball stays moist while the roots are spreading out beyond it, build a small, temporary basin that's slightly larger than the root system. Water every other day for the first ten days in hot weather.

Balled and Burlapped Plants

Prepare the hole and backfill soil as you would for bare-root plants (page 38). Set the plant on a cushion of soil mix so the top of the ball is slightly higher than the surrounding ground.

Leave the burlap on. Cut the twine after the hole is half filled with soil.

Build a watering basin, as with a bare-root tree. Since the water may drain faster through the soil in the backfill than through the rootball, keep the rootball watered by building a small dike a few inches from the trunk, and trickle water near the trunk for 15 to 30 minutes. Repeat weekly for the first month. As soon as the roots enter the soil around the rootball, remove the inner dike and fill the large basin with water every two weeks. Adjust your watering schedule according to the amount of rainfall.

Balled and Burlapped Plants

Remove any burlap extending above soil. Build water basin and soak well. Leave burlap on—when hole is about half filled, cut twine and loosen burlap at top of ball. Hole for balled burlap plant should be about twice as wide as ball. Set rootball slightly higher than soil level.

Tools carefully chosen to meet the
gardener's needs and kept sharp, clean,
and well-oiled will be ready for any task.

GENERAL MAINTENANCE

Proper pruning, weeding, and general grooming give the garden greater immunity to some insects and diseases.

There is a fine line between doing a task routinely and regarding it as mere drudgery. Anyone who goes to the effort of planting a garden will see that effort thoroughly wasted if they don't take the care to maintain that garden. But popular conceptions aside, routine maintenance gardening needn't be dreary if you approach the subject as a labor of love. Cleaning up, pruning, mulching, and weeding may not be as exciting as planning and planting, but they will keep what you've planted in healthy, vigorous condition.

Sanitation Practices

You can give your plants greater immunity to some insects and diseases by carrying out certain sanitation practices. For example, keep the ground beneath trees free of debris by burning or hauling off any old leaves, hulls, or dead twigs in fall or early spring. When mowing your lawn, rake up the clippings so that they don't mat down on top of the grass and form thatch. And if you plan to use the clippings for compost, be sure to turn them over every few days to keep them from rotting and attracting flies.

Tools

As painters value a sable brush, so gardeners value good tools. A good tool is sturdy, suited to a particular type of job, and has a good feel in the hand. It is worth buying quality tools and spending a bit more, if need be. Good tools last longer and make the job more enjoyable. Particularly in tools that need to be sharp to do their work, the quality of the steel in the cutting edges determines the quality of the cuts.

Choosing your tools. As the foregoing advice suggests, steer clear of cheap tools—they will cost you more in the long run. Go for quality every time. Get a personal sense of the tool—lift it, touch it, make an appropriate gesture (e.g., digging, raking, cutting) with it to get the feel of it. Check out the weight of a tool, and the feel of the handles, for ease of use.

Caring for your tools. Your work will go more smoothly if you keep your tools sharp and clean. After each use, dry the blades and rub in a few drops of oil to prevent rust. If the tool has joints, oil them also. If your shears have been tearing plants instead of cutting them, try tightening them. If they won't tighten, they probably have sprung, in which case they are useless and should be thrown away.

It's rare that good-quality shears get out of alignment. It happens only when they are used on branches that are larger than they were designed to cut.

Clean off, dry, and store rakes after use.

Wash, dry, and store shovels and hoes to keep them from getting rusty and dull. For best results, sharpen before each use.

Hoes. You can choose from among a very wide assortment of hoes—the

Garden hoe, 2-1/2"

Garden hoe, 6"

Onion hoe

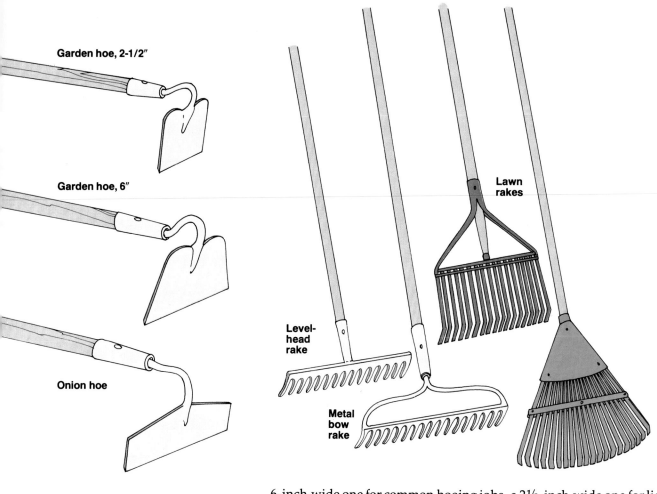

Lawn rakes

Level-head rake

Metal bow rake

Hand pruner

Wide-blade saw

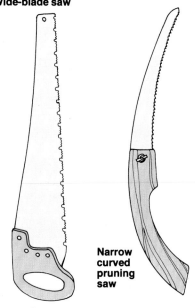

Narrow curved pruning saw

6-inch-wide one for common hoeing jobs, a 2½-inch-wide one for light jobs in narrow places, and even a special scuffle hoe to use with shallow-rooted plants. And for a combination hoe/weeder, there's the weeding hoe. Sharpen your hoe each time before using.

Pruners. *Hand pruners.* These can be used on wood up to ¾ inches thick. Two main types are available: scissor style and anvil style. *Scissor-style pruners* have sharpened blades that overlap when they make the cut. If forced, this type of pruner may make a jagged cut, injuring the plant. However, if you keep them sharp and use them properly, scissor-style pruners will give a close, clean cut.

Anvil-style pruners. These have a sharpened top blade that snaps onto a flat plate of softer metal. This type is lighter and easier to handle than the scissor type, but it always crushes the bark on the anvil side, and it cuts less closely than the scissor type.

Rakes. *Level-head rake.* The flat-topped rake is good for leveling seed beds and making seed furrows, but not for heavy-duty raking.

Metal bow rake. This is what you use for the heavy work: leveling soil or gravel, or making mounds.

Lawn rake. This is the standard rake for raking up grass clippings, leaves, and other lightweight material. Lawn rakes are made of metal and bamboo.

Saws. *Pruning saws.* Used for heavier work, these will cut wood with a diameter of 2 inches or more. Smaller pruning saws have narrow backcutting teeth on a curved blade, which makes them good for working in narrow spaces. The double-edged saw has teeth on both sides: one for coarse cuts and one for fine cuts. However, while you cut with one side, the teeth on the other side may tear the bark of nearby limbs.

Wide-blade saws. Use these for the biggest limbs. They are about the same

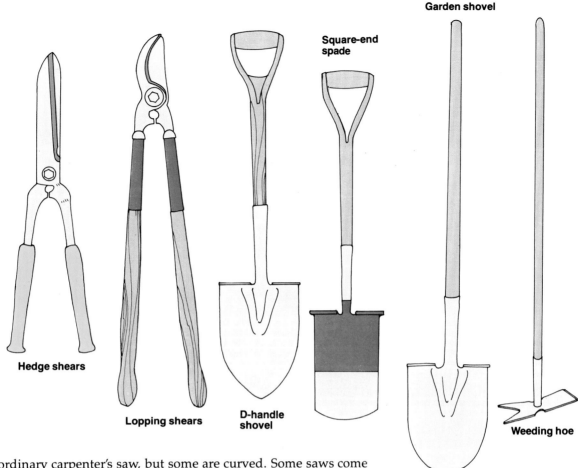

Hedge shears

Lopping shears

D-handle shovel

Square-end spade

Garden shovel

Weeding hoe

size as an ordinary carpenter's saw, but some are curved. Some saws come with both cutting teeth and rakes, such as the Tuttle tooth saw.

Shears. *Hedge shears.* With their long, scissorlike blades, these will trim and shape bushes. But use shears with one notched blade; this will keep the foliage from slipping away. Manual shears are fine for shorter jobs, but for any lengthy pruning task they may be tiring. Instead, consider electric hedge shears, which are faster and easier to use, and allow greater accuracy of line.

Lopping shears. These are actually pruners with long handles that give extra leverage when cutting wood up to 1¼ inches thick. For cutting through wood 1¾ inches thick, use heavy-duty loppers.

Shovels. Shovels come in different sizes, lengths, and shapes.

Long-handled, round-pointed shovel. This popular shovel is used for digging and scooping.

Garden shovel. A near relative of the long-handled, round-pointed shovel, this is also used to dig and scoop, but it is slightly smaller and lighter.

Scoop shovel. Use this to move sawdust or any lightweight material.

D-handle shovel. Use this to move soil, sand, and gravel.

Square-end spade. Used for edging, digging, and cultivating, the square-end spade comes with a long handle or a shorter D-handle. Always sharpen a spade before you use it.

Transplanting spade. Used for transplanting shrubs and moving perennials.

Trowel. It's worth trying out a number of trowels for fit before you buy. Get one that's easy to hold and handle.

Weeders. *Weeding hoe.* This combination tool has a hoe on one side and a weed puller on the other.

Asparagus or dandelion weeder. This special tool is for pulling out taprooted weeds such as dandelions and for weeding in narrow places.

Trowels

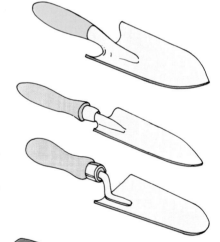

Asparagus or dandelion weeder

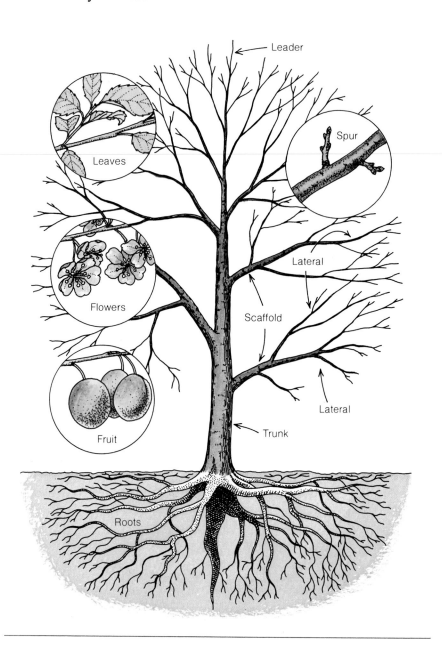

Leader

Spur

Leaves

Lateral

Flowers

Scaffold

Lateral

Fruit

Trunk

Roots

Pruning

When you prune a plant, you are giving it more than just a well-groomed appearance; pruning directs the plant's growth, improves its health, and increases production.

It pays to have some basic knowledge of the parts of a plant. Despite varying appearances, all plants have the same parts: roots, stem or trunk, branches, leaves, flowers, and fruits.

Roots. Roots serve two purposes: they anchor the plant in the soil, and they absorb water and necessary mineral nutrients.

Stem or trunk. A stem or trunk has two pipelike parts. The inner one carries water and minerals from the roots up to the branches, leaves, flowers, and fruit. The outer one carries food down from the leaves to the rest of the plant. In addition, the stem or trunk supports the branches, leaves, flowers, and fruit.

Branches. These bear and support the leaves, flowers and fruits. Branches are named according to where they are on the trunk. The *leader* is the central, highest branch. *Scaffold* branches are the main side branches. *Lateral* branches grow horizontally from scaffold limbs. *Hangers* are lateral fruit-tree branches that drop after bearing the weight of the previous year's crop. The word also refers to unnaturally drooping branches and broken branches that remain in the tree. *Spurs* are the short twigs or branchlets that bear fruits and flowers. *Suckers* are leafy shoots that sprout at the tree's crown or roots. *Water sprouts* are shoots that grow above the pruned parts of a tree.

Leaves. The leaves are where food is manufactured, using energy from the sun.

Flowers and fruits. Flowers are the sexual portion of plants that produce seeds for reproduction.

When to prune. "Prune when your shears are sharp" is one way to answer the when-to-prune question; but in a more serious vein, how *do* you know when it's time to prune? Should it be done in winter or in spring? Before flowering or after?

The answer depends on (1) when the plant flowers, and (2) which kind of growth it flowers on—shoots from the current season; wood from the previous year; or wood two or more years old.

Shoots from the current season. Prune plants that bloom on new shoots *before* the plants bloom. Most roses, for example, begin growing on shoots grown during the current year. If you prune them in the spring before they begin to bloom, this will encourage new growth and more roses.

Wood from the previous year. Many plants, including forsythia, bloom on year-old wood. Prune them *after* flowering. Otherwise, you would be pruning away flowering wood. Indeed, cutting away *all* of last year's wood would mean no flowers at all this year.

Wood two or more years old. You don't need to be as selective in pruning a tree that flowers on wood several years old. Just cut to shorten and strengthen the fruit-bearing branches.

Pinching. Once you have pruned a plant for the year, "pinch" to reduce the amount of pruning needed the following year. "Pinching" is shortening those shoots you don't want for branches by pinching out the tips. This diverts the plant's strength into the branches or buds you want to develop.

Pinching creates denser growth and a more compact plant that may later require thinning.

Where to cut. There are two kinds of buds: terminal and lateral. Terminal buds grow at the tip of a shoot. Lateral buds grow off the sides of the shoot.

Always prune just above a bud. Most of the growth normally takes place in the terminal bud. When you cut off a terminal bud just above a lateral bud, that lateral bud is now at the tip of the stem and will inherit this strength. This situation is called *apical dominance.*

For cutting, choose a lateral bud that points outward. This will cause the new branch produced by the bud to grow out from the trunk, and will open up the plant to receive light and air and grow in an orderly pattern.

For example, if you wanted to prune a 6-foot grandiflora rose bush down to 4 feet and also train it to grow wider and fuller, you would first prune all the stems down to 3 feet, cutting at outside lateral buds. This would cause the branches to stay at a height of about 4 feet for the year. It would grow taller the next year, but you could trim it back again.

Whatever pruning decisions you make, don't make a cut unless you have a good reason, and understand clearly the probable results.

Weeding

Despite all your tender loving care, weeds are likely to crop up in even the best of gardens. Even though some weeds are actually rather attractive, you don't want uninvited plants muscling in on your garden. The best time to

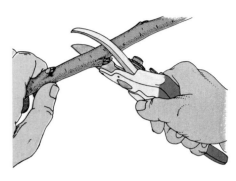

The Correct Cut

Hold the branch below where the cut will be made. Put the cutting blade of your hand pruners under the branch. Cut at an upward angle. The slant of the cut should be in the direction you want the new branch to grow.

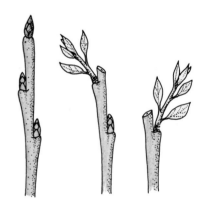

Choosing the Right Bud

Prune by the lateral bud that will produce the branch you want. An outside bud will usually produce an outside branch. The placement of that bud on the stem indicates the direction of the new branch.

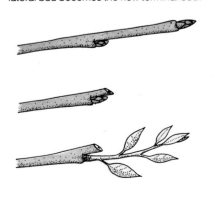

Cutting Off a Terminal Bud

Generally the strongest growth goes into the terminal bud. When you cut it, the closest lateral bud inherits its strength. In fact, that lateral bud becomes the new terminal bud.

Cutting grass with a higher setting on the lawn mower will help keep weeds down.

Above: Crabgrass
Right: Bermudagrass
Top right: Quackgrass

deal with weeds is after spring germination has occurred. And as for the best way to control weeds, you have a choice.

Mulching. The use of an organic mulch will keep the weed population down, but it must be thick enough to keep weed seedlings from going through it on their own stored food. An organic mulch will take care of annual weeds, but not perennial weeds. However, a black plastic mulch will effectively control *all* kinds of weeds and grasses. (For more on mulches, see pages 67–71.)

Hand weeding. Pull up shallow-rooted weeds by pinching them between your fingers at ground level and lifting up firmly. For deep, tap-rooted weeds such as dandelion, dig up the root with a special asparagus or dandelion weeder (see page 45) or a screwdriver. Hand weeding works well if there are only a few weeds. But if you have acres of them, use a more efficient, less time-consuming method.

Mowing. For lawn weeds such as crabgrass, putting your lawn mower at a higher setting will help keep young weeds from becoming established (the taller the grass, the less likelihood there is of sunlight reaching the weed seedlings).

Deep, infrequent watering. To cut down the survival of most weed seedlings, water your lawn and plants deeply and infrequently.

Chemical control. Chemicals can be applied as needed in spot treatments, sprayed to cover the entire garden or a particular group of plants, or put into the soil as a "pre-emergent" weed killer. Of these alternatives, spraying is the least desirable; it should be used as a last resort, and then only on a day without wind.

Left: Chickweed
Above: Dandelion

Common Weeds

There are two kinds of weeds: grassy and broadleaved. Grassy weeds can be killed with pre-emergent weed controls that destroy the seed as it germinates. Broadleaved weeds are killed by chemicals that cause their hormones to speed up growth until the weeds are dead.

Grassy weeds include:

Bermudagrass. This weed outgrows cool-season grasses when the weather is hot.

Control: Set lawn mower at a higher setting, or apply Dalapon carefully (it also can kill the very grasses you want to remain in your lawn).

Crabgrass. This prolific annual weed thrives in hot weather and crowds out other grasses. In fall it turns reddish-brown and dies, but its seeds remain in your lawn, ready to come up the following spring.

Control: Set your lawn mower at a higher setting; or avoid wearing the grass down to dirt; or water deeply and infrequently, as mentioned; or apply a product containing azac, balan, betasan, or dacthal in winter. In spring, treat residual seedlings with a product containing methyl arsonate, disodium methyl arsonate, or calcium methyl arsonate.

Quackgrass. This weed spreads by underground, rooting stems, spreading seeds as it goes, and poisoning other grasses.

Control: Treat infected areas with amino triazole. If so much area gets infected that it requires professional help, ask your local nurseryman to recommend someone.

Broadleaved weeds include dandelions and chickweed, and are best controlled by spot treatments of weed oil (however, keep the oil away from other plants or it will kill them, too). Chemical sprays also can be used. Buy 2,4-D or 2,4,5-TP. Handle it carefully. Spray on a windless day so wind will not carry these hormone sprays to other plants that you don't want killed.

Some lawn fertilizers contain controls for leafy weeds. If you use them, be sure to follow the directions carefully.

SOIL, FERTILIZER, MULCH, AND WATER

A basic working knowledge of these four subjects is essential for successful gardening.

Nongardeners may think of soil as just "dirt"—the stuff you find in playgrounds, under cracked pavement, and (incidentally) in gardens—but to a gardener, soil has a significance and a reality all its own. It is a porous, living structure that enables a plant to spread and anchor its roots, absorb water, ingest food, and breathe air.

There are all kinds of soils, and you want the right kind—the kind that will let you grow the type of plant you want to grow. A favorable soil makes the difference between a successful crop and built-in frustration. Little else can so effectively dampen a gardener's enthusiasm as hard-to-manage soil. Perhaps a firm knowledge of soil, rather than a magical "green thumb," accounts for gardening success.

Although you are likely to find at least some plants that will grow in whatever kind of soil presently exists in your garden, having to meet this condition will limit your selection appreciably. It's not worth trying to live with an unfavorable soil when it's so easy to modify it. For all but the very worst soils, it's relatively simple to change the soil so that it will support a wider variety of plants. Most gardeners try for a happy medium: plants that will grow well in a soil that may require a bit of modification but not a grand-scale conversion.

Soil Defined

Geologists look at soil as the interface between the rock shell of the earth and the living things on its surface. No matter what the soil's color, texture, or composition, soil is something that humans are dependent on for life itself.

Soil scientists focus more specifically on the thin layer of loose material covering the earth's 20- to 30-mile-thick shell. The soil can be anywhere from a few inches to a few feet thick. This layer is composed of mineral elements from weathered rocks, dead and living organic matter, air, and water. It lies on top of a thick layer of solid rock and is constantly changed by the weather, chemical processes, microbes, plants, and humans.

Soil Composition

Soil begins as solid rock exposed at the earth's surface. Over time, the weathering process crumbles the rock into loose material. This material is further broken down by: frost action; expansion and contraction due to temperature changes; the grinding action of streams, glaciers, and wind; and the force of large tree roots. In addition, chemical weathering processes dissolve the rock minerals and bring about chemical changes.

Soil is made up of two types of particles: inorganic and organic, often referred to as the "mineral component" and the "organic component." These particles are composed of weathered and unweathered mineral grains from the original rocks, new minerals that have formed in the soil, living microorganisms, and organic matter in various stages of decay.

Many things can be determined by the "feel" of the soil. A handful of soil that falls apart after being squeezed is dry enough to be spaded or tilled easily.

The mineral component. The mineral component varies in particle size. The largest particle size is found in sand; the smallest is in clay. Rarely is a soil composed of purely one particle size; most often, it is a mixture.

If you want to get an idea of the proportions of particle types in your soil, wet the soil and then rub some of it between your thumb and fingers to determine its "feel." At one extreme is clay, which can be squeezed into a smooth smear. A clay loam smear is not as smooth as a clay's, nor as broken as a silt loam's. Loams give only a very rough smear; sandy loams give scarcely any. At the other extreme are the harsh, gritty sands whose particles scarcely hold together at all. (Loamy sands are gritty, too, but the particles cling together when moist.)

Particle size does more than give the soil a specific texture; it also affects: water percolation; water retention; aeration; supply, release rate, and storage of nutrients; and resistance to chemical and temperature changes.

The mineral component also is what gives a plant most of the essential nutrients it needs for growth.

The organic component. Organic matter, which makes up the organic component, consists of decomposed vegetable and animal matter that makes soil dark colored. Organic matter includes living soil microorganisms, plant roots, manure, animals, insects, leaves, stems, sawdust, and other substances.

All soils contain some organic matter, but in widely varying proportions. No matter what type of soil is in your garden, organic matter will improve it. The beneficial property of organic matter is due largely to the countless microorganisms that inhabit the soil. These microorganisms use the organic matter for food, as a source of energy. First they use the nutrients; then they pass them on in a form that plants can use. Although the organic matter that is naturally in the soil contains nitrogen, plants can use virtually none of it until the microorganisms have converted the organic matter into a form of inorganic "available" nitrogen.

It takes newly added organic matter from months to years to finish undergoing its chemical changes. The end result is humus, a mixture of partially decomposed vegetable matter and available mineral elements.

Organic matter influences the structure as well as the fertility of the soil. When mixed into clay soils, organic matter improves drainage and air flow, which warms the soil earlier in spring. When mixed into sandy soils, organic matter increases the moisture- and nutrient-holding ability of the root zone. Indeed, no matter what the soil type, adding organic matter makes the soil easier to work by giving it a soft and loamy consistency— what the old-timers refer to as a "mellow" soil.

Texture. The texture of a soil is determined by the size and proportion of the mineral component—sand, silt, and clay, from largest to smallest. Since soil is rarely 100 percent sand, silt, or clay, scientists have created hybrid categories to help gardeners classify their soils. Determined by the percentages of sand, silt, and clay they contain, these categories are: loamy sand, sandy loam, silty loam, loam, sandy clay loam, clay loam, silty clay loam, sandy clay, and silty clay.

The easiest soils to handle are those with intermediate textures—that is, sandy loams, loams, and silt loams. These also make the best garden soils. Sand, silt, and clay occur in the right proportions to balance their effects on water retention and drainage, aeration, and nutrient supply. These properties enable loam soils to support a wide variety of crops.

To find out the texture of your soil, try this simple experiment: Fill a quart jar about ⅔ full of water. Add soil until the jar is almost full. Screw on the jar top and shake the jar vigorously, then let the soil settle. Soon the heaviest sand particles will sink to the bottom and the sand layer will become visible. However, the silt and clay particles will take hours to settle out. The very fine

An easy way to determine your soil structure is to fill a quart jar two-thirds full of water and then add soil until the jar is nearly full. Shake the jar and let the soil settle. The heavy sand particles will soon sink to the bottom, but the lighter and finer clay and silt particles will take considerably longer to settle. The stratification in the jar will give you a general idea of the composition of your soil.

Note: To achieve the best stratification, use about 1 teaspoon of a wetting agent or liquid detergent per quart of water. Or add a little water softener which contains such an agent.

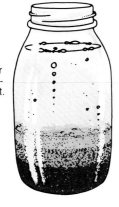

Soil Texture

Sand, silt, and clay are designations based on the size of mineral particles found in soil. The texture of soil is determined by the proportions of these various-sized particles (here enlarged about 30x).

Diameter of Particles

	Clay	Silt	Sand
Clay	60–100%	0-40%	0-20%
Loam	20–30%	30–50%	30–50%
Silt	0–15%	85–100%	0–15%
Sand	0–10%	0–10%	80–100%
Loamy sand	10–15%	10–15%	70–80%
Sandy loam	15–25%	15–25%	50–70%
Silty loam	5–20%	70–85%	10–25%
Sandy clay loam	30–40%	5–30%	40–55%
Clay loam	30–60%	35–60%	5–35%
Silty clay loam	30–40%	40–55%	5–30%
Sandy clay	40–55%	0–15%	45–60%
Silty clay	40–60%	40–60%	0–20%

Clay
Less than 1/12,500 inch

Silt
1/12,500 to 1/500 inch

Fine Sand
1/500 to 1/250 inch

Medium Sand
1/250 to 1/50 inch

Coarse Sand
1/50 to 1/12 inch

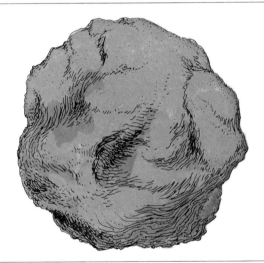

clay particles are so small that the molecular action of water itself will keep them in suspension indefinitely. (To hasten stratification, add about 1 teaspoon of water softener to the jar.)

Do this test several times with soil from different places in your garden. Then chart each soil sample by marking off the layers on a piece of paper held up to the jar. Finally, compare your results with the chart shown here. If the particles divide into about 40 percent sand, 40 percent silt, and 20 percent clay, you have loam and don't need to modify your soil. If your soil falls into another classification, you may want to amend it with organic matter (see pages 57–61).

Clay soil. Clay soils have the smallest-sized particles, and thus retain moisture well—too well, in fact; unable to let water drain through sufficiently, they can puddle up and become compacted. Consequently, the roots of plants growing in clay soil frequently do not receive sufficient air. In such cases, the plants simply die.

If your soil is clay, you can improve its texture by adding large amounts of organic matter. This will cause the particles of clay to form small granules and crumbs, and make the soil easier to work. In addition, it will improve drainage and air flow, and allow the soil to warm up earlier in spring.

Sandy soil. Sandy soils are at the opposite extreme from clay soils—their particles are so large that water rushes right through them. This robs plants of water and nutrients, and discourages roots from taking hold.

Again, the answer is to add organic amendments. The more organic matter you add to a sandy soil, the more you increase its ability to retain moisture and nutrients.

Loamy soil. Loamy soil is considered the ideal gardening soil. It has a balanced proportion of particle sizes, which makes for good water retention and drainage, aeration, utilization of nutrients, and general plant vigor. Loamy soil is good for growing many different kinds of plants.

A loam that has a dominant proportion of sand is called a sandy loam. A loam that has more clay in it is called a clay loam, and so on. The more the loam loses its balance—that is, the more a particular particle size predominates—the less strictly "loamy" the soil becomes, and the more it needs organic matter to restore the balance.

Acidity and Alkalinity

Soils can be acid, neutral, or alkaline. Most plants do well in a slightly acid soil, but a too-acid soil needs to be neutralized with lime or gypsum. Since each garden soil can rarely be suited to all plants, choose the acid/alkaline value that will do for most of your plants. With container plants, however, give each individual plant the kind of soil it likes best.

The task of balancing a soil's acidity or alkalinity is fairly simple. In the past, veteran gardeners simply added ground chalk or marl (a limey clay) to correct a "sour" (acid) soil, left highly alkaline soils unfarmed, and added acidulous organic matter (for example, pine needles or certain peats) to

Soil Acidity Chart (pH)

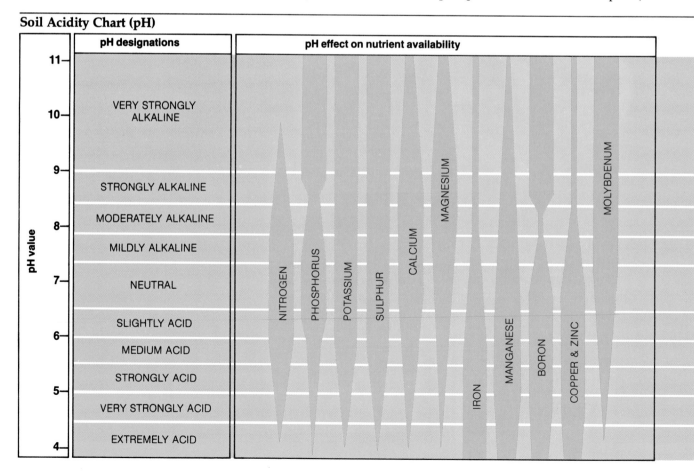

moderately alkaline soil. Modern technology offers us more sophisticated solutions, but they are based on the same principles as they were long ago.

pH tests. The measurement of a soil's acidity or alkalinity is called pH (pronounced pee-aitch). A soil's pH will affect plant growth in terms of four factors: (1) availability of essential nutrients; (2) growth of soil microorganisms; (3) efficiency of root cells (which affect the root's ability to absorb water and nutrients); and (4) solubility of toxic substances.

The pH scale indicates the relative acidity or alkalinity of a given substance. 0 means "extremely acid," 14 means "extremely alkaline," and 7 means "neutral." In order to know whether to tamper with your soil's acidity or alkalinity, you first need to know what its pH is and what it should be. As a general rule, garden vegetables, most of the common annual flowers, most lawn grasses, and many perennials and shrubs do best in slightly to very slightly acid soil (a pH of about 6). Most garden soils have a pH of between 4.5 and 7 (above 7 in much of the arid West).

To find out the pH of your soil, you can have a professional laboratory do a soil analysis. Or you can use a commercial kit that you can purchase through your nursery, a scientific supply store, or catalogs. Or you can get a rough idea by means of the following experiment.

Go out into your garden and dig up some soil from under the surface. Dig in two or three locations. Mix the collected samples together in a clean bucket. Over this pour distilled water purchased from the market. Into this mud place several pieces of blue litmus paper and wait about 10 seconds. Now remove one piece of paper and rinse it off with distilled water. If it is already pink, your soil is very acid.

If the first piece of litmus paper is still blue, wait another 5 minutes, and then remove a second piece of litmus paper. If it shows pink, it means that your soil needs to be made less acid, but not as drastically as if the color had changed immediately.

Soil Acidity Chart (pH)

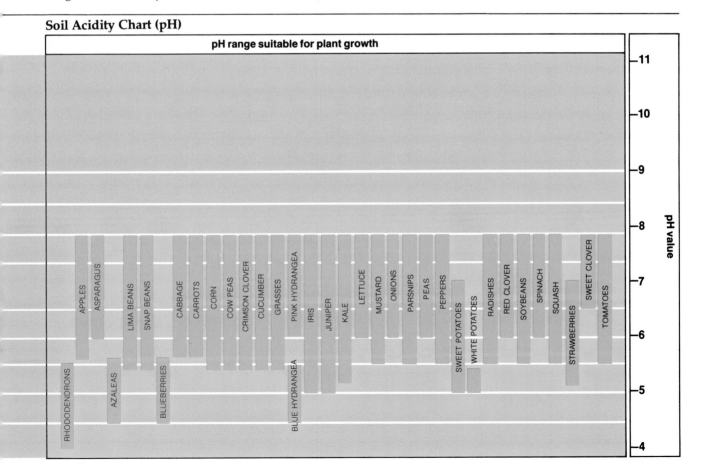

Raised Beds

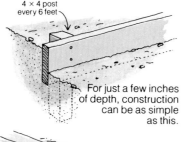

4 × 4 post every 6 feet

For just a few inches of depth, construction can be as simple as this.

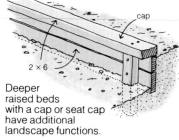

cap

2 × 6

Deeper raised beds with a cap or seat cap have additional landscape functions.

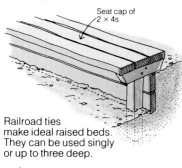

Seat cap of 2 × 4s

Railroad ties make ideal raised beds. They can be used singly or up to three deep.

Railroad ties

Rock walls are less stiff and harsh than wooden raised beds—and you can plant in the cracks.

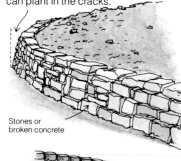

Stones or broken concrete

Short lengths of logs, poles or grapestakes driven into the soil

Another 10 minutes later, remove a third piece of litmus paper. If it is still blue or nearly blue, your soil probably does not need to be limed.

Acid soil. Acid soils are most prominent in areas that experience heavy rainfall, such as the Pacific Northwest and the eastern seaboard. The sulfuric acid in rain is good for plants, providing mineral nutrients. Some plants love acid soil—for example, blueberries, camellias, azaleas, rhododendrons, pieris, ternstroemia, and hydrangeas—but for the most part plants prefer a soil that is only slightly acid, or neutral. For a too-acid soil (a pH of 6.0 or below), the most frequent cure is to "lime" the soil by adding finely ground dolomitic limestone. The heavier the soil, the more lime you will need. Follow application instructions, and check the pH level every two or three years. If necessary, apply more lime at that time.

Alkaline soil. Alkaline soils are found in arid desert regions, and are caused by too much calcium and sodium. To correct a moderately or mildly alkaline condition, add powdered sulfur or an acid mulch (pine needles, sawdust, or acid peat). Or you might add fertilizers containing ammonia, such as ammonium sulfate.

However, if your soil is extremely alkaline, the best remedy is to use raised beds or containers filled with a synthetic soil mix (see page 60).

Improving Soils

If your soil is less than ideal in terms of particle size, pH value, or drainage capability, it's worth your while to make the necessary modifications. An improved soil equals an improved crop. It's as simple as that.

Drainage and water retention. A soil must do more than just receive water; it must also allow the water to drain through it. When water flows through the soil, roots get a continuous supply of nutrients and oxygen. But when water remains stationary in the soil, plant roots suffocate. A well-drained soil lets water carrying dissolved nutrients move through, and also lets adequate air reach the root zone.

As with most aspects of gardening, however, balance is the objective. You don't want water to move through too slowly, as it does in *clay* soils, which have a high water-retention capacity. Nor do you want the water to move through too rapidly, as it does in *sandy* soils, which have such a low water-retention capacity that the water frequently washes the nutrients right out of the soil. The ideal drainage situation is illustrated by *loamy* soils, which absorb almost all the water they receive and, if there is an excess, allow it to drain away.

Determining the drainage capacity of your soil. To find out how much water and air your soil will hold, try the following tests:

To determine the soil's *water-holding capacity:* Gather three different samples of soil and let them dry completely. Then put them in three clay pots, filling them to within an inch of the top but without tamping down the soil. Position each pot over a jar with a funnel in its opening (see illustration). Now pour a pint of water into each clay pot and observe how long it takes for the water to start dripping into the jars below, and also how much water appears in the jar. Compare the water-retention capacity of soils from different parts of your garden by comparing how much water is left in the soil (that is, what has not dripped through) once the dripping has stopped.

To determine the soil's *drainage capacity:* Wait until the pot has just stopped dripping. This means that the soil is completely saturated—it can't hold any more water. Now pour another pint of water into the container, and see how much time it takes the full pint of water to move through the soil and collect in the jar beneath.

Raised beds. A soil that drains poorly needs to be improved, but if you don't want to modify all the soil in the garden you can save yourself time and expense by building a raised bed and putting improved soil into it. The raised bed offers a variety of advantages, not the least of which is that since it is above ground level, it won't get waterlogged by rain or hose water.

Amendments. Adding amendments to a soil enriches the soil and makes it more able to hold moisture and nutrients. You can use organic amendments or mineral amendments.

Organic amendments. The only way to change a heavy clay soil or a light sandy soil into a rich, loamy soil is to add lots of organic matter. Many materials that can be used as mulches on top of the soil can also be mixed into the soil; for example, compost, peat moss, manure, sawdust, and ground bark. (See pages 68–69 for more on these materials.) The addition of organic matter will make clay soil more porous, improving its drainage and air flow, and will make sandy soil more able to hold moisture and nutrients in the root zone. Indeed, although some soils require the addition of organic matter, it never hurts to add it to any kind of soil.

However, don't confuse adding large quantities of organic matter with doing long-term soil improvement. It's the latter that causes organic matter to break down into true humus—the final, black, sticky material that holds soil particles together in crumbs.

Garden waste material is collected and treated to form the black, crumbly, fragrant, partially digested organic residue called compost. The advantages

An example from the Old Westbury demonstration gardens in New York reflects the advantages of the raised bed for the gardener with soil and water problems: it establishes a structure in which the gardener can effectively apply basic gardening laws and within which soil conditioning can be concentrated.

Water Retention and Drainage

The following two tests can be used to determine the water-holding capacity of a given soil, as well as its drainage potential (see text for details):

1. Clay pots filled with different mixtures of soil and amendments—use the same size of jar to measure results accurately.

2. The coffee can test is carried out directly on the soil.

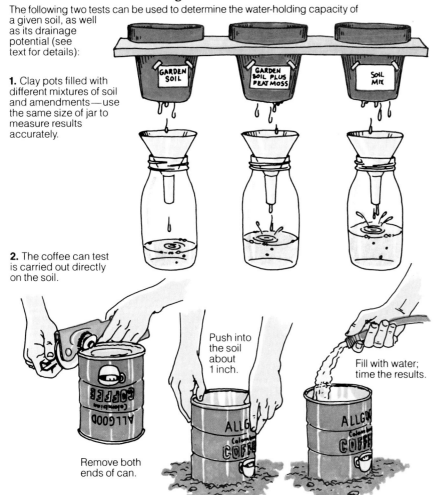

Remove both ends of can.

Push into the soil about 1 inch.

Fill with water; time the results.

This compost bin provides compartments for daily waste, fast-working compost, and compost ready or nearly ready for use. It also provides the air circulation so important for proper decomposition. A board or two across the top provides a shelf for plant display.

of using compost are many: microorganisms that attack the compost produce nitrates, which are an important element of plant food; humus, the end-product of composting, is an excellent soil conditioner; and the ingredients for making a compost heap are easy to come by—kitchen waste, plant clippings, twigs, and so forth.

However, there are also disadvantages: you can't count on compost to provide all the trace elements necessary for plant growth (it depends on how long the heap stands before you apply it to the soil); and you need to pay attention to a compost heap—you have to turn the ingredients over periodically, especially if grass clippings are included.

To build a compost pile you can use a mixture of moist and dry materials. Moist materials include grass clippings, green weeds, lettuce leaves, pea vines, and other succulent materials. The sugar and proteins in these materials provide excellent nutrients for the bacteria that break down the soil, and they decompose quickly. Dry materials include sawdust, dry leaves, small twigs, and prunings. These contain very little nitrogen, and when composted alone they decompose very slowly. This is why a mixture of moist and dry materials works best.

How quickly dry material decomposes depends on its size. Large leaves and pieces of wood material take longer to decompose. You can speed up the decomposition process by shredding the material first.

When composting grass clippings, mix them thoroughly into the composting material to avoid odor and fly problems. Then spread a layer of soil or old compost over the top of the pile.

The most convenient way to compost is to make three piles or compartments. The first is for the waste products you collect daily, such as vegetable scraps from your harvest, vegetable matter from the kitchen, coffee grounds, egg shells, shredded paper, small prunings, wood ashes, green weeds, and dry weeds. The second is for the fast-working compost (make no additions here), which gets turned often. And the third is for the finished or almost finished humus.

In building the compost pile, many gardeners prefer to put a layer of mixed fertilizer, manure, and garden soil between each layer of waste material. First spread a layer of waste material about 6 to 8 inches deep. Then apply a layer of the manure-fertilizer-soil mix (for fertilizer, use about 2

Soil amendments: **1.** Vermiculite **2.** Sand **3.** Bark **4.** Perlite **5.** Peat moss. **6.** One of several synthetic soils available is Jiffy-Mix.

cups of ammonium sulfate or blood meal per square foot—more with dry material, less with green).

Now wet down the fertilizer layer—but sparingly, just enough to carry the chemicals through the layer.

Now add another layer of waste material, spread another layer of manure-fertilizer-soil mix, and wet it down again. Repeat this process until you run out of material, or until the pile is 4 to 5 feet high.

Keep the pile as wet as a wrung-out sponge. If the climate is warm and dry, you may have to water the pile every four to five days.

Under normal conditions, turn the pile in two to three weeks, and then about every five weeks after that. It should be ready to use in three months.

Mineral amendments. Mineral amendments include vermiculite, perlite, sand, lime, and gypsum. They are used to make a heavy soil (fine particle structure) more porous. Once added, they are fairly permanent and do not need to be replaced. Mineral amendments are heavy, bulky, and expensive, but for small areas and containers they can be worth the effort and expense.

Vermiculite, a flaky mineral, resembles mica as it is mined. When expanded by heat it increases its volume by twenty times. Vermiculite helps the soil receive air, water, and nutrients. It decomposes more quickly than perlite.

Perlite, initially a granitelike volcanic material, expands to roughly twenty times its volume when heat-treated. Like vermiculite, it helps aerate the soil and absorbs water.

Sand helps to aerate the soil. Among the varieties of sand available, washed and screened quartz sand is preferable for gardening use.

Lime is used to make a too-acid soil more alkaline, and can be obtained from a variety of materials. The best of these, however, is finely ground dolomitic limestone (also called magnesium limestone).

Gypsum, like lime, is used to neutralize acid soils. It also helps break up heavy clay soil to let water drain through.

How to add amendments. You must add enough soil amendments to physically change the soil's structure. This means that at least one-third of the final mixture should be amendments.

Wait until you are ready to prepare the soil for planting. Then, on top of the soil you want to improve, spread a layer of amendment material that's at least 2 inches thick. Over that, spread fertilizer (see pages 62–67). Then work it all in to a depth of 6 inches.

If you find it too expensive to treat the entire garden in this manner, you can treat only the area where you intend to plant, add the amendment to the individual planting holes, or use a raised bed.

Digging. Amendments can be added manually or by machine. For small areas, dig with a spade to turn the soil over. Use your feet; balance with one foot and push the tool straight down into the soil with the other. For best results, keep the blade sharp.

Once the soil is loosened, use a scoop-shaped shovel to mix or turn loose material such as soil and amendments. Because the shovel is pointed, it can easily slide into the material; because the blade is concave, it can hold the material securely.

Tilling. For large areas, digging by hand may prove too tiring. In that case, consider using a power tiller. You can buy or rent large or small tillers that range from hand-held to tractor models. Whichever type you end up using, be careful not to overuse it or else the soil particles will become so fine that the first rain will produce a garden full of mud. Then the soil will dry and the surface will crust over.

In addition, make sure not to till when the soil is too wet. Feel the soil with your fingers; if you can crumble it apart with your fingers, it's tilling time.

Synthetic soils. An alternative to using either organic or mineral amendments is to add a synthetic soil to your garden soil or replace it entirely. "Synthetic," in this context, does not mean "artificial" but "put together by humans." The ingredients are wholly natural.

Synthetic mixes are available under such names as Jiffy-Mix, Pro Mix, and Redi-Earth. Jiffy-Mix, the most widely obtainable, is made up of 50 percent peat moss and 50 percent vermiculite. It contains just enough nutrients to sustain a plant's initial growth. Use it to germinate seeds, to grow flower and vegetable transplants, and for container plants.

Such mixes provide rapid drainage, good aeration, and a reservoir of water in the soil after drainage.

Air and water retention. The amount of air left after drainage, as well as the water-retention properties of various mixes and their ingredients, has been measured. The figures shown in the table indicate percent by volume. For comparison, physical properties of clay are also shown.

Additional advantages. Synthetic mixes are free of disease organisms, insects, and weed seeds. Many of the disease problems presented by regular soil never crop up when you use a synthetic mix.

Also, synthetic mixes are lightweight—about half the weight of regular soil. This comes in handy if you are gardening in containers, on roofs, or on balconies.

How to use. You can use the mix straight from the bag, but be sure to wet it thoroughly before using. Especially if your mix contains dry peat moss, try putting the desired amount into a plastic bag, adding warm water, and then squeezing and mixing the bag by hand. Better yet, add the water and let the bag sit overnight before using the mix.

One 4-cubic-foot bag will fill the following number of pots:

2½-inch-square Jiffy pots: 1,144
3-inch-square Jiffy pots: 388
3-inch-round Jiffy pots: 427

One 4-cubic-foot bag will fill a planter box 24 inches wide by 36 inches long by 8 inches deep.

Jiffy pots are molded from a mixture of 70 percent peat moss and 30 percent wood fiber, to which soluble fertilizers are added. Transplants grown in Jiffy pots can be set out in the garden, pot and all. There is no transplant shock or check in growth.

Air and Water Retention

Material	% Total Porosity	% Water Retention	% Air Space After Drainage
Clay loam	59.6	54.9	4.7
Sphagnum peat moss	84.2	58.8	25.4
Fine sand	44.6	38.7	5.9
Redwood sawdust	77.2	49.3	27.9
Perlite, 1/16″–3/16″	77.1	47.3	29.8
Vermiculite, 0″–3/16″	80.5	53.0	27.5
Fir bark, 0″–1/8″	69.5	38.0	31.5
1:1, fine sand: fir bark	54.6	37.4	15.2
1:1, fine sand: peat moss	56.7	47.3	9.4
1:1, perlite: peat moss	74.9	51.3	23.6

1. Begin by gathering all the basic ingredients you'll be using.

2. Measure each ingredient into a separate pile.

3. Start the blending process by combining all the ingredients into a single pile.

4. Rebuild the pile three to five times until all the ingredients are thoroughly distributed.

If you are using the mix in large containers, try adding sand (about 10 percent) to give it enough weight to keep plants from tipping over in a wind.

Many gardeners add topsoil to the mix when planting shrubs and trees in containers. Although this creates a soil of good physical properties, it destroys all the advantages of the sterile mix. If you grow tomatoes in containers to avoid damage from soil-borne disease, don't add any topsoil to the mix.

If you need a large amount of soil mix—for example, to plant a number of trees and shrubs, or to fill a raised bed, try making your own. Choose either of the following proportions:

5. The final mix is ready to use or can be stored if it is completely dry.

9 cubic feet of fine sand
18 cubic feet of ground bark or nitrogen-stabilized sawdust
or
9 cubic feet of fine sand
9 cubic feet of peat moss
9 cubic feet of ground bark.
Add to either of these:
5 pounds of 5-10-10 fertilizer
7 pounds of ground limestone
1 pound of iron sulphate

Mixing soils. To mix sand, peat moss, ground bark, and fertilizers:

1. Dampen the peat moss, then pour it, the ground bark, and the sand in a rough pile. Sprinkle the fertilizer and lime on top.

2. Shoveling from the first pile, make a cone-shaped pile by pouring each shovelful directly on top, so that the ingredients dribble down the sides.

3. Shoveling from the second pile, again make a cone-shaped pile so that the ingredients dribble down the sides.

4. Repeat this process once again. When the third cone-shaped pile is ready, it can be used.

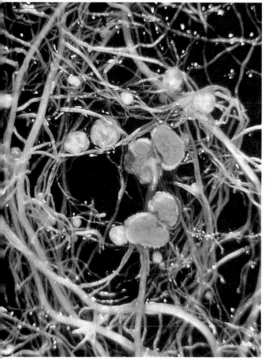

Top: Nitrogen is "fixed" in the roots of certain plants within the nodules. The process involves a symbiotic relationship between the plant and specific strains of bacteria in the soil which provide the plant with nitrogen.

Bottom: This garden plot was planted in the fall with a cover crop that was power tilled under the following spring. This process returns nutrients and organic matter to the soil.

Fertilizing

Like humans, plants need food—and on a fairly regular basis. While it's true that most soils already contain organic and mineral nutrients, for the most part these nutrients exist in forms that plants cannot use. And where they can, the nutrients are not supplied at a fast enough rate to keep the plants growing adequately. Therefore, gardeners add fertilizers to keep their plants healthy and vigorous.

No matter what their form, all fertilizers contain some or all of the nutrient elements that plants need in order to grow. There are 16—possibly 17—chemical elements that plants need for growth, and all must be present; the absence of even a single one of these elements will keep the plant from growing. The elements are grouped into four categories: (1) carbon, hydrogen, and oxygen (which come primarily from the atmosphere and water); (2) nitrogen, phosphorus, and potassium (the "macronutrients"); (3) calcium, magnesium, and sulfur (the "secondary nutrients"); and (4) boron, chlorine, copper, iron, manganese, molybdenum, and zinc (the "micronutrients"). A fifth category is made up by the seventeenth element, cobalt, which is thought to be needed by some plants.

Of all these, it is nitrogen, phosphorus, and potassium that are considered the three mineral elements that plants most need to grow. A fertilizer is said to be "complete" when it contains a percentage of each.

Nitrogen. Plants usually absorb more nitrogen from the soil than they do other elements. It's nitrogen that produces rapid plant growth and gives the leaves and stems a healthy, deep green color. If a plant has insufficient nitrogen, the newer shoots will use up whatever nitrogen there is, causing the older leaves to turn yellow. To right this imbalance, add a fertilizer. There are both organic and inorganic nitrogen fertilizers (see pages 63–65).

Phosphorus. Plants need phosphorus during all phases of their growth. However, this element is particularly needed by crops at the time of early maturity, during the formation of seeds and fruit. It increases root growth and encourages the development of disease resistance.

If a plant lacks enough phosphorus, the younger tissues will steal whatever there is from the older tissues. Insufficient phosphorus is indicated if the lower (therefore older) leaves are too light (lack of chlorophyll) or too dark (a green or reddish color).

To give your plants enough of this element: (1) keep soil pH at levels between 6.0 and 7.0 (see page 54); (2) apply phosphorus in "bands" below soil level, near the root zone (phosphorus doesn't move down to the roots but rather is fixed at the place where it is added); (3) when planting trees and shrubs, mix a phosphorus fertilizer or complete-formulation fertilizer into the soil dug out for the planting hole, and return the soil back to the root-zone level; (4) water well to maximize the available phosphorus; and (5) add phosphorus in early-spring plantings, since it is least available in cool weather.

Potassium. Potassium, or potash, is essential for plants, which absorb large amounts of this element from the soil. Potassium helps plants in a variety of ways: in some plants, it increases disease resistance; it helps oil-bearing plants form oil-bearing seeds; it improves stalk rigidity; it helps plants overcome poor weather or soil conditions; and it generally makes plants more vigorous.

Unfortunately, plants cannot make much use of the potassium in most soils; indeed, whatever potassium is in the soil is easily leached out, especially if the soil is lightweight and fast-draining, as in container plants. To replace the potassium that is leached out from the soil, add potassium on an annual basis.

Often it is hard to tell whether your plants have a potassium deficiency.

The most common symptom—a general reduction in growth—is just about invisible unless you compare the size of the plant with the size of others that are growing in a similar place and that are getting sufficient potassium. And a reduction in growth doesn't necessarily point to a potassium deficiency; it can just as easily mean other nutrient deficiencies. Unfortunately, once potassium deficiency is severe, it is already too late: further applications won't help, especially with short-season, fast-growing annuals and vegetables.

To supply your plants with adequate potassium, use a complete fertilizer and follow a general fertilization procedure (see page 65).

Organic Fertilizers

Organic fertilizers improve soil structure and release plant nutrients slowly, which reduces the possibility of overfertilizing (a definite advantage for new, overzealous gardeners). However, those with a low percentage of nitrogen are bulkier and heavier to handle, since they must be applied in greater quantities. How well they work depends on how warm the soil gets and the level of soil-microbe activity, so the schedule on which these fertilizers work is unpredictable. Liquid forms, such as fish emulsion fertilizer, are used for container plants. Compost and manure are used on lawns, roses, and vegetables.

Bone meal. Bone meal decomposes slowly and releases phosphorus slowly. Use it for bulbs that don't sprout until several months after planting, or dig it into the loose dirt at the bottom of a hole where a bulb is planted.

In addition, its alkalinity helps neutralize the acidity of peat-based synthetic soil mixes, and is useful for alkaline-loving plants such as cacti and succulents.

Cottonseed meal. This somewhat acidic by-product of cotton manufacturing is used to fertilize acid-loving plants such as azaleas, camellias, and rhododendrons. For general garden use, apply 2 to 5 pounds per 1,000 square feet.

Blood meal. Dried, powdered blood from cattle slaughterhouses is a rich source of nitrogen—indeed, almost too rich; be careful not to overuse it. Blood meal also supplies certain of the essential trace elements, including iron.

Fish emulsion. This blend of partially decomposed, finely pulverized fish is high in nitrogen, and also contains several trace elements. Boost plant growth by applying it in late spring, when plants have already sprouted. Be careful not to use too much of it, or it can burn your plants.

Manures. Horse, cow, pig, chicken, and sheep manure are all usable. Fresh manures have more nutrients, but aged or composted manures have fewer salts, which means that the plants are less likely to be burned. Do not use fresh manure where it will come into contact with tender roots. Chicken manure is particularly strong, so use it sparingly.

Compost. The end product of the compost pile is called "humus." Mature humus is a mixture of partially decomposed vegetable matter. Organic wastes containing nitrogen are broken down by microorganisms to produce nitrates and ammonia. Green plant material makes especially good compost. If your starting compost material lacks sufficient nitrogen, sprinkle a few handfuls of a high-nitrogen commercial fertilizer into the compost heap to start things off.

Green manure. Also known as a "cover crop," green manure plant material is grown just so that it can be tilled back into the soil to improve the soil's physical structure, increase the organic-matter content, and increase soil fertility. Cover crops include alfalfa; ladino clover; sweet clover; red clover; kudzu; white clover; ryegrass (in the northern states); crimson clover, horse

One of the most apparent signs of potassium deficiency in plants is a general slowing of growth. However, it is difficult to tell if a plant is suffering from such a deficiency unless you compare it to a similar plant that is growing normally. In the photograph, the leaf on the left is from a healthy plant; the other leaf indicates a plant's potassium deficiency.

bean, and rough pea (in the southern states); and bitter vetch and common vetch (in the West). Till any of these crops into the soil shortly before they reach full maturity. If the soil has very low fertility, apply a commercial fertilizer during the growing season.

Inorganic Fertilizers

All commercial fertilizers are labled with the percentages they contain of nitrogen, phosphorus, and potassium. There are many listings—for example, 24-4-8, 5-10-10, 12-6-6, and 16-16-16—but the listings are always in the same order: nitrogen, phosphorous, and potassium. In general, the percentage of nitrogen in the formula tells you how much fertilizer to apply.

Common fertilizer forms. Inorganic fertilizers come in different forms: dry, liquid, slow-release, pelleted, and soluble, among others. Both the variety of forms and the variety of formulations lets you choose according to your own preferences. You may like a dry fertilizer to mix with a soil mix, or a liquid fertilizer to apply from a hose sprayer. Still others may opt for a slow-release fertilizer that needs to be applied only infrequently. No particular kind of fertilizer is better than another; the decision depends on what kind of plant you are growing and what kind of application preference you have.

Simple or single-nutrient fertilizers. Actually, these should be used only by experienced gardeners: if too much is applied, plants will be damaged, and other nutrient needs may tend to be overlooked. When a specific nutrient is needed, however, these fairly inexpensive, concentrated, low-bulk fertilizers are practical. They usually are sold in dry form. Popular examples include ammonium sulfate, urea, superphosphate, triple superphosphate, ammonium nitrate, and muriate of potash.

Slow-release fertilizers. These labor-saving fertilizers let you apply more at once, thus reducing the frequency of applications. And since the plants absorb the food gradually, they do not suffer from shock. Slow-release fertilizers are expensive, however, and nutrients may be released at an inconstant, somewhat unpredictable rate. Popular examples include Osmocote, MagAmp, IBDU, and ureaform. Use Osmocote and MagAmp with container plants and hanging baskets; use ureaform and IBDU for lawns.

Fertilizers combined with insecticides or herbicides. These convenient fertilizers let you fertilize and kill weeds or insects at the same time. However, timing can pose a problem: when it's time to fertilize, it isn't always the best time to control weeds. Therefore, use this type of fertilizer for problems that require pesticide treatment. Many popular lawn fertilizers are available in this form.

Soluble complete fertilizers. Because these fertilizers are 100 percent soluble in water, the nutrients they contain are ready for the plant to use right away. Apply these fertilizers in early spring, while the soil is still cool. However, be careful: applying too much can burn the leaves, and applying too infrequently will starve the plants between feedings. Follow label directions carefully. Popular examples include Hyponex, RapidGro, Spoonit, Miracid, Ortho's House Plant Food, and Ortho-Gro Liquid Plant Food 12-6-6. Use for hydroponics, and for container plants in which nutrients are leached out by frequent waterings.

Partially soluble complete fertilizers. These fertilizers are applied most often for general garden use. There are formulations for specific plant groups: rose food, vegetable garden food, orchid food, citrus food, lawn food, houseplant food, and so on. They supply nitrogen, phosphorus, and potassium in a single application. Because they are partially insoluble, they can supply some nutrients over a longer period of time than simple or single-nutrient fertilizers. Available forms include liquid, dry, slow-release, spikes, pellets, tablets, and granules. The high-nitrogen kinds are for lawns, the high-phosphorus kinds are used as starter fertilizers, and there are many

If you think you have applied too much fertilizer or are concerned about salt buildup within a pot, the excess fertilizer or salts can be leached out. Simply run a hose on low pressure in the pot for 10 to 15 minutes. The excess materials will drain out.

special-purpose complete fertilizers in between. Partially soluble complete fertilizers are the most commonly used of all the forms, especially for vegetables or flower annuals.

When to Fertilize

Apply nitrogen fertilizers in accordance with the plant's natural growth rhythm—that is, when the plant is *already* growing, not to *make* it grow. However, it is safe to use formulations that do not contain nitrogen, such as 0-10-10, during the nongrowing season—for example, with citrus plants, azaleas, cymbidium orchids, and other evergreen plants to promote healthy flowering and fruiting.

Applying Fertilizers

Few plants require really individual fertilization care; for the most part, they will grow well if the soil provides them with sufficient nutrients right from the start. The need for nitrogen, phosphorus, and potassium is high in vegetables; medium to high in lawns; medium in fruits and annual flowers; medium to low in herbs, perennial flowers, deciduous shrubs, and deciduous shade trees; and low in evergreen shrubs and evergreen shade trees. In applying any fertilizer, follow the directions on the label. Don't try to outguess the manufacturer by adding more than the recommended amount. Too much of any fertilizer is dangerous.

There are four basic ways to apply fertilizers: (1) incorporating them into the soil; (2) side banding; (3) applying liquid; and (4) foliar feeding.

Incorporating into the soil. For an overall application, apply dry fertilizer directly into the soil. Spread it over the soil evenly and at the rate called for on the label. Then work it into the soil with a spade or power tiller. This method works well for vegetables and trees.

To fertilize lawns, you can broadcast dry, pelleted fertilizer by hand; however, since this is difficult to do evenly, do it only in small areas or in the absence of other alternatives. A drop spreader works well for small lawns. Be sure to overlap the wheel marks just enough so that all the grass gets covered on one pass or another. Or you can use a broadcast spreader (hand-held or on wheels) that throws the fertilizer pellets over a wide swath.

Side banding. To put fertilizer in more localized areas—just where you want it—apply narrow bands of fertilizer 2 to 3 inches from the seed row and 1 to 2 inches deeper than the seeds or plants will be. If you must err, leave too *much* space between the seeds or plants and the fertilizer; if the

Side Banding

Side dressing fertilizer on established plants

Work fertilizer into soil, and water.

Fertilizing Vegetables
Fertilizer banding when planting seeds

A hose-end sprayer is indispensable for applying liquid fertilizers to lawns and gardens. Several models are available.

Broadcasting dry fertilizers by hand sometimes has uneven results. When using the hand method, apply fertilizer in a criss-cross pattern to reduce spottiness.

Drop spreaders are the most popular tools for applying dry fertilizer to average-sized lawns. These spreaders are fast, easy to use, and accurate.

fertilizer gets too close to the seeds, it will burn the roots of the seedlings. Vegetables and flowers can be fertilized in this manner.

Liquid feeding. Liquid fertilizers can be mixed with water and applied by means of a sprayer attached to an ordinary garden hose. Be sure to follow the directions on both the fertilizer label and the sprayer. Also make sure that all parts of the sprayer work well and are attached securely, so that the fertilizer, as well as the water, gets to your plants or lawn. Liquid fertilizers can also be used for watering houseplants.

Foliar feeding. When foliage receives fertilizer directly, it quickly absorbs and uses the nutrients. Foliar feeding is recommended only in cases where (1) insufficient fertilizer was used before planting; (2) you are after rapid plant growth; (3) the plant cannot utilize the micronutrients locked in the soil; or (4) the soil is too cold to convert nutrients into usable forms. A foliar spray is particularly useful at transplanting time, and—for perennial plants—in early spring, to promote growth.

Fertilizing Vegetables

For vegetables, you have the choice of a 5-10-10 formula (applying 3 to 4 pounds per 100 square feet) or a formula with a higher nitrogen content (but be sure to reduce the rate of application to avoid nitrogen burn). A high-phosphorus fertilizer such as 6-18-6 often is recommended for vegetables as a starter food.

Dry fertilizers require a three-step application:

(1) Spread the fertilizer evenly over the soil at the rate called for on the label, and work into the soil with a spade or power tiller.

(2) Apply narrow bands of fertilizer 2 to 3 inches from the seed and 1 to 2 inches deeper than the seeds or plants are to be placed. Space carefully—if the fertilizer gets too close to the seeds, it will burn the roots of the seedlings.

(3) Once the plants are up and growing, apply dry fertilizer as a side-dressing, scattering the fertilizer on both sides of the row 6 to 8 inches from the plants. Rake it into the soil and water thoroughly.

Fertilizing Lawns

There are four ways to apply fertilizers to lawns:

Hand broadcasting. Broadcasting dry, pelleted fertilizer by hand is possible but difficult, and should be used only in very small areas or if no other method is possible. To get the most even coverage, apply half the total amount of fertilizer by walking in rows in one direction, then apply the remaining half by walking in perpendicular rows.

Hose-end sprayers. Apply liquid fertilizers with a sprayer attached to a hose. Follow the directions on both the fertilizer label and the sprayer carefully, and make sure all parts of the sprayer work well and are attached securely, so that the fertilizer (as well as the water in the sprayer jar) gets to your lawn.

Drop spreaders. This popular method is good for applying dry fertilizer to small lawns. Be sure to overlap the wheel marks so that all the grass gets covered on one pass or another; don't overlap too much, however, or the lawn will get burned.

Cover the ends first. Then go back and forth the long way. Gradually shut off the spreader as you approach the end strips, and keep it closed while you are turning around, backing up, or stopped (this will prevent double applications).

Broadcast spreaders. Providing the easiest way of applying dry fertilizer, broadcast spreaders are available in hand-held and wheeled models, both of which throw the fertilizer pellets over a wide swath. Find out the width of the swath thrown by the spreader so that you can tell how far apart to space your passes. Avoid using the spreader when it's windy.

Fertilizing Trees

When young, trees may need a complete fertilizer to get established, but once mature, they need only nitrogen, and not much of it. In fact, mature trees usually need little or no fertilization, as long as they have good leaf color and grow reasonably well.

Apply fertilizer at a rate of 2 to 4 pounds of actual nitrogen per 1,000 square feet. You can use a simple nitrogen fertilizer such as ammonium nitrate, ammonium sulfate, calcium nitrate, or urea, or you can use a complete fertilizer. Another way of figuring how much to apply is to measure the diameter of the tree trunk. For trees over 6 inches in diameter, use 2 to 4 pounds of a fertilizer that contains 12 percent nitrogen (such as 12-6-6) for each inch of diameter. For smaller trees, use 1 to 2 pounds of 12 percent nitrogen fertilizer for each inch of diameter.

Apply half the needed amount in spring, and the other half in summer. Keep the fertilizer at least 12 inches away from the trunk to avoid injuring it, and apply the fertilizer as far out from the trunk as the tips of the branches (the drip line). Water the area thoroughly.

Let the tree itself tell you how much to apply. If young trees show excessive growth, use less fertilizer for the next application, or skip a year altogether. If shoots are shorter than you want and the leaf color is pale, double the fertilizer rate. As the tree matures, fertilize only if growth or leaf color is below expectation.

Mulching

Mulches are materials that are put on top of the soil to modify the growing environment of the plants. Although often decorative, they have a functional purpose: "to protect the roots of plants from heat, cold, or drought, or to keep fruit clean. Specifically, mulch modifies the soil microclimate in which a plant is growing," according to Dr. J. W. Courter, an extension specialist in small fruit and vegetable crops at the University of Illinois.

There are three kinds of mulches: organic, mineral, and synthetic. The organic and mineral types are used to keep the soil cool; synthetic mulches are used to warm it up.

Organic Mulches

Organic mulches are made from plant material (such as leaves, straw, and compost) or the residue of plant materials (such as buckwheat or nut hulls, and sawdust). Depending on how much mulch you need, you can recycle plant material you already have, or purchase new material from your local garden center.

Advantages. Organic mulches will keep your soil cool and moist, and help the plants grow. In addition, they can also give the garden an attractive appearance. Other benefits include:

Weed control. If you make the organic mulch thick enough, annual weed seedlings will not grow through the mulch. Perennial weeds, unfortunately, will not be stopped by organic mulches; however, black plastic will stop them. It can be hidden under any other mulch.

Conservation of moisture. An organic mulch will keep moisture in the top 6 to 8 inches of soil by reducing the speed of water evaporation by as much as 70 percent. Not only do these mulches save water, but they also keep an even supply of water in the upper layers of the soil.

Reduction of crop loss. If the soil in your vegetable garden tends to develop a hard surface crust after a rain or a watering, an organic mulch will break the fall of the water drops; this will keep the soil from compacting and the pore spaces in the soil open. A mulch beneath unstaked tomatoes, summer squash, and cucumbers will make the crop less likely to rot.

Making use of the soil's richest layers. Organic mulches insulate the upper

Fertilizing Trees

Measuring a tree trunk diameter with calipers

Feeding a young tree with a root feeder

layer of the soil from the sun's heat, and keep the moisture on the surface of the soil even. This allows the plant roots to spread out in the soil's richest layers, where they develop an extensive root system.

Improved soil texture. Adding such mulches as peat moss or shredded bark to soil quickly improves it: clay soils experience improved aeration, and sandy soils are better able to retain water. In addition, organic mulches protect the soil structure during heavy rains.

Disadvantages. There are fewer cons than pros to the use of organic mulches, but there are a couple. Organic mulches increase the danger of frost hazards by reducing solar radiation into the soil. And, as mentioned, by themselves they won't make a dent in the growth of perennial weeds.

Applying organic mulches. Apply the mulches only in summer, when they will maintain reduced soil temperatures and save water. Do not apply in early spring, or they will slow up the natural warming process of the soil.

Fine mulches such as sawdust should be applied 1 to 2 inches thick; coarse or fluffy mulches should be put on 3 to 4 inches thick. (If using untreated sawdust, increase the amount of fertilizer by an extra one-fourth. This is to replace the nitrogen the sawdust will take from the soil as it decomposes.)

Apply the mulch evenly, leveling it with a rake or your hands. If you are using a kind of mulch that gets soggy when it gets wet, be sure to leave room around a plant's stem or trunk; don't pack it down. To ensure adequate air circulation to the base of the plant, wet the mulch thoroughly and then pull it back a few inches from the stem or trunk.

Kinds of organic mulches. Many materials that used to be considered "waste" matter are now considered mulches—sawdust, bark, manure, and so forth. The list that follows is a pretty standard one for most parts of the country, but you might investigate to find out whether there's any material particular to your own area. If grapes are pressed locally, then there will be pomace. If nuts are shelled, there will be shells and hulls; when ground or pulverized, those will make a useful, attractive mulch. And, a cider mill will yield apple pomace.

Buckwheat hulls. Don't use this fine-textured material in windy places, or it may blow around. In relatively windless areas, however, it is useful for landscapes: it is long-lived and has a good neutral color. Hot, humid weather may produce some odor.

Chunk bark. Redwood and fir are the most popular forms. This long-lasting material is available in various sizes to fit many landscape needs.

Compost. As well as improving the soil, compost makes an excellent mulch. Various kinds of nonwoody plant refuse can be used, such as plant tops from the vegetable and flower garden, grass clippings, and leaves. Although compost may not be the most attractive mulch, it is one of the best. (See pages 57–59 for more on compost.)

Lawn clippings. Let the clippings dry before applying them. If you must put them on fresh, be sure to spread them loosely; otherwise they will mat down, produce heat during decomposition, and give off an offensive odor. If the lawn has been treated with a weed killer such as 2,4-D or related compounds, do not use the grass clippings for mulch.

Leafmold. If you do a good job of composting leaves in the fall, the material should be partially decomposed by spring. Although this makes a good mulch, it is hard to apply evenly and is not particularly attractive.

Leaves. This is a useful mulch in areas with many trees. Leaves are the least expensive mulch you will find. They work best if composted. Nitrogen additions probably will be needed.

Manure. Make sure that this excellent mulch has not been treated with odor-reducing chemicals, which could harm growing plants. When using manure, you don't have to apply additional nitrogen.

Top: A mulch of bark chips not only benefits the roses by cooling the soil but also improves the soil structure as it gradually breaks down. It should be replaced yearly.

Bottom: The attractive color and texture of ground pecan shell mulch makes it decorative as well as effective as a weed control. Regular users report some problems with birds and rodents, however.

Left: A straw mulch is used here in a vegetable garden. As such material decomposes, soil microorganisms secrete a sticky substance that plays an important role in soil granulation. When adding a mulch to change soil structure, add enough to change the top six inches of the soil.

Bottom left: Tar paper and newspaper, several layers thick, are satisfactory mulches but deteriorate quickly. Plastic jugs provide early frost protection.

Bottom right: Grass clippings must be spread thinly and evenly to prevent rotting and the resulting bad odor. Allow them to dry out before using. Avoid grass treated with weed killers.

Peanut hulls. You can buy this excellent, often attractive mulch in some local garden centers, especially in areas where peanuts are processed.

Peat moss. This popular mulch looks quite rich when used properly. However, its cost can be prohibitive if large areas must be covered. Peat must be kept moist; when it's very dry, it sheds water rather than letting it soak in.

Pine needles. Pine needles make a light, airy, attractive mulch. Since they are moderately acid, they are especially desirable for acid-loving plants such as azaleas and blueberries.

Sawdust. If you use a sawdust mulch, apply fertilizer to prevent nitrogen deficiency.

Shredded hardwood bark. This popular material makes an excellent mulch: it is easy to apply and very attractive in landscaped settings. Shredded bark usually lasts longer than peat moss, and also adds valuable organic matter to the soil.

Straw. This is useful both for winter protection and as a summer mulch. However, it is both unattractive and highly flammable.

Wood chips or wood shavings. This material is available in large quantities. The slow-to-decompose wood chips may cause nitrogen deficiency. Therefore, apply additional fertilizer.

Mineral Mulches

Mineral mulches are composed of inorganic, natural materials such as vermiculite, perlite, and sand (see page 59). Although these materials can be used as soil amendments, they also work well as mulches.

Pebbles, rock, and gravel also make useful and attractive mulches that cool the soil and conserve moisture. However, because they don't shut out light entirely, they do not stop weed seeds from germinating beneath them. If you want to use a mineral mulch but you have an actual or potential weed problem, first cover the ground with black polyethylene plastic, and then spread the mineral mulch on top of that.

Plastic Mulches

A variety of synthetic mulches are used to increase crop yields, help control weeds, and warm up the soil. Included in this category are clear plastic, black plastic, brown paper, aluminum-coated plastic, and aluminum foil.

Of these, the plastic (polyethylene) films are used most frequently. Initially, only commercial farmers and university researchers used them, but recently home gardeners have joined the ranks as well.

Advantages. Plastic film mulches offer many advantages: they warm up the soil temperature, conserve soil moisture, control weeds, keep roots from being injured by too-close cultivation, maintain good soil temperature, and allow for economical irrigation.

Black plastic versus clear plastic. Each type of film has its own strengths. Which one to use depends on your gardening needs. Black film keeps out light, so it prevents weeds from growing underneath. It also can increase crop yields and speed up the ripening time of melons, eggplant, peppers, and summer squash. Make sure to dampen the soil before applying black film; this will give the moisture-retaining film some moisture to retain.

Clear plastic, on the other hand, warms the soil to a greater degree, which makes it good for germinating early vegetables. However, make sure to remove the film as soon as the seedlings emerge from the soil.

Some specific recommendations come from extension specialist J. W. Courter:

"We promote the use of black film rather than clear film for home gardens. The exception would be where we would want to promote early development of sweet corn or some other early-seeded crop.

"Clear polyethylene film also can be used to promote germination of early vegetables. I have seen it used very successfully for covering lettuce, radishes, and even early potatoes. The film is removed after the seedlings emerge from the soil. So you can see that both clear and black may be used as long as the gardener understands the advantages and drawbacks of each."

Disadvantages. For all the praises sung of plastic mulches, there are a few undeniable disadvantages as well. They are harder to apply than organic mulches. All planting must be done by hand through the plastic. Since most plastics are not biodegradable, they must be removed at the end of the season, which is bothersome, messy, and a possible disposal problem. In addition, no plastics enthusiast—no matter how ardent—will deny that synthetic mulches are far less attractive than organic or mineral mulches.

Plastic plus organic mulches. Combining plastic and organic mulches can be very effective. For example, use a plastic mulch to warm up the soil in early spring. Then later on, when the sun's direct rays get hot enough to damage your plants, cover the plastic with an organic mulch.

Watering

On the face of it, watering would seem to be the easiest task a gardener could have. However, more is involved than just turning on a hose. It isn't for

How to Install Plastic Mulches

These photos (from various university experiment stations) show a typical installation of black plastic mulch. **1.** Dig a shallow furrow or trench on each side of the row, approximately as wide as the plastic. **2.** Secure the end of the plastic at the end of the row. **3.** Roll out the plastic evenly along the row. Secure the plastic's edges by burying them in a trench and covering them with soil.

4. A "bulb-planter" is an excellent tool to cut plastic and dig small transplanting holes. (Sharpen the tool's edges with a file.) Or cut a cross-shaped slit in the plastic and manually dig a small hole (this alternative is as effective, but less fast). The size of the slit will depend on the size of the root-ball you intend to plant.

5. Here, a finished planting hole awaits a transplant in a Jiffy 7 pellet. In hard soil, a small amount of soil substitute can be used in the hole to give the transplant's root system a good start.

6. Transplant as usual.

7. The look of the planted row. Water the trench on either side of the row. Side seepage irrigates the row.

8. Properly done, the results should look like this.

Hose-end nozzles

nothing that water is called "the hazardous necessity": too much of it will suffocate a plant's roots; too little will starve the roots and put the plant under "water stress." And even simple-sounding jobs, such as determining how frequently to water, become frustrating without a dependable formula.

Happily, however, except for extreme overattention or extreme neglect, most plants tend to tolerate careless watering practices. But why not give your plants what they need? Good watering habits can be learned.

Drainage

If your soil has a loamy consistency (whether naturally or because of amendments you have added), your watering task will be the easiest of all. But if you have sandy or clayey soil, you will have to take these characteristics into account. Clay soils have a high water-retention capacity, which means that water moves through them slowly, requiring only infrequent watering of plants. Sandy soils, on the other hand, have a low water-retention capacity, so water moves through them rapidly, necessitating frequent watering. A loamy soil—the ideal garden soil—absorbs almost all the water it receives, holds much of it within its fine pores, and lets any excess drain away.

However, if you have amended your soil up to loamy-soil standards, you can water at a much more even rate; sandy soils will be more water-retentive and heavy clay soils will open up to admit more air and water.

To find out how long your soil takes to drain, try the simple drainage test on page 57.

How Much Water and When?

Much as a formula would be desirable, there just isn't any. However, there is a rule of thumb that may prove useful: Apply water until the root zone is filled; then wait until the soil begins to dry out before watering again.

Be careful not to water too often or too deeply, or all the air spaces in the soil will fill up. This will stop root growth, which in turn will damage the roots. And damaged roots are susceptible to rot-causing microorganisms.

But watering too seldom and too lightly is not the answer either; it leads to shallow-growing roots. And because a shallow-rooted plant has no access to deeper reserves of water in the soil, the plant cannot survive even brief periods of drought or high temperatures.

The best gauge is your own experience; water your plants well, and find out how long it takes for your soil to dry slightly between waterings.

There are many opinions about *when* to water, but aside from one specific recommendation, your own common sense will easily see you through. The specific recommendation is that you water in the early morning. Because this gives plants a chance to dry off before night, the risks of plant diseases are reduced (leaves that are wet at night are more susceptible to attack by disease-causing organisms).

When do you stop watering? When the water has seeped down into the top three or four inches of soil. But until you can do this by feel, dig into the soil with a shovel or trowel and see whether the water is moving into the soil below the top layer.

Methods of Applying Water

There are many ways to water plants, some of which are described and illustrated here. Whichever method you choose, be sure to follow these general rules:

Water well, and let the soil dry out somewhat before you water again.

Water early enough in the day so that the leaves are dry by nighttime.

Water in early morning, when the sun and wind both are low.

In really hot, dry weather, give plant leaves a cool shower.

When irrigating clay soils, apply water over short periods. In between, let the water soak in for at least twice as long as it takes to apply the water—for example, 10 minutes on, 20 minutes off, 10 minutes on. Use a sprinkler that releases water as slowly as possible.

When irrigating sandy loams or other open soils, apply water in one continuous period.

Set sprinklers to avoid waste on sidewalks and driveways.

Keep sprinkler heads clean to assure even distribution of water.

Irrigation. *Flooding.* Flooding is used most often where summer heat is extreme. Lawns and some vegetables and fruit trees can be flooded over a large area to ensure complete saturation.

Furrow irrigation. This is probably the most common way to water vegetables and berries. The irrigation water is confined to the root zone of the plants, and weed growth in unwatered areas is inhibited. Dig furrows for dry walkways between rows.

Sprinkler systems. *Hose-end sprinklers.* These come in many shapes and sizes to match the wide variety of irrigation needs. Although they are less convenient than a permanent sprinkler system, they are also much less expensive. To avoid wasting water, choose the sprinkler that best fits the space you've got.

Hose-end nozzles. These watering devices can make clean-up and watering chores easier. There's a hose-end nozzle for virtually every need.

Underground sprinkler systems. If your garden has large expanses of lawn, these systems will give you good, even coverage with a minimum of guesswork. For even further convenience as well as regularity, you can have a timer installed. In general, weigh the expense of such systems against the ease they offer.

Drip systems and soaker hoses. Several drip systems are available, with different nozzles to suit different growing situations. Most of these systems provide small, steady, precise amounts of water exactly where needed, and require a filtration unit to avoid clogging. Drip irrigation hardware lets you water plants in a variety of ways. Here, plastic pipe with drip spitters attached to a number of spaghetti tubes delivers water in the small amount the containers hold. It's a good way to "vacationize" your garden.

Soakers. These offer the advantage of releasing water slowly and economically, without disturbing the soil structure or causing crust formation (common with overhead sprinklers). Many gardeners leave soakers in place throughout the season.

Wetting agents. Wetting agents make water wetter. They are particularly useful when you're trying to get organic matter, such as peat moss or ground bark, to absorb water. Wetting agents come in liquid and dry forms. You can mix the dry form directly into synthetic soil; you can put the liquid form into a hose-end sprayer or mix it in a watering can to wet container-plant soil.

Flooding

Furrow Irrigation

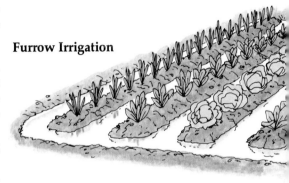

Drip Irrigation

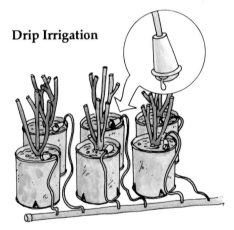

Soakers

Localized Watering

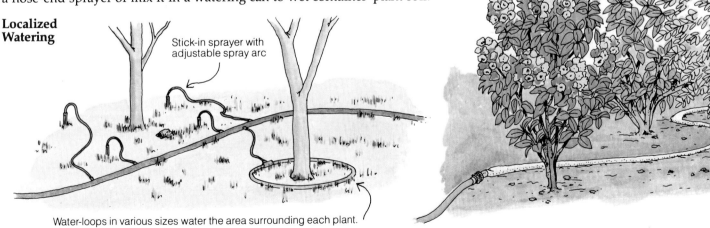

Stick-in sprayer with adjustable spray arc

Water-loops in various sizes water the area surrounding each plant.

TREATING FOR PESTS AND DISEASES

There are many basic gardening practices and controls that will minimize the effects of pests and diseases and perhaps eliminate them altogether.

Although some insects and diseases can't be avoided completely, keeping the garden clean will help reduce plant problems. In the fall or early spring, burn or haul away old leaves, hulls, unharvested nuts, and dead twigs. During the growing season, get rid of any nuts that fall prematurely (they may have worms inside). After a harvest, clean up all vines, leaves, and fruit, and spread them on the compost pile or spade them into the soil. Remove any plants that are obviously infected.

Insects

Insects can damage plant growth and render your crops unattractive and inedible unless preventive measures are used. The most commonly found insects—and the controls to use against them—include the following:

Aphids. Aphids, which come in several colors and sizes, suck plant juices, stunt growth, pucker and curl leaves, deform buds and flowers, and generally disturb your garden. The honey-dew they secrete attracts ants and is a medium for the growth of black sooty mold fungus.
  Hosts: All plants.
  Controls: Diazinon, Malathion, Sevin.

Beetles. Within this huge, diverse group of insects are many beneficial as well as destructive insects. The benign ones include ladybird beetles (ladybugs) and black ground beetles, which are predaceous and feed on aphids, grubs, and other harmful insects. These should not be harmed.

The damage done by the destructive beetles varies in almost as many ways as there are beetles. The larva of the elm leaf beetle eats everything but the veins of leaves; weakened trees thus become fair game for the elm bark beetle, which carries spores of the Dutch elm disease fungus. Flea beetles eat a shot-hole pattern into leaves of young plants, and spread a disease-causing virus. The larva of the striped cucumber beetle feeds on the roots of cucumbers, muskmelons, and winter squash; the adults feed on the leaves and blossoms of many plants. These beetles also spread such diseases as bacterial wilt and cucumber mosaic.
  Controls: Diazinon, Malathion, Sevin.

Bugs. Nongardeners think of any insect as a bug, but to a gardener, "bugs" are a suborder of insects—generally unpleasant, destructive, and difficult to control. Bugs have an incomplete metamorphosis. Nymphs resemble adults, but are smaller and lack wings.

As bugs suck juices, many inject a toxin that causes unsightly spots on the plant and wilting.
  Hosts: General feeder throughout the garden.
  Controls: Diazinon, Malathion, Sevin.

Caterpillars. For the most part, these are the larvae of moths and butterflies.

Aphids

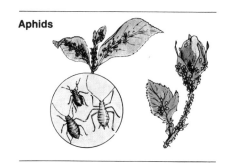

Beetles

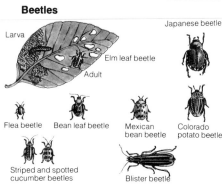

Larva
Japanese beetle
Elm leaf beetle
Adult
Flea beetle | Bean leaf beetle | Mexican bean beetle | Colorado potato beetle
Striped and spotted cucumber beetles
Blister beetle

Bugs

Squash bug | Harlequin bug | Boxelder bug

Nymph
Adult

Four-lined plant bug | Tarnished plant bug | Lygus bug
Brown, green stink bugs

Caterpillars

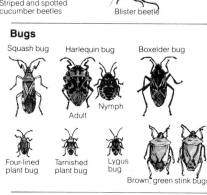

Leaf tier
Leaf roller
Cankerworms

Tussock moth larva

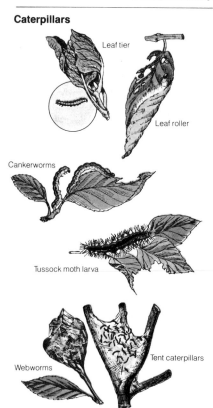

Webworms
Tent caterpillars

They come in all sizes and colors; some are naked, others hairy; some are decorated with tufts or spines. All feed on foliage. Many have a spinneret with which they make silk thread. Their names are derived from their appearance, hosts, or way of life—for example, leaf rollers, bagworms, hornworms, pickleworms, and leaf skeletonizers.

Banded woolybear. This is the larva of the tiger moth. When touched, it rolls into a ball. It feeds on many garden plants.

Hornworms. These are big (2½ to 3 inches long) worms with big appetites. Most destructive on tomatoes. Leaves seem to disappear overnight.

Leaf rollers and tiers. These are caterpillars that feed inside rolled or tied-together leaves. Hosts include basswood, canna, elm, honeylocust, honeysuckle, locust, oak, redbud, willow, and others.

Loopers, inchworms, measuring worms, and canker-worms. Many kinds of caterpillars all have the same movement, doubling or looping as they crawl. On trees, they feed on new foliage in spring and are known as cankerworms. In the vegetable garden, the cabbage looper eats ragged holes in the leaves of cabbage and lettuce.

Tussock moths. Their larvae feed on many deciduous shade trees, and are notorious for skeletonizing the leaves. In the East, the first generation feeds from April to June, the second in August and September.

Webworms and tent caterpillars. They don't all use the same approach. Some build unsightly "tents" in forks or crotches of trees and crawl from them to feed. Others web together needles or leaves (usually at the ends of branches) and feed beneath the webs. Many trees and shrubs are hosts.

Controls for caterpillars: Diazinon, Sevin.

Corn earworm. Corn earworms (also called tomato fruitworms) enter into the tip of the corn's ear and damage the kernels.

Control: Sevin spray or dust (apply 1, 4, and 7 days after the silks appear). Repeat weekly until the silks are brown. Be sure to read the label for instructions about the minimum time between the last application and harvesting.

The European cornborer, another borer, damages both stalks and ears, from the base or side.

Control: Sevin spray (apply in the center of the leaf whorls when ear shoots form). Repeat at least three times at 5-day intervals. Spray until runoff occurs at the base of the plant.

Cutworm. This dark caterpillar hides in the soil during the day and feeds at night. Cutworms cut off tender young plants just above the soil surface, leaving the wilted tops undisturbed and the stub of the plant emerging from the soil. One way to protect new plants is to remove both ends from ordinary cans, and sink the cans 1 or 2 inches into the soil (leaving 2 or 3 inches above the soil), making a collar around the new plants. Remove the cans once the plants are well established.

Control: Diazinon dust.

Leafhoppers. These small (⅛- to ½-inch-long), wedge-shaped insects have piercing/sucking mouthparts and feed on all kinds of plants and trees, usually sucking sap from the undersides of leaves. As a result, the plants lose color, look stippled and wilted, and generally lose their health and vigor. Some species inject a toxic substance as they feed, causing leaves to wilt. Leafhoppers also carry many plant virus diseases. They are easy to see, and hop away quickly when disturbed.

Hosts: General feeder on all plants.

Controls: Diazinon, Malathion.

Leaf miners. The larvae of several kinds of flies, midges, and moths lay eggs on or within leaves. When the eggs hatch, they feed between the leaf surfaces, creating ugly blotches or serpentine trails. Leaf miners attack

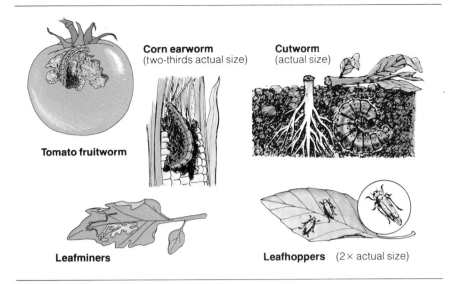

Tomato fruitworm

Corn earworm
(two-thirds actual size)

Cutworm
(actual size)

Leafminers

Leafhoppers (2× actual size)

conifers as well as broadleafed plants.

Hosts: Spruce, white fir, pine, arborvitae; flowering cherry, azalea, aspen, birch, holly, and other trees; many flowers.

Controls: Diazinon, Sevin.

Mealybugs. These close relatives of scale insects have soft, segmented bodies up to ¼ inch long, covered with powdery white wax that extends in filaments beyond the body. Mealybugs may be found singly or in groups on twigs and undersides of branches, but mostly in crotches. They damage plants and trees by sucking sap and secreting large amounts of honey-dew, which in turn is fed upon by an unsightly black mold. They mostly live on the interior branches and leaves of plants, where they may go unnoticed until the plant loses color, wilts, and even partially or completely dies.

Hosts: Gardenias, amaryllis, camellia, catalpa, cineraria, cycas, crotons, ivy, lantana, oleander, magnolia. Mealybugs also like soft-stemmed plants such as coleus, begonias, geraniums, and ferns.

Controls: Diazinon, Malathion, dormant oil spray.

Mites. Not really insects, mites belong to the Arachnida, along with spiders, ticks, and scorpions. Many species damage plants by sucking sap from lower leaf surfaces. Then the top surface of the damaged leaf turns pale or yellow and is covered with tiny yellow specks. Turn over suspicious-looking leaves—use a hand lens to look for small webs, many dark specks of excrement and discarded skins, and mites themselves. Mites that attack leafy plants become more active in hot weather. Those that damage conifers start in the cool of early spring.

Hosts: Many flowers; cucumbers and melons; ivy; oak, elm, spruce, fir, pine, and many other trees.

Controls: Diazinon, Malathion, dormant oil spray.

Onion maggots. By the time the damage done by the onion maggot is discovered, it's too late to do anything about it.

Control: Diazinon dust or granules before planting onions and radishes.

Scale insects. There are two groups of scale insects: armored and soft. Armored scales live beneath an outer shell of molted skins and waxy secretions. The soft scale shell is part of the scale, as the shell is part of the turtle; although it is called "soft," often it is as hard as armored scale. Soft scales usually secrete honey-dew, causing unsightly blackening of foliage and sticky drippings on cars and walks beneath. A scale's mouth is a needlelike tube that uncoils to six to seven times as long as its body. Reaching deep into plant tissue, it sucks out the juices, reducing the plant's

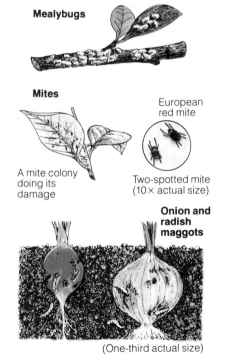

Mealybugs

Mites

A mite colony doing its damage

European red mite

Two-spotted mite
(10× actual size)

Onion and radish maggots

(One-third actual size)

Scales

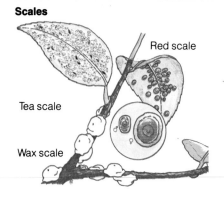

Tea scale

Red scale

Wax scale

Juniper scale

San Jose scale

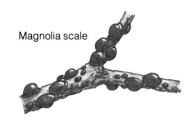

Magnolia scale

Slug

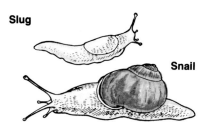

Snail

Thrips

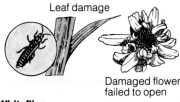

Leaf damage

Damaged flower
failed to open

Whiteflies

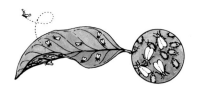

vitality. Foliage pales, and leaves or needles drop prematurely. Heavy infestations may kill branches, and sometimes entire trees or shrubs. Except when in their "crawler" stage, scales are immobile. Their shells protect them from predators and most insecticides.

Tea scale. A tangle of white males and threads dotted with brown females infest the lower leaf surface.

Red scale. Infest leaves and fruit of some plants.

Wax scale. Form waxy globs on stems.

Juniper scale. Tiny white scale infest needles, then turn brown or black.

San Jose scale. Encrust bark and fruit.

Magnolia scale. The largest of all the scales, these encrust bark.

Hosts: Most shrubs and trees.

Control: Orthene.

Snails. Snails and slugs are night feeders that hide during the day under a ground cover of ivy, under pots and planter boxes—in short, any place that is dark, cool, and moist.

Slugs wait until the weather warms up in spring to do serious damage, reaching a peak population in early summer.

Control: Slug and snail bait, with special attention to their favorite hiding places. Around food crops, use a bait that is especially formulated for use in the vegetable garden.

Thrips. The tiny thrips, barely visible without a lens, enter the garden as adults in massive flights, scraping and scarring foliage and feeding inside buds; consequently flowers are deformed or fail to open. Usually, thrips are discovered only when damage has already been done. They can be seen slithering for cover when the infested flower is examined or shaken over paper.

Hosts: Shasta daisies, gladiolus, roses, and some foliage plants.

Controls: Diazinon, Malathion, Sevin.

Whiteflies. Adult whiteflies are small (1/16 inch long), wedge shaped, and pure white. When disturbed, they fly like little clouds of snowflakes. The damage is done by the nymphs, who are scalelike, flat, oval, and pale green, brown, or black, depending on the species. Some have a white, waxy fringe. All species suck juices from the underside of leaves and secrete honey-dew. Infested leaves become pale and mottled and may turn yellow and die. In warm-winter areas they are an all-year pest; in cold-winter areas they are summer pests only.

Hosts: Especially serious on tomatoes, beans, ixora, gardenia, and privet. Infests many others.

Controls: Diazinon, Malathion, dormant oil spray (for larvae).

Diseases

All plants are susceptible to diseases, but vegetables suffer most severely. So look for disease-resistant varieties when planting some vegetables. In some localities, many vegetables—for example, tomatoes and cucumbers—can be grown with little attention to disease problems. In other places, scab, mosaic, powdery mildew, downy mildew, anthracnose, and verticillium and fusarium wilt will frustrate your hopes for a crop. When growing cucumbers, tomatoes, or other vegetables bothered by these diseases, you might consider a disease-resistant variety.

The following vegetables are troubled with the diseases listed:

Tomatoes—fusarium, verticillium.

Cucumbers—scab, mosaic, downy mildew, powdery mildew, anthracnose.

Muskmelon—fusarium, powdery mildew.

Snap beans—mosaic, powdery mildew, root rot.

Cabbage—virus yellows.

Spinach—blight, blue mold, downy mildew, mosaic.

Some plant diseases that affect flowers and trees as well as vegetables include the following:

Black spot. Leaves have black spots.

Control: Get rid of badly infected plants.

Damping off. A stem rot develops on newly sprouted seedlings near the soil surface, and the seedlings fall over or fail to sprout.

Control: Sow seed in a sterile soil mix and water the newly sown seed with an appropriate fungicide.

Powdery mildew. Powdery mildew shows up as a blue-white dust on leaves and flower buds.

Control: Get rid of infected annuals. Cut off damaged parts of any plants.

Rust. Leaves form blisters, which scatter reddish or yellow spores.

Control: Get rid of infected leaves.

Wilt. Tomato wilts from bottom up, gradually yellows and dies. Tomatoes often are attacked by this disease, which lives in the soil.

Control: Buy resistant varieties.

Animal Pests

The objective is not to kill animals that might compete for your plants, but to let them know your plants are hands (or paws, or feathers)-off. Following are some preventive measures to use to protect your plants from animals.

Birds. Delightful as they are, birds sometimes can pose a big problem in the vegetable garden or orchard. Many vegetable seedlings and most fruits need protection from bird damage.

You can stake and stretch plastic netting over newly planted corn, peas, beans, strawberry plants, grapevines, and fruit trees. The netting is available in sizes from 4½ × 36 feet to 9 × 200 feet—enough to cover a row crop or an entire tree.

Nylon netting, available in 72-inch widths and unlimited lengths at department stores and yardage shops, is equally effective.

To keep birds from eating corn kernels out of the tip of the ear, slip a paper bag over each ear after it has been pollinated. To protect large clusters of grapes, tie a plastic bag around the cluster.

There are additional ways to keep birds from damaging vegetable seedlings and fruits. One is to make a cover of aluminum fly screen. Build portable frames to fit the dimensions of your crops—for example, 14 inches

Damping off

Powdery mildew

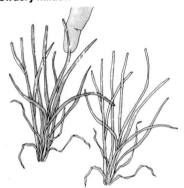

Rust

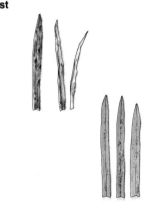

Protection from Birds

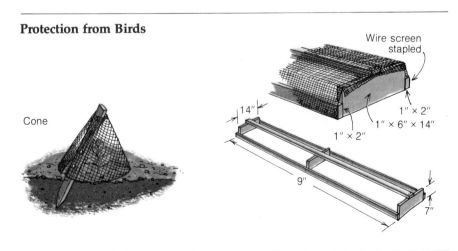

Cone

Wire screen stapled

14"

1" × 2"

1" × 6" × 14"

1" × 2"

9"

7"

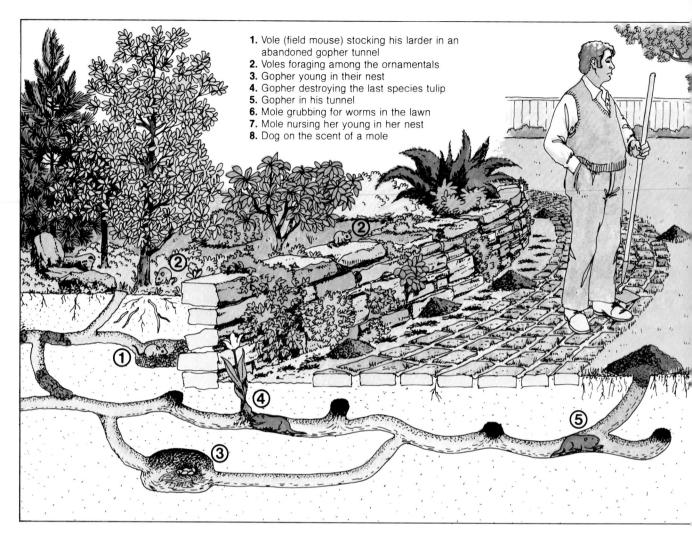

1. Vole (field mouse) stocking his larder in an abandoned gopher tunnel
2. Voles foraging among the ornamentals
3. Gopher young in their nest
4. Gopher destroying the last species tulip
5. Gopher in his tunnel
6. Mole grubbing for worms in the lawn
7. Mole nursing her young in her nest
8. Dog on the scent of a mole

Protection from Gophers

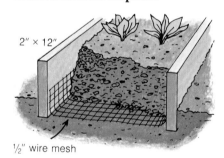

2" × 12"

½" wire mesh

wide, 7 inches high, and 9 feet long for peas and beans; smaller ones for carrots, beets, lettuce; and so forth. Store these frames in winter, and begin using them for the first sowing of seed.

Make the length ½, ⅓, or ¼ the length of a full row, stapling the wire to the frame afterwards.

A cone of wire screen or plastic hardware cloth tacked to a stake will not only protect a plant from birds but also offer some wind and frost protection.

Deer. To keep deer away from your garden, choose among any of these methods: build chicken-wire cages around young plants; build tall (6 to 8 feet) fences; use blood meal fertilizer on the soil, or hang it up in small bags; scatter moth balls on the soil; plant daffodils, holly, mahonia, rosemary, and zinnias—all of which deer dislike—in strategic places.

Gophers. Gophers eat roots, including bulbs, tubers, roots of trees, vines and shrubs, and occasionally entire plants. Gophers tunnel from 6 to 12 inches under the soil and push the excavated dirt out to the surface, leaving small mounds of fine-particled dirt.

Gophers, therefore, seem to have the advantage—they can tunnel underground and get your plants from underneath. To keep the upper hand, try any of these methods: (1) build a 12-inch-deep raised bed, and line the bottom with ½-inch mesh wire; (2) plant in plastic cans (with holes in the bottom), and sink them into the soil to protect the main roots from gophers; or (3) use raised beds (see page 56).

Moles. Mole habits resemble those of gophers, but moles burrow close enough to the surface to leave traces of their route. In the process of

tunneling, moles break off tender root systems, snap stems, and uproot seedlings. The soil pushed out onto the surface is in small, compact plugs. The remedy is the same as for gophers.

Field mice and voles. These do less damage than gophers and moles because they attack the aboveground (that is, visible) portion of plants. Often, they "girdle" the base of trees and shrubs by gnawing the bark off. This can cause trees to die with the first spurt of spring growth. Therefore, protect the lower trunk (especially in winter, when field mouse and vole attacks are common), with a cylinder of hardware cloth. Check occasionally to make sure it doesn't get too tight as the tree grows.

Rabbits. Remember how fond Peter Cottontail was of greens? His real-life counterparts are equally fond of them—so much so that just a few rabbits can quickly deplete your vegetables. To protect your garden, make a fence of fine chicken-wire, and anchor the bottom in a trench that's 6 inches deep.

Squirrels. Squirrels often can be a bigger obstacle to successful nut production than plant diseases and insects are. If there are enough tree squirrels, they can steal most of your filberts, pecans, hickories, and Persian walnuts before you harvest them.

To reduce losses caused by squirrels, try placing a smooth metal shield around the tree's trunk. If the tree is isolated, squirrels should not be able to climb up it or get to it from other trees, buildings, or wires. Make the shield 24 inches wide, and place it on the trunk about 5-6 feet up from the ground.

Or try this method: shake the tree limbs, and pick up whatever mature nuts fall off as often as you can.

Nursery shopping is both fun and difficult.
Doing your gardening homework will make
it easier to select the plants, seeds, shrubs,
or trees that will thrive in your climate and soil
for the most attractive and productive garden.

CHOOSING PLANTS

The following pages describe the characteristics and care of the most commonly planted annuals, perennials, bulbs, shrubs, trees, vegetables, fruits, and berries.

No matter what part of the country you live in, what the climate, or what the soil conditions, there is a plant to suit your needs and preferences. *Annuals* complete their entire life cycle in a year or less, while *biennials* live for 2 years. They offer the gardener flexibility in color, texture, and flowering season.

Perennials live more than 2 years and provide a more permanent background and continuity to the landscape.

Climate variations play a great role in determining whether a plant is perennial in any given area.

The entries that follow form a suggested but not exhaustive list of varieties. *AAS* indicates that the variety was an All-America Selection. For additional information on selections suited to your area, consult your local nursery, and see pages 18–24.

Annuals and Perennials Used as Annuals

Sun versus shade. There are many kinds of shade—shade that occurs for part of the day, filtered shade, light shade, filtered sun, and deep shade. Most plants tolerate or welcome shade. Plants that set bud in full sun will bloom in shady areas.

If you live in a cold northern area, you can still have flower color in late fall and early winter. Annuals such as fibrous begonia, balsam, impatiens, and geranium will keep blooming if you cut them back, pot them up, and bring them indoors before the first frost. However, they will need lots of sunlight while they are indoors.

If you live in the Sunbelt, you can do fall plantings of pansy, viola, calendula, primula, sweet pea, and cineraria to get late-winter color. Check your local nursery to find out what transplants will be available for fall.

Seed versus transplants. To find out whether to grow seed directly outdoors or buy transplants, check the "Days to Germination" column on the chart (pages 84–88). The column will also tell you whether seed should be started indoors (I) or direct seeded outdoors (D). Unless you have a greenhouse or are well-equipped indoors, you'd do best to buy transplants for plants that must be started indoors.

How many days it takes for seed to germinate also will influence your decision. Some annuals take a long time to start from seed (for example, fibrous begonias take 14 to 21 days), and you may not be able to maintain ideal conditions for that long. Therefore, once again, buying transplants is your best bet.

If you do decide to start from seed, consider the length of time between seeding and flowering. If the chart indicates quite a long time (for instance, geraniums take 16 weeks), buy transplants from the nursery to get the earliest color. Or, if you are set up to handle your own seedlings, start the seeds early indoors and set out the transplants later on.

Name	Form	Color	Season of Bloom	Climate*	Exposure† S	Exposure† PS	Exposure† FS	Days to Germination‡	Seed to Flower (Weeks)	Comments and Uses
AGERATUM	6-12" mounds	Shades of blue and purple; pink and white also available	S, F	W	●	●		8(I)	10	One of the few annuals with true blue color; use for compact edging or hanging bouquets. Transplants are best. Can be brought indoors for fall and winter bloom. Good varieties include: 'Blue Blazer' (6"), deep blue; 'Blue Angel' (6"), mid-blue; 'Blue Mink' (12"), light blue; and 'Royal Blue' (6"), purple.
ALYSSUM	3-8" low trailing mat, 10-15" spread	White, purple, and rose	Sp, S, F	W	●			8(D)	8	Good as edging or a small-scale ground cover. Fast-growing, profuse bloomer, tough, and versatile. Faintly fragrant; shear for second bloom. Try 'Tiny Tim' (2-3"), white, for hanging bouquets. Other good varieties include: 'Carpet of Snow' (4"), white; AAS 'Rosie O'Day' (4"), deep rose; AAS 'Royal Carpet' (3-5"), violet purple; and 'Oriental Night' (4"), deep purple.
AMARANTHUS	24-60" erect, very vigorous, may spread 48"	Wide range of bright foliage colors on variously cut leaves	Sp, S	W	●	●		10(D)	10	Valuable in mass plantings or as a background plant for its vigorous growth and bright leaf colors. Good for hot, dry conditions. Varieties include: 'Early Splendor' (36"), rosy crimson; 'Flaming Fountain' (36"), bright red; 'Joseph's Coat' (Amaranthus tricolor 'Splendens') (36"), yellow, green, and red.
BACHELOR'S BUTTON	10-36" erect, bushy	Shades of blue, red, pink, and white	Sp, S	C	●	●		10(D)	10	Neat and bushy habit; long-lasting cut flowers. Use dwarf forms for edging and pots, taller varieties as borders. AAS 'Snowball' (12"), white, is heat and disease resistant (others may scorch in summer heat). Other good varieties include: 'Blue Boy' (36"), blue; 'Jubilee Gem' (12"), deep blue; and 'Polka Dot' mix (15"), mixed colors.
BALSAM	8-30" erect	Wide range—pink to purple, orange shades, scarlet, and white	S, F	W		●		8(D)	12	Neat plants bear long-lasting flowers resembling small camellias. Take full sun in cool areas. Bring indoors for winter bloom. 'Tom Thumb' (10" mix) has a compact habit and lavish bloom; ideal for pots or edging.
BEGONIA, fibrous	6-14" erect, bushy	Red, rose, pink shades, and white	S, F	C-W	●	●		14-21 (I)	16	This versatile plant is attractive in pots, hanging bouquets, the flower border, or as an edging. Blooming season lasts all summer. Tolerates partial shade. Transplants are best. Favored varieties include: 'Linda' (6-8"), deep rose; 'Viva' (6-8"), white; and 'Scarletta' (6-8"), scarlet-red. 'Galaxy' mix (6-8") and 'Cocktail' mix (6-8") are also valuable for their bronze foliage.
BROWALLIA	8-18" spreading	Blue shades and white	S, F	W		●		15(D)	12	This profuse bloomer has an ideal habit for hanging baskets, pots, or edging a flower border. Transplants are easiest. These varieties have a "no-pinch" habit: 'Blue Bells Improved' (8-10"), lavender blue; 'Silver Bells' (8-10"), white; and 'Sky Bells' (8-10"), sky blue.
CALENDULA	6-30" compact, spreading	Orange, yellow shades, and white	Sp, S, F, W	C-W	●	●		10(D)	8	Best in cool temperatures. Summer sowing will produce bright winter color in mild areas, spring and summer color in cold regions. Good for pots or borders. Variety 'Pacific Beauty' (18"), all shades, is heat resistant, has long-stemmed flowers ideal for cutting.
CANDYTUFT (Annual Iberis)	6-15" mounds	Red, pink, lavender, purple shades, and white	Sp, S	C-W	●	●		8(D)	10	Best in cool-summer areas. Fine for containers or borders. Varieties include 'Umbellata Dwarf Fairy' (8"), many shades, very compact and somewhat heat resistant, and 'Giant Hyacinth' type (14"), white, valued for cut flowers but very heat sensitive.
CELOSIA	6-36" erect	Yellow, gold, purple, pink, red shades, and white	S, F	W	●			10 (D, I)	8	Very vivid, bright colors. Cold sensitive. Pinching and overhead watering reduce flowering. The feathery Plumosa type has varieties 'Fairy Fountains' (14"), mix; AAS 'Golden Triumph' (30"), gold; and AAS 'Red Fox' (24"), red. Favorite Cockscombs types include: 'Jewel Box' (4-8"), mix; AAS 'Toreador' (12"), red and yellow; and 'Fireglow' (20"), red.

*Climate: C = cool; W = warm; †Exposure: S = sun; PS = partial shade; FS = full shade; ‡Germination: D = direct seed outdoors; I = start seed indoors; AAS = All America Selection

Name	Form	Color	Season of Bloom	Climate*	Exposure†			Days to Germination‡	Seed to Flower (Weeks)	Comments and Uses
					S	PS	FS			
CINERARIA	12-15″ erect	Blue, red, pink, purple shades, and white	W, Sp, S	C		●	●	10(I)	8	These beautiful bouquets of daisylike flowers are ideal for pots or a shady border. For winter color in mild areas, sow in fall.
COLEUS	12-30″ erect	Wide range of foliage color combinations in red, pink, green, yellow, and rose shades		W		●		10(I)		Spectacular leaf form and color, indoors or out. Excellent in a shady border. Needs direct filtered light indoors. Carefree series reaches 12″ and is self-branching. Rainbow series (15″) has fringed leaves. 'Magic Lace' (18″) has deeply cut and ruffled leaves.
COSMOS	24-72″ erect	Red, orange, gold, yellow, lavender shades, and white	S, F	W	●	●		5 (I,D)	12	Pinch for best flowering. Start indoors for an early bloom. The Early Sensation series (48-72″), all shades, includes the beautiful crimson-flowering AAS 'Dazzler.' The earlier-flowering Klondike series (30-36″), all shades, includes red-flowering AAS 'Diablo' and vermillion 'Sunset.'
CREEPING ZINNIA (Sanvitalia procumbens)	4-8″ spreading	Gold, yellow	S, F	W	●			7(D)	10	Beautiful, profuse bloom. Fast growing and versatile, this plant is stunning in hanging baskets or as a ground cover.
DUSTY MILLER	6-24″ bushy	Yellow	S	W	●			10-15 (I)	24	Includes many species valuable for their silver-gray foliage and interesting leaf shapes. Transplants do best. Good as an accent plant.
FAIRY PRIMROSE (Primula malacoides)	10-12″ erect	Lavender, pink, red, rose shades, and white	W, Sp	C		●	●	21-28 (I)	28	Delicate, profuse bouquets rise above fuzzy green foliage. Tolerates light frost; at its best in the cool weather of early spring. Use in pots, edgings, and beds, or in combination with spring-flowering bulbs. Transplants are best. 'Rhinepearl' series has best habit and bloom.
FEVERFEW (Chrysanthemum parthenium)	6-24″ mounds	Gold, yellow shades, and white	S, F	W	●	●		15 (I, D)	20	Compact, profuse blooming plant with "mumlike" flowers. Attractive in pots, or as a low border. 'White Stars' (6-8″) completely covers itself with white flowers. Other varieties include: 'Golden Ball' (8″), golden-yellow, and 'Snowball' (6-8″), white.
FORGET-ME-NOT (Myosotis)	6-24″ erect	Many blue shades, white, and pink	Sp, S	C		●		10(D)	6-8	Reseeds heavily. Sow in fall for earliest spring bloom. Beautiful as a ground cover for spring-flowering bulbs.
GAILLARDIA	10-36″ mounds	Gold, yellow, and red shades	S, F	W	●			20(D)	17	Forms profuse-flowering, compact mounds. Heat tolerant. Makes excellent cut flowers, fresh or dried. The Lollipop series (10″), bronze, scarlet, and yellow, is compact and double flowering.
GAZANIA	8″ bushy erect	Cream, yellow, orange, pink, bronze, red, and some with contrasting colors	S, F	W	●			10(D)	10	These large (5″) brightly colored, daisylike flowers have a long bloom period. Thrives in hot, dry locations. Good for edge or low border, colorful in large pots or boxes.
GERANIUM	6-36″ erect	Red, scarlet, pink, rose shades, and white	S, F	W	●	●		14-21 (I)	16	Seed-grown geraniums need no pinching, are compact and uniform, and have large blossoms. If available, use transplants. Great in containers; bring indoors for winter color. Varieties include: Carefree series (24″), all shades, and Sprinter series (18″), all shades.

*Climate: C = cool; W = warm; †Exposure: S = sun; PS = partial shade; FS = full shade;
‡Germination: D = direct seed outdoors; I = start seed indoors;   AAS = All-America Selection

Name	Form	Color	Season of Bloom	Climate*	Exposure† S	PS	FS	Days to Germination‡	Seed to Flower (Weeks)	Comments and Uses
GLOBE AMARANTH (*Gomphrena globosa*)	6-30" erect	Red, purple, blue shades, and white	S, F	W	●			14 (I,D)	10	Very heat and drought tolerant. Use dwarf forms as edging, taller ones in the border. Cut flowers for dried bouquets, Christmas tree decorations. Best to buy transplants, or start indoors in cold-winter areas. Varieties include: 'Dwarf Buddy' (6-8"), purple, and Standard mix (18"), all shades.
HELIOTROPE	12-48" bushy	Purple, lavender, and white	S, F	W	●			21(I)	21	Large fragrant flowers. Heat tolerant. Good potted plant; can be brought indoors. Best as transplants.
HOLLYHOCK	24-72" erect	Cream, pink, red, scarlet, yellow shades, and white	S, F	W	●			14-21 (I, D)	18	Flowers on tall, erect spikes make this a background or high border plant. Buy varieties that flower the first year; transplants are best. Good varieties include: AAS 'Silver Puff' (24-30"), silvery-pink, and AAS 'Summer Carnival' (48-72"), all shades.
IMPATIENS	6-20" mounds	Solid and bicolor shades of red, pink, violet, orange, and white	S, F	W		●	●	18(I)	12	Offers bright color in the shade for pots, hanging bouqets, edgings, and borders. Blooms profusely; cut back for second bloom. Use transplants. Favored varieties include: Elfin series (6-10"), single shades; Baby series (6-10"), single shades; Zig-Zag series (6-10"), bicolored white; and 'Imps' (12-15"), single shades.
LARKSPUR (*Delphinium*)	12-60" erect	Many shades of violet, blue, red, pink, rose, yellow, and white	S, F	C-W	●	●		18(D)	12-16	Use for tall accent in borders and beds. Grows in partial shade in hottest areas. Don't transplant; sow directly as early as possible. Varieties include AAS 'Connecticut Yankee' (30-42"), lavenders, blues, white, and 'Giant Pacific' series (60"), all shades.
LOBELIA	5-8" erect or trailing	Lavender, blue, pink, and white	S, F	W	●	●		18(I)	12	Neat, profuse-flowering plants. Transplants are best. Erect forms include: 'Crystal Palace' (5"), dark blue, and 'Heavenly' (8"), mid-blue, extra large flowers. Favorite trailers are: 'Blue Cascade' (8"), light blue, and 'Sapphire' (8"), dark blue with white centers.
MADAGASCAR PERIWINKLE (*Catharanthus roseus*)	6-24" mounds, some trailing	Red, pink, rose, and white, some with contrasting centers	S, F	W	●	●		15(I)	12-14	Bright, phloxlike flowers show up attractively against glossy foliage in borders, edgings, pots, or boxes. Use transplants. AAS 'Polka Dot' (6"), trailing, white with red centers, makes a fine ground cover.
MARIGOLD	6-36" erect or bushy	Solid and bi-color shades of yellow, red, gold, and orange	Sp, S, F	W	●			7 (I, D)	8-10	This most useful, obliging, and foolproof of all annuals has sizes to fit every need. Start indoors or buy transplants for early bloom; otherwise, sow direct. Favorites include AAS 'Petite Gold' (6-8"), golden-yellow; 'Bolero' (12"), gold/mahogany bicolor; 'Showboat' (13"), yellow; 'Gold Galore' (18"), orange-gold; 'First Lady' (18-20"), light yellow; and 'Happy Face' (26"), deep gold.
MORNING GLORY	Climbing vine to 20'	Violet, blue, red, pink shades and white, some with contrasting throats	S, F	W	●			7(D)	10	This vine will climb up a wall or a trellis, or provide color among your climbing crops. Dwarf forms are good in pots. Too much water or fertilizer reduces flowering. Good varieties include: 'Heavenly Blue' (10-12'), sky blue with light center; AAS 'Pearly Gates' (10-12'), white; and AAS 'Scarlet O'Hara' (10-12'), scarlet.
NASTURTIUM	6-15" bushy or trailing vine to 72"	Maroon, red, orange, rose, yellow, and cream	Sp, S, F	C-W	●			10(D)	6	For quick color and profuse blooms in pots and hanging baskets. Use dwarf, compact forms for edgings or low borders. Varieties include: 'Dwarf Double Jewel' (12"), bushy, many shades; 'Whirly-bird (6"), bushy, many shades; and AAS 'Double Gleam' (24"), trailing, all shades.

*Climate: C = cool; W = warm; †Exposure: S = sun; PS = partial shade; FS = full shade; ‡Germination: D = direct seed outdoors; I = start seed indoors;   AAS = All America Selection

Name	Form	Color	Season of Bloom	Climate*	Exposure†			Days to Germination‡	Seed to Flower (Weeks)	Comments and Uses
					S	PS	FS			
NEMESIA	8-24" erect	Most flower colors except green	Sp, S	C-W	●			10(I, D)	12	Charming for hanging bouquets, in pots, or window boxes; makes a colorful low border or edge. Start indoors for early bloom. 'Carnival' blend (10"), white, red, orange, and yellow, has a base-branching, no-pinch habit.
NICOTIANA	8-36" erect or bushy	Red, rose, lavender, green shades, and white	S, F	W	●	●		10(I, D)	8-10	Abundant, fragrant blossoms make this a favorite for borders, background, containers, and cut flowers. Needs afternoon shade in hot areas. 'Sensation Day-light' (36"), all shades but green, has blossoms that stay open all day; others open only at dawn and dusk.
NIEREMBERGIA	6-10" mat	Violet-blue	S, F	W	●	●		15(I)	16	Forms a compact, dense, flower-covered mat for pots, hanging baskets, rock gardens, or parking strips. Perennial in mild-winter climates. Start indoors, or buy transplants for early color.
PANSY	6-8" erect	Full range, some blotched	Sp, S, F	C	●	●		10 (I, D)	18	An old-fashioned favorite for pots, window boxes, edgings, and hanging bouquets. A cool-season performer; give partial shade in warmer areas. Transplants are easiest to handle. Varieties include AAS 'Imperial Blue' (7"), light blue with violet face and good eyes, and AAS 'Majestic Giants' (6"), wide range of colors with "painted faces." Both have good heat resistance.
PETUNIA	12-15" bushy mounds	Wide range of red, pink, blue, purple, yellow, orange, white, and single bicolor shades	S, F	W	●			12(I)	12-15	Versatile garden color for use in pots, hanging baskets, borders, and beds. F_1 hybrids are the best performers. Grandiflora varieties have large, ruffled flowers and vigorous growth. Multifloras are more compact and weather resistant, and bear smaller flowers in great profusion.
PHLOX, annual	6-15" erect or bushy	Blue, violet, crimson, pink, yellow shades, and white	S, F	C-W	●			12(D)	10-12	Compact, profuse bloomers for pots, hanging bouquets, low borders, beds, and cut flowers. Try AAS 'Twinkle' (7"), all shades, pointed petals, heat tolerant; 'Dwarf Beauty' mix (6-7"), all shades; and 'Globe' mix (8"), all shades, good forms, heat tolerant.
PINCUSHION FLOWER (Scabiosa)	18-36" erect	Many shades of red, blue, maroon, and white	S, F	C-W	●			12(D)	14	These fragrant, ball-shaped flowers are favored by hummingbirds. Disappointing in extreme heat. Pinch to encourage bushiness. Use in the border, bed, or as background for cut flowers.
PINKS (Dianthus)	3-15" erect and bushy	White, pink, salmon, red, rose, and violet	Sp, S, F	W	●	●		7(D)	6-12	Fine sturdy, compact plants. Fragrant flowers are good for cutting. Dwarf forms make a neat edging or hanging bouquet. Use taller varieties for borders. Varieties include: 'Baby Doll' (8"), red, pink, violet, and white; AAS 'China Doll' (10-12"), pink, red, and salmon-edged white; AAS 'Magic Charms' (6"), white, rose, scarlet, and white; AAS 'Queen of Hearts' (15"), scarlet-red; and 'Wee Willie' (3"), red, rose, and white.
PORTULACA	6" trailing	Red, rose, orange, yellow shades, and white	Sp, S, F	W	●			10(D)	8	This profuse, long-season bloomer thrives in hot, dry climates. Great for rock gardens, shallow pots, hanging baskets, or as a ground cover. 'Sunglo' has large double flowers and an excellent habit.
SALPIGLOSSIS	24-36" erect	Purple, red, pink, yellow, orange, buff shades, with contrasting veins	S, F	W	●			14(I)	20	Interesting color pattern; good massed in a bed, border, or as background. Excellent cut flowers. Pinch to encourage bushiness. May need staking. Buy transplants. 'Splash' is a good compact, free-flowering variety.

*Climate: C = cool; W = warm; †Exposure: S = sun; PS = partial shade; FS = full shade;
‡Germination: D = direct seed outdoors; I = start seed indoors;   AAS = All America Selection

Name	Form	Color	Season of Bloom	Climate*	Exposure† S	PS	FS	Days to Germination‡	Seed to Flower (Weeks)	Comments and Uses
SALVIA	6-36" erect and bushy	Scarlet-red, white, pink, and blue	S, F	W	●	●		12-15 (I)	8-10	The height of the variety dictates whether to use it in containers, edging, borders, or background. Avoid full shade and cool temperatures. Buy transplants. Of the many red-flowering forms of *Salvia splendens*, try 'St. Johns Fire' (12"), 'America' (16"), and AAS 'Evening Glow' (16-24"). *S. farinacea* has long, rich blue spikes.
SNAPDRAGON	6-36" erect	Many shades of red, pink, rose, orange, yellow, bronze, lavender, and white	S, F	C-W	●			7-14 (I, D)	14	Many varieties available; choose for height, color, and flower form. Dwarf types are good for pots, tubs, or as an edge. Taller forms are useful as borders, beds, or background. Generally heat sensitive, but AAS 'Bright Butterflies' (32"), many shades, has good tolerance. Other favorite varieties include AAS 'Little Darling' (15") and AAS 'Madame Butterfly' (30").
STATICE	12-36" erect	Red, rose, blue, purple, orange, and yellow	S, F	W	●			15-20 (I, D)	25	Choose varieties for color and height. Excellent cut or dried flowers.
STOCK (*Matthiola*)	12-36" erect	Lavender, purple, pink, rose, yellow shades, and white	W, Sp	W	●	●		14(D)	7-10	Colorful, fragrant flowers are attractive in massed display or border. Needs cool weather. Good varieties include: 'Trysomic 7' (12-15"), and 'Dwarf Ten Week' (12").
STRAWFLOWER (*Helichrysum*)	15-36" erect	Purple, red, rose, salmon, gold, yellow shades, and white	S, F	W	●			7(D)	10	Makes a superb cut flower, fresh or dried. Best as background plant to conceal its rather spindly habit.
SWEET PEA	8-36" mounds or climbing vines to 6'	Many shades of purple, red, pink, lavender, blue, and white	W, Sp, S	C-W	●			15(D)	16	Fragrant flowers in great profusion. Compact bush types are good in containers, borders, or beds. Vining types add color to wall or trellis. Direct seed in early spring. Sow in summer in mild areas for a winter bloom. Varieties with good heat tolerance include: 'Bijou' (15"), bush type; 'Knee High' (30"), bush type; and 'Royal' (6'), vine type.
THUNBERGIA	Trailing vine	Orange, yellow, and white with black throat	S, F	W	●			12(D)	12-16	Best in hanging basket or as a small-scale ground cover. Fast growing. May overwinter in mild areas. Available forms include: *Thunbergia alata* (Black-eyed Susan), and *T. gibsonii* 'Orange Lantern' with large, orange flowers.
TITHONIA	36-60" rather spreading to 4'	Orange-scarlet	S, F	W	●			5-10 (I, D)	16	These tall, robust plants thrive in hot, dry climates. Best used as a background plant. AAS 'Torch' is the available form.
VERBENA	4-20" spreading mounds	Red, pink, blue, purple, and white, some with white centers	S, F	W	●			20 (I, D)	10-12	Beautiful in pots, window boxes, hanging baskets, or as a ground cover. Fragrant flowers bloom in abundant clusters over a long period. Heat loving and drought tolerant. Start indoors for early bloom. Favorites include: AAS 'Blaze' (8"), scarlet; AAS 'Amethyst' (8"), blue; and 'Sparkle' mix (8").
VIOLA	6-12" bushy	Wide range of colors, single and bicolors	Sp, S	C-W		●		14-21 (I)	18	These tough relatives of the pansy have smaller flowers but longer bloom. Excellent for pots, tubs, hanging bouquets, edges, and beds. Buy transplants.
ZINNIA	6-60" erect	Wide range of single and bicolor shades, excluding blue	S, F	W	●			7(D)	8	This versatile old standby has many uses. Showy when massed in containers. Use elsewhere according to size—small ones as an edge, and taller types in borders, beds, or for background. Fine for cut flowers.

*Climate: C = cool; W = warm; †Exposure: S = sun; PS = partial shade; FS = full shade;
‡Germination: D = direct seed outdoors; I = start seed indoors;   AAS = All America Selection

Bulbs

The term "bulb" includes a whole range of fleshy-rooted plants. Not all bulblike plants are true bulbs, however. A true *bulb* is a central stem, surrounded by fleshy, underground leaves that store food in dormant periods. Examples are onions, tulips, daffodils, and lilies. A *corm* looks like a bulb, but here it's the stem, not the leaf, that stores food. Examples include gladiolus, colchicum, crocus, and freesia. A *tuber* is also a swollen underground stem that stores food, but here, new sprouts grow from several eyes on the surface. The tuberous begonia is an example. A *rhizome* still has a swollen underground stem, but it is long, tough, and grows from the leading end. Many iris are rhizomatous. A *tuberous rootstock* is a swollen root (where the food is stored) with a single growth bud. Anemone, canna, and dahlia are examples. A *bulblike perennial* is a fleshy-rooted, often clumping plant, such as the daylily and agapanthus.

Planning for bulbs in the garden. For a natural look, don't line the bulbs up in straight, boring rows—toss or roll them from a basket and plant them wherever they fall.

After blooming, a bulb's leaves must continue growing to store food for the following year. To make these leaves less visible, plant a low ground cover or annuals along with the bulbs. For a natural look, mix informal bulbs such as scilla, crocus, snowdrops, and aconite in a woodsy corner.

Some bulbs require winter chilling to grow and bloom. Tulips need up to two months of chilling at under 40 degrees; hyacinths, crocus, and daffodils need a month of cold. If you live in a mild-winter area, buy these bulbs early, and put them in the vegetable bin of the refrigerator before planting.

Daylilies can function as a kind of ground cover if they are massed. Keep them close to paths or terraces so you won't miss the fragrance.

Tuberous begonias look best in the sprawling, hanging-container forms. Hang them high in the shade of a tree so that the flowers can be seen from below. Guard against mildew by providing good air circulation. Erect kinds also can be grown in pots; when the weather is right, half-bury the pots in the garden—it's easier than transplanting.

Dahlias can be had in a wide range of flower and plant forms, suiting nearly any purpose. The dwarf kinds make fine bedding or pot plants. The taller kinds form a lush background for annuals. All are good for cutting. Try

Above: The violet and yellow of early-blooming crocus gives one of the first color accents to a spring garden.

Left: The colors of the crocus are reproduced on a larger scale in a bed of yellow and pale violet iris. Here, red Oriental poppies have been included and make a lively addition.

Bearded iris   Amaryllis   Bearded iris   Tulips and hyacinths

Crocus   Lily of the Nile   Tiger lily   Anemone

out the giant-flowered dahlias, but make sure to pinch out all but the largest buds and to provide staking to support the heavy heads.

Plant the taller gladiolus in a cutting garden. Cut the spikes when the first bloom opens at the bottom, and let the rest of the blooms open in a vase. Leave most of the leaves on the plant so that the corm can store food. Plant the dwarf kinds along with annuals in a border or bed, massing them for a most attractive effect.

Planting bulbs. To prepare the soil for any bulbs, spade in organic matter and superphosphate. If your soil is already light and rich in humus, just sprinkle a tablespoon of superphosphate into the planting hole and work it in slightly. Check the chart on pages 92–93 to find out how deep to go. Provide space between plants depending on what effect you want.

A few plants need special treatment. For begonias and caladiums, fill pots with moist, light potting mix (or use peat moss and sand in equal parts). Lay the begonia tuber on the surface with eyes (sprouts) up, and barely cover with potting mix. Leave it in a warm place until it sprouts, then bring it into the light. When it's time to set the plants out in a shady place, just plant the pot. Plant three tuberous roots of caladiums to one 8-inch pot. Keep the potting mix moist at all times.

For dahlias, plant after the last frost, digging down about 6 inches, then working a complete fertilizer into the soil at the bottom of the hole. Cover the fertilizer with a little of the dug-out soil, set in the tuber (keeping the long axis horizontal), and cover it slightly. As it sprouts, fill in the hole to keep the shoot barely covered. During planting, set a stake for tall varieties.

Ornithogalum   Tigridia   Canna   Daffodil

Dutch iris   Allium   Ranunculus   Tulips and hostas

Dividing bulbs. Many kinds of bulbs are easy to increase—in fact, many true bulbs (for example, narcissus) simply increase themselves by growing bulblets around the main bulb. Leave them in place; or lift the bulbs after the foliage dies, and break off the bulblets. In the fall, replant them separately. Leave the smallest with the main bulb.

Many kinds of lilies have bulbs that are divided into segments, or scales. To increase a planting, lift the main bulb when the plant dies and break off the largest outer scales. Replant them (and the parent bulb) immediately. They'll reach full size in about a year.

You can increase several kinds of bulblike plants simply by cutting them in pieces. For iris that grow from rhizomes, lift the old plant in late summer and cut off all the new rhizomes at the outer edges of the clump. Throw away the old center and replant the young pieces.

For dahlias, lift the plant when it dies in the first frosts. Cut the tubers apart, leaving a piece of the central stem and at least one growth bud on each. Then store the separated tubers until the spring planting.

Cut gladiolus corms that grow very large in half or in thirds, and dust them with sulfur to prevent rot during storage. If double corms or tiny corms have formed, just break them up. The cormels take two or three years to bloom.

Cut large begonia tubers in several pieces with an eye on each piece, and dust with sulfur to store.

Forcing and pot planting. Some bulbs can be forced to bloom indoors ahead of their normal season. Good forcing bulbs include amaryllis, colchicum, hyacinth, and scented narcissus (for example, the tazettas).

All except amaryllis can be potted or not. Force these bulbs by placing a layer of pebbles about 2 inches thick in a shallow container. Fill with water to just below the pebble surface. Set one or several bulbs on the pebbles and store the container in a cool, dark place until the bulbs root and begin to sprout. Then bring them into the light and let them bloom. Keep the water level just below the bulb base. (Or buy a special vase for forcing that holds the bulb in a cup above the water.) After the forced bulb blooms, discard it—it cannot store food for another year.

Large pots massed with bulbs such as tulips or hyacinths make striking displays. To make them grow and bloom together, fill pots with light potting mix and set the bulbs tightly together in the upper portion, planting 6 or more of the same kind and color. Set the pots outdoors and bury them in peat moss so that the tops of the bulbs are at the planting depth indicated on the chart. When the leaves are well grown and buds appear, lift the pots from the peat moss and set them in a display area to bloom. Buy new bulbs each year for pot displays, and discard the old.

Bulb Chart

Name	Height	Planting Depth	Exposure* S PS FS	Planting Season	Flowering Season	Comments
AUTUMN CROCUS (Colchicum)	6-12"	3-4"	●	August	September	Blooms without leaves, sprouts leaves in spring. Blue-pink or white flowers. Set on pebbles in water for forcing.
BEGONIA, tuberous	12-20"	Barely covered	● (PS)	Late winter	Summer	Trailing kinds make ideal hanging plants. Grow erect kinds in pots, sink in garden after frost. Need rather cool, moist shade. Good in containers.
CALADIUM	9-30"	Just covered	● (PS) ● (FS)	Spring	Bloom is inconspicuous	Plant them for their leaf color. Use them like begonias. Can grow indoors. Dormant in winter.
CANNA	18-60"	5-6"	●	After frost	Late summer, fall	These tropical-looking, bronze or green plants have spikes of bloom like limp gladiolus. Cut down when flowers fade; dig and store where ground freezes.
CROCUS	4-5"	2-3"	● (S) ● (PS)	Fall	Fall to spring by species	Need cold winter. Chill in refrigerator 1 month before planting in mild regions. Flowers are blue, purple, gold, and white.
DAFFODIL (Narcissus)	5-20"	Twice width of bulb	●	Fall	Spring	Big yellow trumpet is a favorite, but try tiny dwarfs, scented tazettas, and bicolors. Flowers face the sun. Force tazettas.
DAHLIA	6-60"	6"	●	After frost	Summer	Size ranges from little daisies to enormous 12-inch pompoms. Many petal shapes. No blue. Store tubers when plants die.
DAYLILY (Hemerocallis)	12-72"	1"		Early fall or early spring	Summer to fall	Grassy perennial with striking red, orange, yellow, or green bloom. Needs some shade in hot afternoons. Can be used as ground cover.
FLOWERING ONION (Allium)	9-60"	2-4"	●	Fall	Spring, summer	Balls of stars, often on giant stems. Need perfectly drained soil. Small species best in containers or rock gardens.
GLADIOLUS	18-72"	4-6"	●	Spring, summer	Late spring to fall	Plant some every two weeks in cutting garden. Dig up corms when tops are yellow. All colors. Dwarf kinds are good for bedding plants.
GRAPE HYACINTH (Muscari)	6-12"	2-3"	● (S) ● (PS)	Early fall	Spring	Leaves appear early but survive the cold. Flowers are blue or white, some with a strong grapey scent.

*S = sun; PS = partial shade; FS = full shade

Daylilies

Daffodils, candytuft, and violas

Bulb Chart

Name	Height	Planting Depth	Exposure* S PS FS	Planting Season	Flowering Season	Comments
HYACINTH	6-18"	5-6"	●	Early fall (needs cold)	Spring	Fragrant columns of pastel bells. Bulb size relates to bloom size; medium-sized bulbs should be planted, large-sized bulbs can be forced in winter.
IRIS	6-48"	Bulb 4"; Rhizome half covered	● ●	Summer or fall	Spring, summer	Two main flower forms: floppy bearded (rhizomatous) and stiff Dutch (bulbous). Many colors and heights. Remove dead leaves; mulch for cold.
LILIES (Lilium)	18-60"	3-6"; Madonna 2"	● ●	Fall	Spring, summer	Must have good drainage, constant moisture, and some shade in hot summer. Keep root zone cool. Many colors and forms.
LILY OF THE NILE (Agapanthus)	18-48"	Top at surface	●	Fall or spring in South, fall in Northeast	Mainly summer	This evergreen tender perennial forms clumps of strap-shaped leaves—tall clusters of blue, white bloom. Dwarf 'Peter Pan' is good for pots. Plant in containers in cold-winter areas; move indoors in winter.
SNOWDROP (Galanthus)	6-12"	3-4"	● ●	Fall	Late winter, early spring	Plant bulbs quickly or they may fail. Inadequate in warm-winter regions. White with green inner tips.
SNOWFLAKE (Leucojum)	12-18"	4"	●	Fall	Spring, early summer	Plant in drifts for mass display of white, green-marked flowers. Best in woodsy, natural-looking landscape.
SQUILL (Scilla)	5-15"	2-4"	● ●	Fall	Late winter, spring	Similar to loose hyacinths. Try English, Spanish bluebell with blue, pink, or white bloom. The earliest are for cold regions only.
STAR OF BETHLEHEM (Ornithogalum)	10-14"	4-5"	● ●	Early fall	Spring	Clusters of green-striped flowers, grassy leaves. May naturalize in some areas.
TIGRIDIA	18-30"	3-4"	● ●	Early spring	Mid to late summer	Treat like gladiolus, dig up when tops die. Speckled red, pink, yellow, or white bloom.
TUBEROSE (Polianthes)	12-15"	2"	● ●	Late winter	Late spring, summer	Plant outdoors only in warmest regions. Fragrance is their outstanding feature. Plant several to a pot, move them outside in warm weather.
TULIP	5-30"	2½ times bulb width	●	Fall (needs 8 weeks cold)	Spring	Chill in refrigerator in mild regions. Many kinds; bloom lasts through spring. Try tiny ones, use in pots.

*S = sun; PS = partial shade; FS = full shade

Azaleas and rhododendrons

Euonymus fortunei

Shrubs and Trees

Shrubs. Unassuming as they first may seem, shrubs can be the most important feature of your landscape because they form the permanent structure of your garden—as background, foundation planting, screen, espalier, or formal hedge. In addition, they may offer displays of seasonal color with flowers, fruit, or foliage.

One of the best ways to choose shrubs for your garden is to observe other gardens that you find attractive. Take a notebook, even a camera if possible. You may not be able to describe it by name, but if you show a color snapshot of its foliage to your local nurseryman, no doubt you will be led right to the shrub you want.

Look at shrubs as part of a landscape design. How can forms, textures, colors, and spacing be blended harmoniously? Consider what kinds of uses will fit your own landscape plans.

The following pages list a few of the many good shrubs that exist, and answer such questions as: How tall will they grow? Do they require sun or shade? Do they need any special attention? Do they have some striking feature, such as flowers, fruit, or fragrance? Even if you end up with plants other than those mentioned here, be sure to ask yourself these same questions about them.

Mature height is so important that the list is arranged by size. However, since size can vary in different climates and soils, the categories overlap.

Plants from 2 to 4 Feet

Shrubs in this height range can be used as foundation plants, low hedges, and borders; flowering kinds can be massed for display, or extended to line a drive or walk.

Azaleas. In the South, azaleas grow up to 4 feet (in the Northeast they range from 3 to 6 feet). All azaleas need similar growing conditions: morning sun or filtered shade; constant moisture; a great deal of air around the roots; and, preferably, acid soil. In alkaline or heavy soils, grow azaleas in pure peat moss, or even in raised beds. In lighter, more acid soils, use a mixture of half soil and half peat moss. For the lower South, plant Southern Indica and Kurume types. Southern Indicas include 'Brilliant' (spreading, red), 'Perfection' (spreading, light pink), and 'Ivoryana' (spreading, white with rose flecks). Kurumes include 'Appleblossom' (pink with white throat), 'Hese' (crimson red), and 'Ward's Ruby' (ruby red).

In the colder middle South, plant Kurume, Glenn Dale, and Gable varieties such as 'Rosebud' (violet pink) and 'Herbert' (deep purple).

In the upper South, plant Gables and Kaempferi hybrids that can take the winters. Kaempferi cultivars include 'Fedora' (clear pink) and 'Kathleen' (rosy red).

Boxwood. Clip it for a tight formal hedge, or let it grow naturally as a border. Korean boxwood (*Buxus harlandii*) is dense and stands up to seashore conditions. Japanese boxwood (*B. microphylla* var. *japonica*) is slow and dense, turns bronze in winter, and is hardy to 0° F. Common boxwood (*B. sempervirens*) is a familiar hedge plant. Prune it to keep it low, or else it will reach 15 to 20 feet.

Euonymus. Use as a small shrub; several varieties are available, including *E. fortunei* 'Golden Prince' with yellow leaf edges, 'Emerald Cushion', and 'Silver Queen' with white leaf edges. These plants will make low hedges, clipped or informal, and need sun for best leaf color.

Floribunda roses. These bloom in masses for five months of the year, and are striking as massed borders or foundation plantings, or along drives and walks. They require sun and a program of spraying, feeding, and pruning.

In cold-winter areas, they may require some winter protection.

Juniper. The junipers that fit this height range are hardy in all but the coldest northern climates. Allow sufficient space between plants—if air circulation is blocked, hot, damp, summer weather may cause disease problems. Try the cultivars 'Nick's Compact' and 'Nelson Blue'.

Plants from 4 to 8 Feet
Plants of this size range are excellent as single-accent shrubs. Some can be massed or planted in rows for screens and borders.

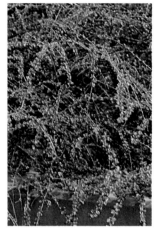
Cotoneaster

Abelia. An old-fashioned but still useful shrub in the warmer regions of the South, abelia can be used in sun or half shade as a screen, corner planting, or informal hedge. White or pink flowers attract lots of bees. Cut old wood to the ground in spring. Good forms are *A. grandiflora* 'Sherwoodii', a white-flowered dwarf, and 'Edward Goucher', with pink bloom.

Azaleas. In the Northeast, deciduous azaleas can stand milder winters (lows above 20° F.), but they need protection from extreme cold and extreme heat. (For growing conditions, see "Azaleas" in *Plants from 2 to 4 Feet.*)

The Knap Hill-Exbury hybrids that bloom in late spring include 'Berry-rose' (fragrant pale pink with orange center), 'George Reynolds' (large butter-yellow flowers with gold blotches and green throat), and 'Toucan' (creamy white with yellow flare and fragrance).

Mollis hybrids bloom a bit earlier and show foliage colors in fall. These include 'Adriaan Koster' (deep yellow) and 'Koster's Brilliant' (red vermillion).

Flowering quince

Cotoneaster. Two varieties, *C. apiculata* and *C. divaricata,* produce interesting pink flowers, red berries, and autumn color. The former is smaller and will make an informal hedge. The latter has long, fountain-shaped stems and does best as a screen. It will hold its berries into winter.

Firethorn (*Pyracantha***).** This shrub gives one of the finest displays of fruit, bearing dense clusters of orange or orange-red berries in late summer and fall. The varieties of *P. coccinea* are the hardiest. Use them in full sun as sprawling, thorny hedges; train them against fences; or espalier them on a wall. After a branch fruits, cut it back to a lateral to force more fruiting wood.

Flowering quince (*Chaenomeles speciosa***).** This is a good deciduous shrub for the sun. In early spring, the bare branches are covered with red, pink, or white flowers, followed by red new growth. In summer, quincelike fruit ripens among glossy green leaves. This shrub can be clipped into fairly formal shapes for small hedges, or grown naturally (prune out flowering branches to force new flowering wood).

Heavenly bamboo (*Nandina domestica***).** Its fragile foliage and frothy bloom make a pleasant tracery against a wall. It takes sun or shade, but is hardy only in the mild climates. Old stems are leggy and ugly—cut them to the ground. If a whole plant is leggy, cut half the stems; let new growth start, then cut the rest.

Juniper

Japanese holly. The small varieties are a good choice. The stiff growth makes them useful as a barrier plant, whether sheared or informal. Try the cultivar 'Convexa', or the more vigorous and larger 'Hetzi'.

Junipers. There are several Pfitzer varieties and varieties of *J. sabina* in this height category. In pruning, don't lop off branch ends; cut back to a main stem to preserve the graceful layered shape.

Mugho pine (*Pinus mugho***).** This valuable, slow-growing accent shrub takes shade. The shape is always interesting and it takes well to bonsai-style pruning. Or you can hold it at a given size by snapping off new growth (candles).

Forsythia × intermedia 'Spectabilis'

Ligustrum hedge (Privet)

Lagerstroemia indica (Crape Myrtle)

Plants from 6 to 12 Feet

Many of these grow wide as well as tall. Use them as hedge and screen plants, or as background to hide walls and fences.

Fatsia japonica. Sometimes sold as *Aralia sieboldii.* This pattern plant has huge, many-fingered leaves that are striking in partial shade. Use for a tropical effect in the ground or in a container. It is hardy only to 18° F.

Forsythia. This fountain-shaped shrub is covered with clear yellow flowers in early spring. Use it as an espalier on a sunny wall, or blend it into a shrub border for splashes of winter color. Good cultivars are 'Beatrix Farrand', with deep yellow flowers marked orange; *F. intermedia* 'Karl Sax', 'Lynwood', 'Spectabilis', and 'Spring Glory', with flowers from deep to pale yellow.

Japanese privet *(Ligustrum japonicum).* Hardy to 10° F., this makes a fine hedge plant for the middle and lower South and is one of the best plants for formal pruning. The plants take sun or part shade, and produce odd-scented white blooms and black berries that attract birds. Some of the cultivars, notably 'Texanum', grow lower than others.

Lilacs. These provide both bloom and fragrance. They like sun, but in very hot weather they need some afternoon shade. They prefer an alkaline soil. Don't prune too heavily or next year's bloom will be lost. Colors range from white through pinks to lavenders and purples. Among species under 12 feet tall are *Syringa* × *chinensis*, with rose-purple flowers ('Alba' is white); *S. josikaea*, with fragrant purple flowers; and *S.* × *swegiflexa*, with pink flowers.

Plants for Tall Screens, Hedges, Windbreaks, or Summer Protection

These are the tallest shrubs or branching trees. They will grow to 20 feet for windbreaks, or screen out unwanted views. To cut a strong prevailing wind, keep enough open space in your screen to let a little wind through. By creating turbulence, this pushes the main flow of air well above your head. Beware of dense or solid barriers—they may create a wave effect, inviting the wind to swoop down into your garden.

Arborvitae *(Thuja occidentalis).* This shrub makes an excellent evergreen screen or hedge plant, especially where icy wind is a problem. The variety 'Columnaris' (also called 'Fastigiata') is a good choice, growing to about 25 feet on the naturally columnar plant. Trim or clip it if desired.

Cherry laurel *(Prunus caroliniana).* This will grow to 20 feet, and will stay compact if pinched or lightly trimmed. It is widely adapted in the South.

Crape myrtle *(Lagerstroemia indica).* Give this deciduous shrub or small tree abundant sun and heat or it may mildew. It grows 8 to 20 feet and produces profuse summer bloom. (There are new dwarf forms that fit the lower-height categories.)

Irish yew *(Taxus baccata* 'Stricta'). This conifer has no cones, and it grows naturally into dark-foliaged, 20-foot columns. Odd-shaped, scarlet, fleshy fruits are poisonous. If you plant it as a windbreak, leave a little space between each plant for wind to pass through and create turbulence. Clip formally, if desired.

Especially for Entrances

If what you need is a single, striking plant that behaves well and won't block passages or spread out of bounds, consider the following:

Burford holly *(Ilex cornuta* 'Burfordii'). This spineless form grows naturally to 15 feet, but it can be pruned to any height from about 4 feet. In a sunny spot, it produces red berries on dark foliage.

Cornelian cherry *(Cornus mas).* This small, deciduous dogwood is interesting for its bloom, fall color, and fruit. In March, it bears abundant, very early yellow flowers on bare twigs; then it has yellow or red leaves in fall. The edible red fruit hangs on from September until some hungry birds (or humans) eat them.

Leatherleaf mahonia *(Mahonia bealii).* This bold-looking plant has large leaves divided into many spiny leaflets. It will grow to as much as 10 feet, but pruning will hold it down. It takes sun or part shade, and produces spikes of purple fruit at the tops of its stems.

Twisted juniper *(Juniperus chinensis 'Torulosa').* This slow-growing plant becomes a columnar plant 10 to 15 feet tall that needs sun. The Pfitzer group of junipers grow to from 2 to 10 feet high, and can fill spaces from 10 to 15 feet across. Foliage color ranges from gold to green.

Mahonia

Trees

The selection of trees offered below is limited to only a few small or slow-growing kinds that provide something special in a small garden—a display of flowers, colorful or interesting foliage, or the ability to grow well in large containers.

Try to suit the tree to its use. A tree that drops fruit or whose roots push up through pavement won't do for a patio; a spreading, low-branched saucer magnolia won't fit a narrow space.

Some flowering trees (such as dogwood or goldenrain) look best at a distance; others (such as delicate crabs and cherries) look best close up. If possible, inspect mature trees before making your decision.

If you have a special interest in trees, consider joining the International Shade Tree Conference. It will give you current information about the selection, care, and planting of trees suitable for your area. Membership includes a subscription to the *Journal of Arboriculture,* and a special rate on publications on landscape trees and shrubs. For membership information, write to ISTC, P.O. Box 71, Urbana, Illinois 61801.

Bradford pear

Bradford pear *(Pyrus calleryana 'Bradford').* Deciduous. An upward-sweeping branching pattern creates a pyramidal tree that is 30 to 35 feet high. It grows at a moderate rate, and it has oval, 1½- to 3-inch, wavy-edged leaves.

Use. Indispensible in the lawn, near the patio for shade, or along a pathway.

Distinctive features. Good in all seasons. White flower clusters in spring are followed by small, inconspicuous russet fruits that attract birds. Beautiful deep green, lustrous leaves dance with the slightest breath of wind, turn a dazzling bronzy-scarlet in fall. Even when bare in winter, the fruit-dotted branches present a bold picture.

Crape myrtle *(Lagerstroemia indica).* Deciduous. Trained as a single-trunk tree, it has a vase-shaped or round form. Grows slowly to 15 to 30 feet, with glossy, deep green, oval (1- to 2-inch) leaves.

Use. A lawn or street tree. Plant in front of a woodland area. Best in hot summers.

Lagerstroemia indica (Crape Myrtle)

Distinctive features. Long (up to 12 inches) clusters of crinkled, crapelike flowers extend from the ends of the branches. Blooms over a long period in summer in shades of white, pink, rose, and lavender. Leaves are orangish-red in fall. Mottled tan bark and interesting branching pattern make the bare tree attractive in winter.

Drawbacks. Susceptible to mildew in cool summers.

Varieties. Indian Tribe crape myrtles, recently developed by the National Arboretum, Washington, D.C., are superior in performance, hardiness, and mildew resistance.

Cercis canadensis (Eastern Redbud)

Eastern redbud in flower

'Red Jade' crabapple

Flowers of *Cornus florida* (Flowering Dogwood)

Eastern redbud *(Cercis canadensis).* Deciduous. Although it starts slowly, the redbud eventually becomes a wide-spreading, round-headed tree, varying in height from 20 to 30 feet. Rich green, heart-shaped leaves are 3 to 6 inches long.

Use. Combines perfectly with dogwood. Makes a pleasant shade tree.

Distinctive features. Small, pealike clusters of pinkish-purple, red, or white flowers cloak the branches in spring, turn bright yellow in fall. Brownish-red seed pods decorate the bare limbs in fall and winter.

Varieties. 'Forest Pansy' has pinkish-purple flowers and purple foliage on red stems; 'Alba' is a profuse white-flowering variety; 'Oklahoma' is a red one.

Flowering crabapples *(Malus* **species).** Deciduous. Of the over 200 varieties of flowering crabapples, here are half a dozen that fill at least two of the three requirements listed here: 1. beautiful spring flowers; 2. resistance to disease; 3. a fall show of fruit.

Use. Bring them in close, on patios, in containers, in entries, or arching over paths or driveways.

Varieties. 'Red Jade' is also the color of the fruit; it has white flowers, and weeping branches. 'Katherine' has large, double pink flowers, grows to 15 feet, and bears yellow fruit; 'White Angel' has a white bloom and tiny scarlet fruit that cling into winter; *Malus sargentii* is a broad, 8-foot shrub with red buds opening white, and red fruit; 'Van Eseltine' has clusters of red buds opening pink and fading white, and golden fruit; and 'Snowcloud', growing to 25 feet, has double flowers, pink buds opening white, and dark green foliage.

Flowering dogwood *(Cornus florida).* Deciduous. The horizontal branching pattern forms a rather flat-topped globe about 20 to 30 feet high. Slow to moderate growth. The oval, 6-inch-long by 2-inch-wide, bright green leaves are characteristically veined.

Use. Wherever you want one of the best spring flower shows. Fine specimen tree. Cooling summer shade for the patio.

Distinctive features. One of the most beautiful American natives. Spring flowers (often fragrant) clothe the naked branches in shades of red, pink, rose, or white. Leaves turn glowing red in autumn, accompanied by bright red berries.

Drawbacks. If used as a lawn tree, it may be severely harmed if lawn mowers bump the trunk.

Varieties. Many are available, including the red-flowering 'Cherokee Chief' and the white 'Fragrant White Cloud'.

Flowering plums *(Prunus* **species).** Deciduous. This very versatile group of trees has many different species and varieties. Most grow rapidly.

Use. Use according to their form—near the patio, in the lawn, in containers, or along the street. Prune high to allow room for walking under.

Distinctive features. Beautiful spring flowers covering the naked branches, and purple foliage. Several forms of *P. cerasifera* 'Atropurpurea' (also called *P. pissardii*) are widely available. 'Thundercloud' is a round-headed tree that reaches 20 feet high and wide. 'Newport' grows a little higher (25 feet) with the same spread. The more graceful *P.* × *blireiana* (25 feet by 20 feet) is a popular fruitless tree. Reddish-bronze in foliage, it bears double pink flowers, in contrast to the single pink clusters of the 'Atropurpurea' varieties.

Goldenrain tree *(Koelreuteria paniculata).* Deciduous. This open-branching, round-headed tree grows slowly and rarely reaches 35 feet, commonly 20 to 25 feet. Long (15-inch) leaves are divided into 7 to 15 pointed leaflets.

Use. Valuable as a lawn or street tree.

Distinctive features. Dense summer bloom is a fine feature of this tree. Long (12- to 18-inch) clusters of lemon yellow flowers bloom in billowy

Left: *Koelreuteria paniculata* (Goldenrain Tree)

Above: *Acer palmatum* (Japanese Maple)

masses. Interesting, papery, Japanese-lanternlike fruits follow the flowers and last long into winter. New foliage opens salmon-pink, gradually turns dark green. Twisted branches and bark add winter appeal. The tree is strong, takes wind, heat, drought, and cold.

Japanese maple *(Acer palmatum)*. Deciduous. This usually multitrunked tree has an open, irregular habit, and is somewhat weeping, with a domed appearance. It grows slowly, rarely to more than 15 to 20 feet. Leaves are 2 to 4 inches long, and deeply cut into 5 to 9 serrated lobes. Foliage is red, purple, or green.

Use. Not only is this one of the finest specimen trees for patios or entranceways, but it also thrives in containers. Grows best in partial shade.

Distinctive features. The artistic branching pattern and leaf structure present a light, airy, oriental feel. Brilliant scarlet fall color. Young growth glowing red. Valuable leaf and branch color.

Varieties. 'Burgundy Lace', soft, lacy effect, deeply cut and serrated burgundy leaves on green stems; and 'Dissectum', low, weeping habit, finely cut, fernlike green leaves.

Thornless honey locust *(Gleditsia triacanthos* **var.** *inermis)*. Deciduous. These fast-growing trees vary according to variety from wide and spreading to pyramidal, and range in height from 35 to 75 feet. Leaves are 10 inches long and divided into many small leaflets.

Use. Fine as a lawn tree. Gives light summer shade.

Distinctive features. Although it is extremely tough, it has an attractive, light, airy form. In fall, the leaves turn soft yellow, then drop, dissolving and filtering into the lawn (which means that you don't have to rake the leaves). Available in colorful leaf forms.

Varieties. 'Imperial' has the densest foliage, is upright and symmetrical to 35 feet; 'Sunburst' has young yellow foliage against older green leaves, giving the appearance of a yellow bloom in spring and summer. Forms an irregular, broad pyramid, 30 to 35 feet high.

VEGETABLES

In growing vegetables, there are a few basic rules to follow: keep the moisture supply constant and uniform; make sure that nutrients are available to the plant every day during the growing season; don't wait until a short-season plant shows distress to feed it; plant vegetable varieties that mature from seed or transplant in 40 to 60 days in soil that has enough fertilizer to last their season.

The 12-month harvest. Storing, freezing, and canning your home-grown produce can give you a year-round harvest. To keep production rolling, pick all crops as they reach usable size, or else the rest of the crop may suffer. For example, one fully ripe cucumber will stop the set of new ones, and a few old pods of peas or beans left on the vine will reduce the set of new ones.

Some vegetables will have to be stored in the ground. One experienced year-round gardener says, "When winter is about to set in, we have an ample supply of root crops and other crops left in the ground to see us through to next year's first harvest. We give carrots, leeks, onions, salsify, Jerusalem artichokes, and parsnips a few inches of mulch to keep the ground from freezing (snow is a bonus mulch), and dig them out when needed. And they are as fresh as can be."

Beets. For storage, plant the variety 'Long Season' or 'Winter Keeper'. These beets will grow to an amazing size (three-fourths the size of your head) and stay sweet and nonfibrous into spring.

With timely planting, prompt picking to encourage bearing, and winter mulching of root crops, the garden harvest can extend throughout the entire year.

Onions. The best storage varieties are the late-maturing pungent onions (with short, shriveled necks) such as 'Southport White Globe', 'Southport Red Globe', 'Red Granex', 'Early Yellow Globe', 'Ebenezer', and 'Yellow Spice'.

Turnips. Harvest early varieties, such as 'Tokyo Cross' (35 days), when they are about 2 inches in diameter (before they get pithy). Sow 'Purple Top White Globe' (60 days) to use in fall and winter.

The roots of 'Purple Top' are crisp when they are 4 inches across. Turnips and rutabagas both store well in the ground for winter use. (However, don't store them in the basement or garage—they give off odors.)

Squash. Winter squash varieties can be stored for a long period, if allowed to mature fully. Pick them before a hard frost. Be sure to cut the stems from the vine—fruits without stems don't store well. To test fruits for ripeness, use your fingernail; if they feel hard, they are ripe.

Winter squash varieties are divided into three classes: *Acorn or Danish type.* 'Table King' (80 days), a bush type; 'Table Queen Ebony' (85 days), with large vines.

Maxima type (small to large squash). 'Gold Nugget' (85 days) has small fruit, is a bush-type vine; 'Buttercup' (100 days) has medium-sized fruit and a large vine; 'Hubbard' (110 days) has large fruit and a large vine; 'Banana' (110 days) has large fruit and a large vine.

Butternut type. The variety 'Butternut' (95 days) produces small fruits on a large vine.

Asparagus

"After the harvest." For a long storage life, each vegetable needs optimum temperature, humidity, and air circulation. But the right storage temperatures are hard to find, even in the coldest climate.

However, most vegetables and fruits will store well at home if you can provide two climatic situations: cold and humid, and cool and dry. For the cold, you can use an old refrigerator (lower it to 33° F.). If you put green vegetables (for example, lettuce, Brussels sprouts, cabbage, broccoli, and kale) in a plastic bag with a few holes punched in it, and then place the bag in the refrigerator, such vegetables will last a month or even longer.

For winter squash, you need the driest, cool (50°–60° F.) spot in your garage or basement. If possible, put them on a ventilated shelf, with a little air space between them to get the winter squash to last from two to three months.

Low temperatures (32°–40° F.) and high humidities are best for beets, carrots, celery, celeriac, kohlrabi, parsnips, rutabagas, salsify, and turnips.

Green tomatoes need warmth (55°–70° F.) and little air circulation.

Store potatoes at 45°–50° F., away from all light. This temperature range needs to be adhered to rather strictly: if it goes above 50°, the potatoes will begin sprouting and shriveling; if it goes below 40°, the potatoes will develop a sweet taste as the starch turns to sugar.

Asparagus

If the first planting is done carefully, you will get 10 to 15 years' production with little effort on your part from one year to the next.

Transplants or seed? It takes three years from seeding for asparagus to produce a full crop. Planting transplants or crowns (year-old plants) from a nursery will save one year in crop production. For thick spears, plant deeply.

Don't forget. Since the fernlike foliage manufactures the food needed by the roots, allow it to develop each year; then cut it back when dry in fall. The first year, let all but a few stalks grow; take more spears the second year. The third year will give several weeks of cutting.

Feed twice a year—once before growth starts, and again after harvest. If space is limited, use the flower border to plant a 4-foot-wide row of asparagus.

Varieties. Rust-resistant 'Mary Washington' or 'Waltham Washington'.

Yellow wax beans

Broccoli

Beans

Warm-season green bush beans and green pole beans are easy to grow.

Transplants or seed? You can use peat pots or seed the beans directly into the soil. If direct seeding, wait until the soil has warmed up to at least 60°, or else some of the seed will rot. If heavy rains or watering make the soil crust over, the beans will break their stems trying to break through the heavy or crusted soil. To prevent this, cover the seed row with a light mulch, or fill the seed furrow with a lightweight mix before planting. For the first early crop, you can plant in peat pots and set them out after the true leaves have developed. However, seed directly for succession plantings.

Don't forget. Inconsistent water supply will reduce the yield. Water stress at blossom time will make blossoms drop from the plant. Water stress while the beans are forming will produce "pollywogs"—only the first few seeds will develop; the rest of the pod will shrivel to a tail.

Pick snap beans at the succulent stage, not later. It only takes a few overmature pods to reduce yields considerably. Pick the old ones off the plant.

Varieties. *Bush green.* There are many varieties. 'Topcrop' AAS (49 days), 'Tendergreen' (53 days), 'Tendercrop' (53 days), 'Tenderette' (55 days), and 'Bush Blue Lake' (58 days).

Bush wax. Most frequently recommended: 'Early Wax' (54 days), 'Pencil Pod Wax' (54 days), and 'Resistant Kinghorn Wax' (54 days).

Pole green. 'Blue Lake' (60 days), and 'Kentucky Wonder 191' (65 days).

Bush lima. Limas require warm soil and more total heat than green beans do. 'Henderson Bush' (68 days), baby limas, and 'Fordhook 242' (75 days), heat-resistant, large, thick limas.

Pole lima. 'Florida Butter' (78 days), and 'King of the Garden' (88 days).

Horticultural. 'Dwarf Horticultural' (60 days). Large-seeded beans should be used in the green-shell stage.

Fava, or broad bean, or windsor. 'Long Pod' (85 days), a cool-weather plant, is not a true garden bean but is related to each of the above. Plant in spring for a fall crop—it will not produce in summer heat. Substitute them for pole limas, green-shell or dry, in short-season areas.

Garbanzo, or chick pea. This bush-type bean produces one or two seeds in each puffy little pod. Use in green-shell stage or dry.

Soybean. 'Verde' (90 days), and 'Kaurich' (100 days). As easy to grow as bush beans.

Beets

Beets prefer cool weather, but they will tolerate a wide range of conditions. For a year-round harvest in mild climates, make additional plantings over a long period.

Transplants or seed? Direct seed in early spring. Thin early to 1-inch spacing. Thin to 2-inch spacing when the young plants are large enough for greens.

Don't forget. Beets will become stringy and tough if there is insufficient moisture, or competition from weeds or other beets. Beets must grow steadily, without interruption.

Varieties. 'Ruby Queen' AAS (54 days), 'Early Wonder' (55 days), 'Burpee's Golden' (55 days), and 'Detroit Dark Red' (60 days).

Broccoli

A cool-weather crop, broccoli can be grown in the early spring and again in the fall. (Fall plantings tend to be more successful.)

Grow sprouting broccoli as you would grow cabbage. Broccoli is more heat-tolerant than cauliflower. It can be harvested over a long period. After the center cluster of buds has been cut (when it's still compact and before the flower heads turn yellow), then the sideshoots develop. You can harvest these for at least a month.

Transplants or seed? Plant transplants in early spring; plant seed or transplants in the fall.

Varieties. 'Spartan Early' (55 days), 'Green Comet' AAS (58 days), 'Green Sprouting' or 'De Cicco' (60 days), and 'Waltham 29' (88 days).

Brussels Sprouts

A cool-weather crop best grown for a fall or winter harvest, Brussels sprouts are miniature, mild cabbages that grow on the stem. The sprouts mature in sequence as long as weather permits. If you remove the leaves from beneath the lowest sprouts and twist them off, the sprouts above will continue to develop.

Transplants or seed? Use transplants.
Don't forget. For a full harvest in cold-winter areas, pinch out the growing tip in early fall. All the sprouts will be ready at the same time. For sweeter sprouts, wait until after a moderate freeze before harvesting.

Varieties. 'Jade Cross' AAS (80 days), and 'Long Island Improved' or 'Catskill' (90 days).

Cabbage

Cool temperatures and rich soil make the best cabbages. The variation in leaf form and head color make cabbage a favorite for a flower border, as well.

Transplants or seed? Buy transplants for earliest planting. Later on, sow seeds directly or start later plantings in peat pots.
Trouble expected? In warm weather, the heads of early varieties may split soon after maturing. To slow down the splitting, withhold water, or partially root-prune the plant when the heads are formed. To break some of the roots, simply twist the plant.

Varieties. *Early.* 'Emerald Cross' AAS (63 days) is slow to bolt, and 'Golden Acre' (64 days) is yellows-resistant but quick to split.
Midseason. 'King Cole' (74 days) is yellows-resistant and tastes excellent fresh or as kraut, and 'Market Prize' (76 days) is yellows-resistant, vigorous, and gives a heavy yield.
Red. 'Ruby Ball' AAS (68 days), and 'Red Acre' (76 days) are deep dark-red, resistant to yellows and splitting, and make fine pickling cabbage.
Savoy. 'Chieftain Savoy' (88 days) has densely curled, crinkled leaves, and 'Savoy King' AAS (90 days) is resistant to yellows and splitting, and has crinkled leaves.
Late. 'Danish Ballhead' (100 days) stores well and is split resistant.

Carrots

No other vegetable supplies food for as long a time as the adaptable, versatile carrot.

Transplants or seed? Direct seed randomly in a wide swath (see page 32); this makes thinning easier and gives a better crop. Apply a thin mulch of vermiculite, bark, grass clippings, or clear plastic (remove the plastic once the seedlings appear). This prevents the soil from crusting over.

Varieties. *Short to medium.* These are good for wet fall and winter and heavy soils: 'Royal Chantenay' (70 days), 'Danver's 126' (72 days), and 'Spartan Bonus' (75 days).
Long and slender. These need deep, loose soil and do better in light, sandy

Brussels sprouts

Cabbage

Carrots

soils: 'Pioneer' (67 days), 'Nantes' (72 days), and 'Imperator' AAS (77 days).
Midget. Good in heavy soils and containers: 'Baby Fingers' (65 days).

Cauliflower

This cool-weather crop is more demanding than broccoli or cabbage. It will not head up properly in hot weather, nor will it stand as much cold as cabbage.

Transplants or seed? Buy transplants, or start in peat pots.

Varieties. 'Snow King' AAS (50 days), 'Snowball' strains (60 days), 'Self-Blanche' (70–72 days) for fall garden, 'Early Purple Head' (80–85 days), and 'Royal Purple' (95 days).

Celery

Celery needs more attention than most vegetables do: fertile soil; successive, large doses of fertilizer; and a plentiful, constant water supply. Plant in early spring or summer for fall/winter harvest.

Transplants or seed? Buy transplants, or grow seedings indoors in peat pots (10 to 12 weeks before transplanting).
  Don't forget. Celery needs lots of food and water. Mature celery produces great quantities of seeds that can be used for flavoring.

Varieties. 'Fall Green Light' (125 days), 'Summer Pascal' (135 days), and 'Utah 52-70' (135 days).

Chinese Cabbage

A cool-weather crop, Chinese cabbage will bolt to seed in the long days of late spring and summer. Grow as fall and early-winter crops.

Transplants or seed? Buy transplants, or start in peat pots.

Varieties. 'Michihli' (75 days) and 'Burpee Hybrid' (75 days).

Chard, Swiss Chard

Chard is a beet, but it produces edible leaves and stalks rather than edible roots. You can harvest a single planting over many months—just cut the leaves and stalks from the plant as it grows. Very easy to grow.

Varieties. 'Fordhook Giant' (60 days) has wide, thick, white stalks with dark green, fleshy leaves. 'Lucullus' (60 days) has white stalks with light green leaves. 'Rhubarb' (60 days) has crimson stalks with dark green, pink-ribbed leaves, and a more delicate, sweet flavor than other varieties.

Collards

Although related to kale, collards will withstand hot summer weather and take much more cold than cabbage. Collards can tolerate short periods of cold as low as 10° F.—indeed, a light freeze actually sweetens the flavor.

Transplants or seed? In spring, sow seed or set out transplants to stand 10 to 15 inches apart. In summer plantings, sow seed thinly and let seedlings grow until they are large enough for greens; then harvest seedlings to create a normal distance between plants.

Varieties. 'Georgia' (75 days) and 'Vates' (75 days).

Corn

Sweet corn responds well to attention, and requires a constant supply of water and a lot of space and warm sunshine.

Transplants or seed? If you plant seeds every two to three weeks after the soil warms, you will have a continuing supply through summer into fall.

Cauliflower

Celery

'Rhubarb' chard

Another way to get a continuous harvest is to plant early, midseason, and late varieties.

Trouble expected? To foil corn earworms, grow varieties with tight husks and a good tip cover. To keep birds away, slip a paper bag over each ear after it has been pollinated.

Don't forget. For good pollination, plant in a block of three to four rows instead of a single row.

Varieties. A great many varieties exist, ranging from early to late, yellow, white, and bicolor. Some favorites are 'Country Gentleman' (93 days), 'Earliking' (66 days), 'Golden Cross Bantam' (85 days), 'Iochief' (89 days), and 'Merita' (84 days).

Cucumbers

This is a warm-weather crop that grows quickly. There are many new varieties with a high level of disease tolerance, which makes cucumbers easy to grow.

Transplants or seed? For early planting, start in peat pots. When setting out the transplants, cover them with clear plastic to increase the temperature and guard against frost.

Don't forget. As soon as the fruits reach a usable size, pick them off the vine. Even if just one fruit is left to mature on the plant, the set of new fruit will stop completely.

Varieties. *Pickling.* 'Wisconsin SMP 18' (54 days), 'Patio Pik Hybrid' (55 days), 'Pioneer' (51 days), 'Burpee Pickler' (53 days), and 'Salty Hybrid' (50 days).

Slicing. 'Gemini 7' (61 days), 'Marketmore 70' (70 days), 'Burpless Hybrid' (62 days), 'Victory Hybrid' (60 days), 'Burpee Hybrid' (60 days), 'Meridian' (64 days), and 'Triumph' (63 days).

Eggplant

Harvest this warm-weather crop before maturity for best eating.

Transplants or seed? Start seeds in peat pots, or buy transplants.

Varieties. 'Burpee Hybrid' (70 days), 'Early Beauty Hybrid' (62 days), 'Burpee's Jersey King Hybrid' (75 days), 'Albino' (68 days), and 'Special Hibush' (82 days).

Endive

For full fall and winter harvests, grow endive as you would lettuce—plant the summer crop in partial shade to prevent bolting to seed.

Varieties. *Cut-leaf type (chicory).* 'Green Curled Ruffec' (95 days), 'Salad King' (98 days).

Broad-leafed type (escarole). 'Full Hearted Batavian' (90 days).

Kale

This vegetable is so attractive that you can even put it in the flower border. However, you need to know how to cook it—the older leaves are tough, stringy, and have a strong flavor. Use the first new leaves and seedlings in salads, along with lettuce. When using large leaves, always remove the tough stems and midribs, and chop the leaves before cooking. Cook as you would cook spinach.

A hardy plant, kale is at its best in the fall garden: it takes freezing weather—in fact, frost actually improves the flavor.

Transplants or seed? For early planting in the spring, use transplants. For the fall and winter garden, seed directly into the soil.

Varieties. 'Dwarf Blue Curled Vates' (60 days)—these low, compact, short-

Pickling cucumbers

A cubed eggplant

Romaine and 'Salad Bowl' leaf lettuce

'Crimson Sweet' watermelon

Long, hot, sunny growing seasons produce sweet melons. Clockwise, from the upper left, are honeydew, watermelon, crenshaw, and cantaloupe.

stemmed plants have blue-green, finely curled leaves and tolerate cold (below-freezing) temperatures. Use them almost all winter, as far north as Philadelphia; and 'Dwarf Siberian' (65 days)—this spreading kale has thick, broad gray-green, feathery leaves. A hardy variety, it tolerates cold especially well. Plants grow 12 to 16 inches tall, spreading 24 to 36 inches.

Lettuce

Plant this cool-weather crop in partial shade in summer to keep it from bolting to seed.

Transplants or seed? Start head lettuce in peat pots, or buy transplants, or sow seed ¼ to ½ inch deep.

Don't forget. Lettuce needs ample room to grow—12 to 14 inches for head varieties. Thin the rows ruthlessly.

Varieties. *Crisphead (also known as iceberg).* 'Great Lakes' (82–90 days), 'Ithaca' (72 days), and 'Imperial 456' (84 days).

Butterhead. 'Summer Bibb' (62 days) and 'Buttercrunch' (65 days).

Leaf Lettuce. 'Grand Rapids' (45 days), 'Prizehead' (45 days), and 'Bronze-leaf' (45 days) for early varieties; 'Slobolt' (48 days) and 'Salad Bowl' (45 days) for heat resistance.

Cos or romaine. 'Dark Green Cos' (76 days) and 'Paris Island Cos' (76 days).

Melons

Melons need space and warm weather. When the vines are growing vigorously, give them lots of water—but be far more sparing with water during the ripening period. You need healthy, vigorous vines to grow sweet, delicious melons.

Transplants or seed? Start seeds in peat pots indoors, three to four weeks before setting out.

Don't forget. Harvest melons at "full slip"—when only a slight pull will be enough to break the stem away from the melon. Harvest crenshaw and honeydew types when the blossom end feels soft.

Varieties. 'Burpee Hybrid' (85 days) and 'Burpee's Ambrosia Hybrid' (86 days). For resistance to fusarium wilt, try 'Harper Hybrid' (86 days), 'Delicious 51' (85 days), 'Gold Star' (87 days), 'Saticoy Hybrid' (88 days), 'Iroquois' (89 days), and 'Roadside F-1' (90 days).

Mustard

Treat this fast-growing, cool-season crop as you would lettuce. To get tender leaves, give the plants lots of fertilizer and water; for the best flavor and texture, harvest before they are full grown.

Transplants or seed? Sow seed in rows.

Varieties. 'Tendergreen' (35 days), 'Green Wave' (45 days), and 'Southern Giant Curled' (50 days).

Okra

Plant okra as soon as the soil is fully warm and there is no further danger of frost. Harvest regularly—as often as three times a week when production is high. Harvest the pods when they are 3 to 4 inches long, and no longer—if they are allowed to remain on the plant even for an extra day or two, the pods get too tough and fibrous to eat. In addition, mature pods left on the plant will reduce future yields greatly.

Varieties. There are many varieties, including: 'Perkins Spineless'—this dwarf grows up to 3 feet. Mature pods are ridged, green, and 7 to 8 inches long. 'Dwarf Long Pod' or 'Dwarf Green Long Pod' are the same type as

'Perkins Spineless', about 3 feet high, and with mature pods that are ridged, green, and 7 to 8 inches long. 'Clemson Spineless' is of medium height (about 4½ feet). Mature pods are 6 inches long, moderately ridged, and green.

Onions and Their Relatives

Onions need a fairly rich, friable soil, lots of food, and a constant supply of moisture. In cool weather they grow tops; in warm weather they form bulbs. Timing of the bulbing is controlled by temperature and day length. Varieties are classed as long-day and short-day.

Transplants or seed? Start from seeds, transplants, or sets. Sets are easiest—you can start pulling edible onions in only a month.

Trouble expected? Watch for thrips.

Varieties. 'Ebenezer' (105 days)—large bulbs with firm, pungent flesh; 'Yellow Globe Danvers' (110 days)—firm and pungent, medium-sized, flattened globe; 'Early Yellow Globe' (110 days)—keeps well, is a medium-sized globe with firm, pungent flesh; 'Southport White Globe' (110 days)—this medium-sized globe has firm, pungent flesh and is a good keeper; 'White Sweet Spanish' (110 days)—the largest white, this medium keeper has firm, mild, sweet flesh, and plants are available; and 'Yellow Sweet Spanish' (115 days)—this large, yellow bulb with mild, sweet flesh is a medium keeper but a good slicer; plants generally are available.

Green onions. You can use any variety of onion as a green onion, if you harvest it when the bulb is small. Yellow and white sets are available from garden stores and seed companies (yellow include 'Ebenezer', white include 'White Lisbon').

In addition to the bulbing types of green onions, there are several pe-

Okra

The onion family is extensive, including scallions, leeks, garlic—and many varieties of red, white, and yellow onions.

Parsley

Parsnips

rennial bunching types. These produce slender white stalks throughout the year.

Varieties. 'Beltsville Bunching', 'Hardy White Bunching', 'Evergreen Bunching' ('Nebuka').

Leeks. Unlike onions, these do not bulb. Blanch the thickened stems by hilling soil around them. To get long white stems, plant in trenches 4 to 6 inches deep, and hill soil against the stems after the plants are fairly well grown.

Transplants or seed? Buy transplants, or start from seed in peat pots.

Varieties. 'Swiss Special' (120 days) and 'Large American Flag' (129 days).

Chives. This perennial grows in clumps with hollow, grasslike leaves that rarely exceed 10 inches. Round heads of lavender-colored flowers cover the plant in late spring. Worth putting in the flower border as well as in the kitchen.

Transplants or seed? Because seed is slow to germinate, buy plants. Chives are very hardy; once established, they will spread rapidly. Divide clumps to extend plantings.

Plant care. Grow in a sunny window or a fluorescent light garden, as well as in the herb garden.

Snip the leaves off the plant at soil level; the plant will renew itself rapidly. Unless plants are clipped regularly (three times during the growing season), the leaves will become tough and inedible.

Garlic. In all but the coldest areas, set out garlic cloves in the fall. Harvest when the tops turn yellow the following summer. After bulbs dry, cut off tops and roots, and braid into strings or tie in bunches, and hang in a cool, dry place.

Shallots. These multiplying-types of onions divide into a clump of smaller bulbs that look like small tulip bulbs. Harvest when the tops die in summer, and replant smaller bulbs in the fall.

Parsley

One of the most popular herbs, parsley is easy to grow—in the vegetable garden, the flower border, or a container. Although treated as an annual, parsley is actually a biennial. It prefers partial shade and rich, moist soil. Thin, or plant transplants 6 to 8 inches apart.

Transplants or seed? Parsley is a slow starter and may germinate poorly. If you do start from seed, soak them in warm water to improve germination. Or buy transplants.

Don't forget. If you want an attractive garnish, plant one of the 'Moss Curled' varieties. For flavoring, the parsley most often used is 'Plain Leaved' or 'Italian' variety.

Varieties. 'Evergreen' (70 days), 'Plain Leaved' (72 days), 'Perfection' (76 days), and 'Moss Curled' or 'Triple Moss Curled' (80 days).

Parsnips

Parsnips develop long roots (12–18 inches). Add generous amounts of organic matter and dig the soil deeply before planting seeds. Or grow in raised beds with special soil, such as that prepared for long-rooted carrots or salsify.

Freezing won't harm these roots. Indeed, low temperatures are needed to change the starch into sugar, giving the parsnip its famous sweet, nut-like flavor.

Store the roots for winter use, or leave them in the ground and dig them out, as desired.

Transplants or seed? Seeds are slow to germinate. After sowing, cover the row with clear plastic to help speed germination. Remove plastic when the seedlings first appear.

Varieties. 'All-America' (105 days), 'Hollow Crown' (105 days), and 'Harris's Model' (120 days).

Peas

Southern. These are warm-weather crops that you can pick in the green-shell stage, or let ripen and store dried. 'Yardlong' or 'Asparagus bean' produces 24-inch beans; train it on a trellis or wire.

Transplants or seed? Seed direct in warm soil.

Varieties. 'Princess Anne Blackeye' (56 days), and 'California Blackeye #5' (75 days).

Edible-podded peas (sugar peas). Sugar peas have the tender, fleshy, podded qualities of snap beans, and the flavor and sweetness of fresh green peas. Harvest the pods just when the peas become visible—before they enlarge. If you grow the new variety, 'Sugar Snap', let the pods become plump before harvesting. Pods are cooked and eaten whole, like snap beans. If you miss that stage, eat them shelled.

'Sugar Snap' peas

English. Plant this cool-season vegetable early. You can plant several varieties of different maturity dates at the same time to get a long-term supply.

Check frequently to see if they are mature—peas are at peak quality for a relatively short time. Pick the pods when they are green and fully developed, and before the peas start to harden. Use or refrigerate the peas as soon as possible after harvest.

Varieties. □ Early. 'Progress #9' (60 days)—a heavy-producing dwarf vine that's resistant to fusarium wilt; 'Sparkle' (60 days)—a dwarf vine; 'Greater Progress' (62 days)—a dwarf vine; and 'Frosty' (64 days)—gives a large yield, freezes wonderfully, resists fusarium wilt.

□ Late. 'Lincoln' (67 days)—very sweet peas; 'Wando' (69 days)—heat resistant; and 'Green Arrow' (70 days)—gives a high yield, and is resistant to fusarium wilt, downy mildew, and leaf curl.

Peppers

Although peppers are classified as a hot-weather vegetable, early varieties can be grown in cool areas. Blossoms drop when night temperatures fall much below 60° F. and rise above 75° F.

'California Wonder' bell peppers

Transplants or seed? Sow seed in peat pots, or buy transplants.

Don't forget. Pepper plants need constant moisture—any stress from lack of water will cause blossoms to drop.

Varieties. *Sweet peppers.* 'Staddon's Select' (72 days), 'Bell Boy' (70 days), 'Yolo Wonder' (70 days), 'Keystone Resistant Giant' (80 days, resistant to mosaic), 'Sweet Banana' (65 days), and 'Canape Hybrid' (60 days).

Hot peppers. 'Hungarian Yellow Wax' (60 days), 'Long Red Cayenne' (70 days), and 'Red Cherry' (75 days).

Potato

The potato is a shortened, enlarged underground stem. It needs cool nights for good tuber formation, and needs a steady supply of moisture.

Transplants or seed? Buy certified seed potatoes or seed pieces.

Trouble expected? If the soil dries out after tubers begin to form, a second growth will begin when the soil becomes moist again, resulting in knobby potatoes or multiples. Alternate wet and dry conditions will cause "hollow heart" or cavities near the tuber center. Watch for insect invasions.

Don't forget. Start hilling (covering stems with soil) when plants are 5 to 6 inches high. You can pick potatoes rather than dig them if you use shal-

Potatoes thrive in plastic garbage bags.

Sweet potatoes

French pumpkin

low planting and peat moss, sawdust, or straw rather than soil to hill over the plants.

In warm-summer areas, plant potatoes as soon as you can work the soil in the spring. For early potatoes, space closely (30 inches between rows and 12 inches between plants) so the plants shade the soil and prevent excessively high soil temperatures. Or mulch the plants with about 6 inches of loose straw when they are 6 inches high to lower the soil temperature. Always use certified seed potatoes, which are free of disease.

Varieties. *Early.* 'Norland' (75 days)—red-skinned, scab resistant; 'Norgold' (85 days)—russet skinned (Idaho type); 'Superior' (90 days)—white-skinned, the most resistant to scab; and 'Sebago' (100 days)—white-skinned, resistant to late blight and scab.

Late. 'Kennebec' (112 days)—white-skinned, resistant to late blight and mosaic; and 'Katahdin' (120 days), white-skinned, resistant to verticillium wilt and mosaic.

Potato, Sweet

Anywhere there is a frost-free period of about 150 days with relatively high temperatures, you can grow sweet potatoes. They need a light, sandy soil, and lots of space.

Transplants or seed? Sweet potatoes are easy to grow from slips (cuttings)—just place the mature root in moist sand, and slips will grow. Transplant slips when they are 6 to 8 inches, or buy slips from garden centers. Set slips in open ground after the soil is warm.

Don't forget. Too much water tends to elongate the roots. Mound or hill up heavy soil before planting. Too much nitrogen will cause potatoes to develop more vines than roots.

Varieties. 'Nemagold' (120 days) and 'Centennial' (150 days).

Pumpkins

Pumpkins need 10 feet or more between rows, but they will grow in less space if vines are trained or pruned. You can cut off the long runners after the fruit is set, if a good supply of leaves remains to feed the developing fruit.

Direct seeding is best, but in short-season areas, you can get a headstart by starting in individual pots, as with melons. Fertilizing and watering requirements are the same as for cucumbers and melons.

Varieties. 'Funny Face' (95 days), 'Cinderella' (95 days), 'Small Sugar' (100 days), 'Jack-O-Lantern' (110 days), 'Spookie' (110 days), 'Young's Beauty' (112 days), 'Connecticut Field' (112 days), and 'Big Max' (120 days).

Radishes

Although radishes are easy to grow, they have certain requirements. Since the growing season from seed to edible roots is very short—21 to 27 days—a supply of nutrients must be in the soil from start to finish, and the water supply must be constant.

Transplants or seed? The radish gets its easy-growing reputation because of its sure, fast germination in cold soil. For a continuous harvest, sow small quantities frequently.

Varieties. There are many to choose from, including:

Red. 'Cherry Belle' AAS (22 days)—the home gardener's favorite is the size of a cherry and has a mild flavor.

White. 'White Icicle' (28 days)—the roots are icicle-shaped; best when young; very mild and crisp.

Red and white. 'French Breakfast' (23 days)—oblong- to olive-shaped, mildly pungent; 'Sparkler' (25 days)—round roots, 1¼ inches in diameter, snappy flavor.

Rutabagas

These relatives of turnips grow best in cool areas, or after hot weather is over. Most rutabagas are yellow fleshed, although there are white varieties, as well. Rutabagas develop slowly, and can be left in the ground for winter storage and dug as desired.

Transplants or seed? Seed directly.

Don't forget. For best results, water the crop well and keep it growing steadily.

Varieties. 'American Purple Top Yellow' (90 days), 'Laurentian' (90 days), and 'Macomber' (92 days).

Salsify

The flavor of this root has earned it the names of "Vegetable Oyster" and "Oyster Plant." If sown as soon as the soil can be worked in spring, salsify's long, tapered roots (similar to those of carrots) will be ready to harvest in fall. They also can be stored over winter in damp sand or well-draining soil.

Transplants or seed? Seeds only.

Don't forget. Salsify grows best in deep, well-drained, light, crumbly soil. Prepare soil as you would for parsnips.

Varieties. The standard variety is 'Mammoth Sandwich Island' (115 days).

Scorzonera (black salsify). This is a close relative of salsify. It has black skin with white flesh.

Salsify

Spinach

Unfortunately, spinach tends to hurry into its flowering phase, which stops production of usable foliage. Use bolt-resistant (long-standing) varieties in spring; in fall, and in winter in mild areas, you can plant some of the quick-bolting varieties. In northern areas, make spring plantings as early as possible, and make fall plantings about a month before the average frost date. In mild-winter areas, plant any time from about October 1 to March 1.

Long-standing varieties (for spring planting). 'Long Standing Bloomsdale' (48 days)—savoy, dark green; 'America' (50 days)—savoy, dark green; and 'Winter Bloomsdale' (45 days)—smooth leaf, dark green, early.

Other varieties (for fall and winter only). 'Virginia Savoy' (42 days)—savoy; 'Hybrid No. 7' (42 days)—semi-savoy, resists downy mildew and blight; 'Dixie Market' (40 days)—savoy, resists downy mildew; and 'Early Hybrid No. 8'—semi-savoy, resists downy mildew and blight.

Summer "spinach." Since you can't get cool-season spinach in summer, try the following tropicals. They offer fresh "greens" that are just as rich in vitamins and as flavorful as true spinach.

Malabar spinach. This attractive, glossy-leaved vine grows rapidly when the weather warms, producing edible shoots in 70 days.

New Zealand spinach. A low-growing ground-cover type plant, New Zealand spinach spreads 3 to 4 feet across. You can cut the long tender stems and leaves repeatedly throughout the summer.

Spinach

Squash, Summer

Summer squashes can be almost unbelievably productive. Just one or two zucchini plants, for example, will present you with more than your family—and even your neighbors—can use.

All types need space. The bush squash spreads its leaves 3 to 4 feet. The vining types require from 5 to 12 feet of space, depending on the variety.

Fertilizing and watering requirements are the same as for cucumbers and melons. Pick summer squashes continually for a steady supply of young fruit.

Above: Winter squash will keep longer on a ventilated shelf in a cool, dry spot.

Below: 'Golden Nugget' winter squash

Zucchini summer squash

Transplants or seed? Direct seeding is best, but in short-season areas you can start indoors in peat pots 3 to 4 weeks before setting out.

Don't forget. Pick summer squashes when they are young and tender—with undeveloped seeds and a soft rind. Harvest zucchini and crookneck types when they are about 1½ to 2 inches in diameter, and bush scallops when they are 3 to 4 inches across.

Varieties. There are many hybrids, including:

Zucchini. 'Greyzini' AAS (50 days)—this compact bush bears fruits that are cylindrical in shape and medium green with grayish mottling in color, and that should be harvested at 4 to 5 inches; 'Zucchini Hybrid' (50 days)—shiny, medium-green cylindrical fruits should be harvested at 6 to 8 inches; 'Chefini' AAS (53 days)—this strong bush has good coverage and produces glossy, dark green cylindrical fruits, best at 7 to 8 inches; 'Aristocrat' AAS (53 days)—this compact, upright bush makes dark green, smooth, cylindrical fruits; and 'Cocozelle' (60 days)—the dark green fruits with light green stripes are best at 6 to 8 inches long.

Yellow straightneck. 'Early Prolific Straightneck' AAS (50 days)—the creamy yellow fruits are edible from 4 to 6 inches until 12 to 14 inches; 'Seneca Butterbar' (51 days)—smooth, cylindrical, tapered, yellow fruits; 'Seneca Prolific' (51 days)—creamy yellow, smooth-skinned, tapered fruits; and 'Burpee Golden Zucchini' (54 days)—glossy, bright gold, slender, cylindrical fruits.

Yellow crookneck. 'Early Golden Summer Crookneck' (53 days)—these bright yellow fruits with hooked ends have their best flavor at about 4 inches.

Scallop. 'St. Pat Scallop' AAS (50 days)—bell-shaped 'Patty Pan'-type fruits taste best when about the diameter of a silver dollar; 'Early White Bush' or 'Patty Pan' (54 days)—fruits are pale green changing to creamy white, 7 inches across, and 3 inches deep, with scalloped edges.

Squash, Winter

Grow winter squash as you would summer squash and pumpkins. However, wait until they are fully mature before you pick them, or they will be watery and have a poor flavor.

Transplants or seed? Direct seed, or start in pots.

Don't forget. Most varieties put out long runners and need lots of garden space. Favor the newly developed bush types.

Varieties. *Acorn or Danish.* 'Table King' (80 days) and 'Table Queen Ebony' (85 days).

Maxima. 'Gold Nugget' (85 days), 'Buttercup' (100 days), 'Hubbard' (110 days), and 'Banana' (110 days).

Butternut. 'Butternut' (95 days).

Tomato

Tomatoes are fussy about temperature, sometimes refusing to set fruit if the days are warm but the nights are below 55° F. Blossoms drop in summer when days are above 90° or nights go above 75°.

Transplants or seed? Sow seed in moist, disease-free "soil," or buy transplants.

Don't forget. Emerging seedlings need full sunlight—ideally, 12 hours a day. Temperatures should be between 70° and 75° during the day and 60° and 65° at night. Gradually expose young tomato plants to lower temperatures before setting them out in the garden.

Varieties. The rule of thumb in choosing varieties to fit your garden is this: The shorter your growing season, the more you should limit your choices to the "early" and "early midseason" varieties. The variety chart includes varieties that are widely adapted, but you should check with your local nurseries and garden centers for special varieties for your area. Soil diseases of tomatoes build up when tomatoes are grown in the same soil for more than one season. Since it is difficult to find new soil each year in a small home garden, plant breeders are developing disease-resistant varieties. In the chart disease resistance is indicated by "V"—Verticillium, "F"—Fusarium, and "N"—Nematodes.

Also indicated on the chart is the growing habit—determinate or indeterminate. The determinate are the bushy type, generally 3 feet or less high. The indeterminate are the tall-growing varieties, usually grown on stakes or trellises or in wire cages. The number of days to maturity refers to the number of days from setting out transplants to harvest.

'Small Fry' tomato

'Roma' tomato

Variety	Hybrid	Days to Maturity	Growth Habit	Fruit Size	Disease Resistance
'Spring Giant'	X	65	Det.	M-L	VF
'Springset'	X	67	Det.	M-L	VF
'Better Boy'	X	72	Ind.	L	VFN
'Burpee VF'	X	72	Ind.	M-L	VF
'Marglobe'		75	Det.	M	F
'Monte Carlo'	X	75	Ind.	L	VFN
'Beefmaster'	X	80	Ind.	XL	VFN
'Beefsteak'		90	Ind.	L	
Paste					
'Chico'		75	Det.	S-M	F
'Roma'		75-80	Det.	S-M	VF
Patio Types					
'Small Fry'	X	50-55	Det.	1"	VFN
'Patio'	X	70	Det.	2"	F
'Tumblin' Tom'	X	72	Det.	1½"	VFN
'Stakeless'		78	Det.	2"	F

'Springset' tomato

Turnips

Turnips grow quickly and easily in spring or fall plantings. Their leaves are rough and hairy.

Transplants or seed? Direct seeding.

Don't forget. Use turnip roots before they get pithy and fibrous. For the most part, this means up to 2 inches in diameter, but under ideal conditions turnips can be 3 to 4 inches thick and still be mild and solid. For greens, use the turnip leaves when they are young and tender, such as plants from thinnings, or grow special varieties for greens.

Varieties. *Roots.* 'Purple Top White Globe' (55 days).

Roots and greens. 'Tokyo Cross' AAS (35 days) and 'Just Right' AAS (60 days for roots, 27 days for greens).

Greens. 'Shogoin' (30 days).

Watermelon

Grow watermelons with lots of room to spread. They need a long, warm growing season.

Varieties. There are dozens of varieties to choose from. Check with your county agent for local adaptations. "Ice box" types are ideal: 'Sugar Baby' has red flesh, weighs 6 to 7 pounds; 'Sugar Doll' has red flesh, weighs 5 to 10 pounds; and 'Family Fun' is excellent eating quality and weighs 13 to 15 pounds. One All-America Selection winner is 'Yellow Baby'—earlier, more productive, and sweeter tasting than red ice-box types. The 7-inch fruit weighs up to 10 pounds and holds up longer. The outer skin is light green with dark green stripes, and it has fewer seeds and more edible flesh than reds do.

'Spring Giant' tomato

What's a Dwarf Tree?

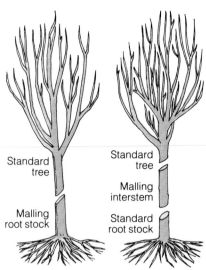

A dwarf tree actually consists of two or three trees. In one type of dwarf, a Malling dwarf tree (named for the East Malling Agricultural Research Station in England, where it was developed) provides the roots, and a standard apple tree provides the fruit. In another type of dwarf, a full-sized tree provides the roots, a portion of a Malling tree provides a section of the trunk (interstem), and the standard tree provides the fruit. The Malling numbered roots, if allowed to grow their own tops, would become slow-growing, shallow-rooted apple trees. When a well-known fruiting apple is grafted to one of these roots, the recalcitrant root doesn't nourish the top as well as ordinary roots might. And since the roots are relatively shallow and don't spread too widely, the mature size of the top is limited. Grafting a Malling trunk section accomplishes somewhat the same results.

FRUITS

Dwarf trees with full-sized fruits. If you want to plant fruit trees but haven't enough garden space, consider dwarf trees. They have certain distinct advantages over standard trees: where standards take five years to bear fruit, dwarfs bear after only a year or two; dwarfs and semi-dwarfs are easier to care for; and spraying and fruit thinning are much easier.

You can grow dwarfs as hedges, or train them as espaliers against fences or walls. Apple and pear dwarf trees are easiest to handle as espaliers; you don't have to do any drastic pruning to produce new fruiting wood, whereas you do with peach dwarfs—indeed, apple and pear dwarfs produce fruit from short fruit spurs that are productive year after year. To espalier, simply build a trellis of wood or wire, and plant and prune an apple or pear dwarf to grow flat against it.

Thinning fruits. Most fruit trees set too many fruits sometimes, which reduces size, color, and quality. This is particularly true for peaches and certain varieties of plums. When the fruits are about ¾ inch in diameter, pull off the excess by hand (between June 1 and 15). Leave 4 to 6 inches between peaches, and 3 to 4 inches between plums.

Apple trees do not usually set heavy crops each year. When some varieties do produce an excessive crop, they may not bear fruit the following year. If a heavy set occurs, thin the fruits to 6 inches apart during early June. Snap the apples from the stem with your thumb and forefinger, leaving the stem on the tree. If you do this no later than 50 days from the time the trees were in full bloom, the trees are more likely to bear fruit the following year.

Apples

Pollination. For really superior fruit—that is, excellent in size and shape—don't plant just one apple variety: cross pollinate, instead. For a quality 'Red Delicious', also plant a variety that blooms at about the same time—such as 'Golden Delicious', a 'Paulared', or a 'Cortland'. The long blooming season of 'Paulared' overlaps that of both the early and late varieties.

Some varieties are not usable as pollinators. These include 'Jonagold', 'Mutsu', and 'Rhode Island Greening'.

Varieties. When you think about which varieties to plant, perhaps your favorite supermarket variety comes to mind. But although taste is a crucial factor, it isn't the only one; you need to examine varieties on a broader base than taste alone. Do you want a good storage apple? A succession of harvests, early and late? A cooking apple for sauces, baking, and pies? Before making a choice impulsively, consider what's available.

'Cortland'. Many apple growers rate 'Cortland' excellent—"better than McIntosh"—as a dual-purpose variety for cooking and eating. It bears heavy, annual crops of red-striped fruit with white flesh. When exposed to the air, the flesh is slow to turn brown, which makes it especially good for salads. Ripens in early October.

'Golden Delicious'. This excellent dual-purpose apple ranks very high and makes a delicious applesauce. The trees bear when they are quite young. 'Golden Delicious' ripens in mid to late October.

'Jonathan'. An early-ripening apple (about mid-September), the standard 'Jonathan' is one of the top commercial varieties in the central states because of its rich flavor and juicy fruit. It is a good choice for snacks, salads, and all culinary uses.

There are two new 'Jonathan' cultivars: 'Jonagold' (named for its parents, 'Jonathan' and 'Golden Delicious'), and 'Jonamac' (a 'McIntosh'-type dessert apple). 'Jonagold' is a dual-purpose apple that's good for cooking and excellent for eating. It stores well. The trees are vigorous and annually

'Golden Delicious' apple

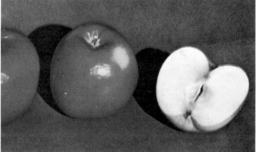
'Prima' apple

'Jonagold' apple

'Cortland' apple

'Melrose' apple

'Jonamac' apple

productive. Ripens in early October. 'Jonamac' is very good for eating, with a milder flavor than 'McIntosh'. Bears annually. Ripens in mid to late September.

'Lodi'. A cross between 'Montgomery' and 'Yellow Transparent', 'Lodi' has medium to large fruit that grows up to 3 inches in diameter. The light green skin sometimes has a slight orange blush. The fine-grained, nearly white flesh has a somewhat greenish tinge and is juicy with a sour taste. It is only fair for eating, but it is excellent for cooking. Because it tends to overset fruit, thin it early and properly, or else it will not bear the following year. 'Lodi' is one of the earliest to ripen—late July through August.

'McIntosh'. A truly great apple, 'McIntosh' fruits are medium to large, white flesh, red, sweet, tender, and juicy. They taste very good fresh, in sauces, in pies, or as a cider variety. Ripens the last week in September.

'Melrose'. A cross between 'Jonathan' and 'Delicious', 'Melrose' resembles 'Jonathan' in color and shape, but is less tart. It is very good for eating out of hand, for use in sauces and pies, and for its exceptional storage qualities. Ripens the last week in October.

'Mutsu'. A cross of 'Golden Delicious' and the Japanese variety 'Indo'. It has large, oblong, greenish fruits that develop some yellow color when mature. It has an excellent, slightly tart flavor when eaten fresh, and is also good in sauces and pies, and as a baked apple. Unlike 'Golden Delicious', 'Mutsu' does not shrivel in storage. The tree is a very vigorous, spreading grower. Ripens in late October.

'Paulared'. The fruit is high in quality and has a popular solid red color. It holds well on the tree, and has a long storage life. The tree is attractive, with angled branches, and it starts bearing heavy annual crops while quite young. Ripens in mid-September.

'Prima'. This variety is scab resistant, which dramatically reduces the need for sprays. 'Prima' is both a good-quality eating apple and a good cooking apple. Bears a good crop every year. Ripens in mid-September.

'Priscilla'. Another scab-resistant variety, 'Priscilla' does well in the same orchard with 'Prima', since it makes a good pollinator. The crisp fruit has a bright red blush over a yellow ground. Eat it fresh; store it for up to three months. Ripens the first week in October.

'Red Delicious'. This is the first choice in the supermarket—its quality as a dessert and out-of-hand apple is superb. The best choices are the red sports such as 'Wellspur' or 'Royal Red'. Thin the tree properly, or else it may produce full crops only every other year. Ripens early to mid-October.

'Rome Beauty'. Known as "the world's best baking apple," 'Rome Beauty' has large, firm fruits. There are many red sports that produce beautiful, solid, medium-heavy, annual fruits. The tree comes into production at an early age. Ripens at the end of October.

'Rhode Island Greening'. This top-quality cooking apple is good for sauces and baking. The fruit is light green to yellow, firm fleshed, crisp, and juicy. Ripens the second week in October.

'Tydeman Early'. This 'McIntosh'-type apple is almost entirely red, shaped like a 'McIntosh', and good to eat. The fruits can be stored much longer than most early varieties. Another benefit: it ripens early, when few other varieties are being harvested. Its drawback is its growth habit: the branches are undesirably long and lanky and need to be controlled by pruning. Ripens at the end of August.

Sports and spur types. Mutations or sports sometimes occur in apple varieties, causing better fruit or a spur habit of tree growth. Why do mutations happen? According to geneticists, they may be caused by cosmic rays that pierce through the growing tip of a shoot and produce a gene or chromosome change. That portion of the shoot which grows after the change occurred contains the new type of tissue. Mutations can happen for many characteristics, including productivity, fruit shape, flavor, and time of ripening. Many changes are so subtle that they are almost invisible. Mutations frequently have been found in 'Delicious' apples—partly because they are the most widely grown apple variety. Mutations also occur often on heavily pruned or winter-injured trees.

Except for 'Northern Spy', the sports generally produce more desirable fruits than the nonsported original variety. 'Delicious' now has more than 150 sports. Other varieties with sports are 'McIntosh', 'Rome', 'Twenty Ounce', 'Northern Spy', 'Stayman', 'Baldwin', 'Ben Davis', and 'Wealthy'.

Trees of spur types generally are smaller than the parent variety from

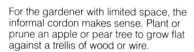

For the gardener with limited space, the informal cordon makes sense. Plant or prune an apple or pear tree to grow flat against a trellis of wood or wire.

which they originated—usually about two-thirds of normal size. This smaller tree size is an advantage, considering that controlling tree size is of interest to many gardeners. Spur-type trees require less pruning.

Other secondary changes may also occur, along with the spur growth habit, including narrower crotch angles, increased winter hardiness, fewer side branches, shorter internodes, thicker twigs, thicker and greener leaves, greater fruit-production efficiency, and greener fruit flesh. Whenever spur types are available, they generally are preferable to the standard growth habit. Spur types are available for 'Delicious', 'McIntosh', 'Rome', 'Golden Delicious', 'Tydeman Early', 'Arkansas Black', 'Earliblaze', 'Winesap', 'Winter Banana', and others.

How much the spur growth habit allows one to control tree size depends on the variety. Trees of 'Starkspur Lodi' are nearly as big as 'Lodi' trees, but trees of 'Starkspur Golden Delicious' sometimes can have less than half the branch volume of nonspur 'Golden Delicious' trees of the same age. Growth suppression in spur types of 'Delicious' is intermediate.

Sometimes spur trees lose their spur character, and the growth habit reverts to the larger, normal type. This means that although an orchard might be planted entirely with spur trees, in a few years the odd tree sometimes would begin to grow as large as the normal, nonspurred parent variety. This has been a problem with spur types of 'Golden Delicious' but not with spur types of 'Delicious'.

Cherries

'Montmorency' is the standard tart cherry for canning, preserving, quick-freezing, and eating right off the tree (but let it ripen fully, first). The fruit is large (largest of the "pie" or "sour" cherries), bright red, and excellent in quality and flavor. This heavy annual bearer needs no separate pollinator. It blooms late enough to escape spring frosts in most areas.

Grapes

There are some grape varieties that you can grow no matter where you live, and others that have distinct regional preferences. The South favors American and hybrid American varieties in the higher elevations and cold-winter areas, and muscadine grapes in the warm-winter area of the coastal plains. The Northeast can support the growth of American, European, and hybrid American-European grapes.

Planting and care. As long as you choose a grape that will grow in your region, all grapes are easy to grow and adapt well to any soil. But do select a variety that fits your climate. Water thoroughly and deeply (to 3 feet) during dry spells to encourage deep rooting. One established vine can produce enough new growth in only one season to cover an arbor, or roof a patio. Vines need to be trained and pruned annually; the shaping depends on how the vine grows.

Plant grapes during the dormant season (November to March). Vines will grow on a trellis or an arbor, but for best fruit production, use a two-strand wire trellis, and train the vines out horizontally in both directions.

Once they have been trained, prune the vines so that they form short fruiting spurs. As soon as the first frosts kill any foliage, cut back laterals from the main stems to two or three buds. If you wait until later to prune, unpleasant-looking bleeding will result; however, it will not hurt the vine. Cut off any side growth on the trunk.

Hoe out weeds, but shallowly—in fact, do not cultivate grapes more than an inch or two deep; the roots are extremely shallow, and cutting them will cause the fruit to drop.

Varieties. Varieties particularly adaptable to the South include 'Scuppernong', 'Dulcet', 'Fry', 'Jumbo', 'Pride', 'Hunt', and 'Higgins'. For cross

Top left: 'Queen Anne' cherry
Top right: 'Montmorency' cherry
Above: Sour cherry

'Aurora' grape (Siebel 5279)   'Baco Noir' grape (Baco No. 1)   'Interlaken' grape

pollination, plant these along with another variety, such as 'Southland', 'Dearing', 'Magoon', 'Carlos', 'Noble', and 'Cowart'.

Bunch-grape varieties include:

'Blue Lake'. Adapted to Louisiana and Florida, this variety bears small fruit in medium-large clusters. It has an unusual aromatic and spicy flavor, and is excellent for juice and jelly.

'Campbell Early'. Adapted to the Ozarks, this vine produces large, purple berries of very fine quality when grown under ideal conditions.

'Catawba'. Large, reddish-blue fruits grow in large clusters. The flavor is very pleasing and distinctive.

'Champanel'. Adapted to Alabama, Georgia, Louisiana, and Mississippi, this late-season variety has long-lived, vigorous vines. The fruits are extremely juicy, large, blue, high in acid, and low in sugar content.

'Delaware'. Hybrid. Early midseason. One of the best-flavored native American grapes, it produces small, light red aromatic berries with a lilac bloom.

'Golden Muscat'. Hybrid. Early midseason. Produces high-quality, sweet, golden fruit in very large clusters.

'Moore's Early'. Very early. Blue-black fruit. One of the first to ripen.

'Portland'. Early. The large, amber berries have a sweet flavor. The vine is moderately hardy.

In the Northeast, you can choose from among numerous hybrids in which the American and European bloodlines have been mixed. For example, the musky, sweet, vat-aged flavor of the frost-susceptible Muscat of Alexandria that grows in hot California valleys can also be had by planting any of the hardy American hybrids, 'Golden Muscat', 'Canadian Muscat', and 'New York Muscat'.

Varieties particularly adaptable to the Northeast include 'Aurora', 'Cameo', 'Steuben', 'Schuyler', 'Suffolk Red' ('Fredonia' × 'Russian Seedless'), and 'Lakemont' ('Ontario' × 'Thompson Seedless'), as well as:

'Buffalo'. Hybrid. Early. This juicy, slipskin variety probably is the best dessert-quality of any early black grape, with its sweet-and-spicy tart flavor. 'Buffalo' is disease free.

'Himrod'. Hybrid of 'Ontario' and 'Thompson Seedless'. Early. This disease-free variety makes for a delicious grape—probably the finest in quality in the seedless series.

'Verdelet' grape (Siebel 9110)   'Steuben' grape   'Seyval' grape (Seyve-Villard 5276)

Grapes adaptable to the entire country include:

'Concord'. Medium-late. This is the well-known American slipskin.

'Fredonia'. Early. Very hardy. Large black berries form in compact clusters. The sweet, spicy flavor is similar to 'Concord', but the berries are larger and earlier.

'Niagara'. Midseason. The best-known of the hardy white grapes, this has sweet, green-gold, medium-to-large, strong-flavored berries. A vigorous grower, it is excellent for arbors.

'Seneca'. Hybrid. Early. The high-quality white berries are sweet and aromatic. Bunches are somewhat loose.

Then there are French hybrid wine grapes, which combine the quality of the classic European varieties with the hardiness and disease resistance of the wild American species, and offer a new and superior class of wine grapes to the home wine-maker in cold-winter areas. Some of them are:

'Baco Noir'. This extremely vigorous, blue-black variety has medium clusters of small berries that ripen three to four weeks before 'Concord'.

Grape Training

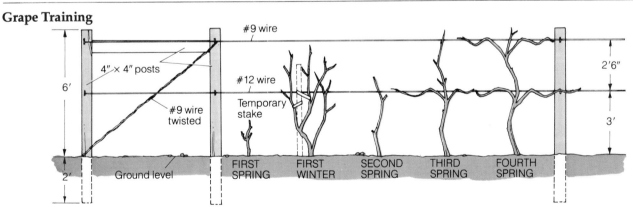

First spring. Set plants 2 inches deeper than they were at the nursery. Cut the shoot back to two buds.

First winter. Tie the shoots to a temporary stake so they aren't broken by wind or snow.

Second spring. Build the wire support as shown. After danger of frost is past, tie the strongest shoot to the lower wire and cut it back to the first bud above the wire.

Third spring. Tie the strongest shoot to the top wire and, again, cut it back to the first bud above the wire. Also tie the two strongest side shoots to the lower wire and cut back to six or seven buds. Remove all other growth.

Fourth spring (and every spring thereafter). Select two strong new shoots near each wire. Tie them to the wires and cut them back to six or seven buds each.

Disease resistant; a good variety for heavy, poorly drained soils. Makes a good Burgundy-type wine.

'Chancellor'. Widely grown in France for red wine, this grape has good body, tannin, and ages well.

'De Chaunac'. Formerly called 'Cameo', this is one of the best black hybrids. Wine samples have consistently received high ratings.

'Interlaken'. This is a California seedless-type grape that will grow in the colder areas (hardy to 15° below zero). The amber-colored berries are crisp, solid, and sweet. Ripens mid to late August.

'Rougeon'. Makes a blending wine of good red color.

'Seyval'. This yellowish-white variety has large, compact bunches of medium-sized berries. Best in areas with longer seasons and less severe winters. Mildew resistant. Plant for both wine and table use.

'Verdelet'. This beautiful, yellow-gold, dessert-type grape also produces a delicate white wine.

Peaches

The best dwarf-tree variety is the red-blushed, yellow, freestone 'Redhaven'. It ripens early (a month before 'Elberta') and has a long harvest season. When a heavy crop occurs, thin it well for full-sized fruit.

Apples and pears bear fruit on long-lived spurs, but peaches bear fruit from buds on new wood. To produce new wood, prune the tree severely after harvest, removing 2/3 of the new growth.

In the warm-winter areas of the South, many varieties of peaches don't receive enough winter cold for the buds to set and so they bloom erratically through the blooming period instead of "bursting" into bloom all at once. Consequently, new foliage may not develop for weeks after the normal time for new growth, and fruit production is poor. Repeated delays of this nature will kill the tree. Fortunately, however, experiment stations in Florida and Georgia have come up with peaches with low chilling requirements. (Send for the University of Georgia Bulletin #657, *Growing Peaches in the Peach State*, Athens, GA 30601.)

'Redhaven' peach

Below left: 'Ventura' peach
Below right: 'Early Elberta' peach

Pears

The pear tree can be trained as an espalier. Most varieties are dwarfed by being grafted onto quince rootstock.

Recommended varieties are 'Bartlett' and 'Clapps Favorite'. For good fruit production, most varieties need cross pollination. Plant two varieties unless the variety you choose is specifically listed as a self-pollinator.

Top: 'Seckel' pear
Above: 'Bartlett' pear
Left: 'Italian Prune' plum

Plums and Prunes

All prunes are plums with a high sugar content. Many people favor the European varieties over the Japanese varieties—the Japanese varieties require separate pollinators, but many European varieties, such as 'Damson' and 'Stanley', are self-fertile and also are good fresh, canned, or dried. 'Stanley' has large, purplish-black fruit whose yellow flesh is sweet and juicy. As a good canning variety, it is similar to, but larger than, the popular 'Italian Prune'.

The beach or shore plum *(Prunus maritima)* is native to the coastal areas of the Northeast, from New Brunswick to the Carolinas, where it grows extensively on sand dunes. If drainage is good, it will also grow on heavier soils. You can make jams and jellies with the fruits. For more information, write for *The Beach Plum* (Bulletin #315, Extension Service of the University of Massachusetts, Amherst, MA 01002).

Top: Mild-climate, trailing blackberry (dewberry)

Above: 'Olallie', the prime California blackberry

Right: 'Marion', Pacific Northwest Coast blackberry

BERRIES

Blackberries

Two kinds of blackberries described in mail-order catalogs are classified differently in different sections of the country. West Coast gardeners call the 'Boysen' berry, 'Young' berry, and 'Logan' berry *blackberries,* but Southerners call these varieties *dewberries.* And what the Midwest, Northeast, Canada, and cold-winter areas of the West mean by the *blackberry* is the stiff-caned, erect kind that is much hardier than the trailing types of the West Coast and South. The 'Young', 'Boysen', and 'Logan' varieties are so large and tasty that gardeners have tried to grow them in areas beyond their hardiness limits. Providing winter protection has enabled some to succeed. But since these berries must be grown on a trellis, it isn't easy to protect them.

Planting and training. If space is limited, plant blackberries in a "hedgerow" type of planting, along with raspberries. You don't need to support the erect growers, but you do need to support the brambles—for example, with a double-wire trellis (see illustration, page 123). Set the erect blackberry bushes 3½ feet apart in the row; red raspberries 2 feet apart; purple and black raspberries 2½ feet apart; and trailing types 6 to 8 feet apart.

Blackberries need a constant supply of water and nutrients. Feed them three times—before new growth appears, in midspring, and in midsummer.

Varieties. These trailing varieties do well in the South:

'Boysen' ('Nectar', 'Rossberry'). California introduction. Late. Very large (1½-inch-long, 1-inch-wide), reddish berries with a "dusty" (not shiny) bloom. Sweet-tart, high flavor, aromatic. Good fresh, frozen, and cooked.

'Gem'. Early. Georgia introduction. These large, round, firm berries have good flavor.

Left: Blackberries
Bottom: Blackberries on a trellis.

'Young' and 'Thornless Young'. Midseason. Louisiana introduction. Similar in size and color to 'Boysen', but the berries are shiny and can be sweeter.

Check at your nursery for other good varieties, such as 'Comanche', 'Cherokee' (Arkansas introductions), and 'Flint'.

These varieties will do well in the Northeast:

'Bailey'. Midseason.

'Darrow'. Vigorous. These giant, glossy black, good-quality berries are over 1 inch long and ¾ inch wide. The disease-resistant canes have few thorns.

'Eldorado' ('Stuart', 'Lowden', 'Texas'). Early to midseason.

'Hedrick'. Early.

'Jerseyblack'. Midseason. Berries are medium to large. Slightly tart. Semitrailing bushes are vigorous and productive. Long fruiting season.

'Raven'. Early. Maryland introduction. The medium-firm, medium-large berries have very good, tart flavor. Moderately vigorous. Short ripening season.

Above: 'Southland' blueberry
Above right: 'Tifblue' blueberry

Blueberries

Rabbiteye. In the South, the native rabbiteye blueberry produces a heavy, delicious crop in warm-winter regions. It is more disease-resistant than the highbush blueberries, and tolerates a wider range of soils. Since it grows naturally in warm areas, it will not grow in inland regions with cold winters.

The rabbiteye is native to streambeds in the lower coastal plain areas of Georgia, but thanks to the work of experiment stations in Georgia and Florida, improved varieties have been created that adapt to the coastal plain from eastern North Carolina to northern Florida, and westward to Louisiana and Arkansas.

Plant care. Although native strains of rabbiteye blueberry will thrive on less acid soils than those required by highbush types, they dislike deep sandy soil, or very poor or wet soils.

The plants require a constant supply of moisture, but they will not tolerate waterlogged soil. To avoid such a problem, plant blueberries in a low raised bed. Put a heavy mulch over the roots to keep them cool—up to 8 inches of straw, pine needles, or old sawdust. Beginning in the second growing season, use a fertilizer recommended for azaleas.

Mulching. Making a 6- to 8-inch-deep mulch of straw, pine needles, or old sawdust will produce better growth and a greater yield.

Varieties. These varieties are especially recommended for home gardens. (Any of them will bear more heavily if you plant another variety beside it.)

'Briteblue'. Late midseason (after 'Tifblue'). Large, light blue berries are of fair flavor; plant is open and spreading.

'Delite'. This variety bears large, excellent-flavored berries that develop sugar early. Plants are upright; many canes form from ground level.

'Garden Blue'. Midseason. Medium-sized, good-quality berries grow on a large, vigorous, upright bush.

'Southland'. Late midseason (with 'Tifblue'). The medium-large, flavorful berries grow on a dense, compact plant that spreads more than 'Tifblue'.

'Tifblue'. Late midseason. These large, light berries may appear ripe before full flavor develops, so taste before harvesting. The plant is large and productive.

'Woodard'. Early midseason. The large, medium-blue berries have a flavor that is said to be the best among the rabbiteyes.

Highbush. In the Northeast, highbush blueberries can be grown wherever rhododendrons, mountain laurel, and *Pieris* can. They need a 160-day growing season, acid soil, and a winter no colder than −20° to −25° F. If you can't match these conditions but want to grow blueberries anyway, do it in almost straight peat moss.

The highbush blueberry does well as a landscape plant, offering handsome foliage, fruit, and autumn color.

In the shrub border, these blueberries will grow to 5 to 6 feet if planted 4 to 5 feet apart. To use them as an informal hedge, plant them 3 feet apart.

For cross pollination, plant at least two varieties. And for a long harvest season, plant two early varieties, two midseason, and two late.

Plant care. Blueberries do best in loose-textured soils, preferably mixtures of sand and peat. They need constant but moderate watering and good drainage, since the roots need lots of air as well as moisture in the soil. If water fills the soil for more than a day, the roots will be damaged badly.

Mulching. To stop weeds, maintain organic matter, and conserve moisture, place a permanent mulch of hay, straw, or similar material 4 to 6 inches deep around and between the plants. Add organic matter each year.

The following varieties are listed in approximate order of ripening:

Varieties. 'Earliblue'. Erect, vigorous. Berries are large and flavorful.

'Collins'. Erect, vigorous growth. Light blue berries have a sweet to mildly tart taste, and are borne in tight, attractive clusters. Not as productive as 'Bluecrop' or 'Herbert'.

'Blueray'. Attractive, tall-growing shrubs produce large, crisp, highly flavored berries.

'Bluecrop'. Unusually productive, this erect, tall-growing bush produces large, high-quality berries.

'Pemberton'. One of the most vigorous-growing and productive varieties. Large, good-quality berries are borne in loose clusters.

'Atlantic'. This sprawling bush produces large, light blue berries.

'Jersey'. This tall, erect-growing bush is not as productive as 'Bluecrop' or 'Collins'. The large, light blue berries taste quite bland.

'Herbert'. One of the best of the late varieties in terms of size, quality, and productiveness.

'Coville'. This productive plant grows vigorously, with an open, spread-

Bird netting draped directly over fruit trees or berry bushes lets birds get to those berries close to the netting. A netting support system (see illustration below) keeps the birds away from all fruit, and it also gives wind and insect protection.

Bird Netting

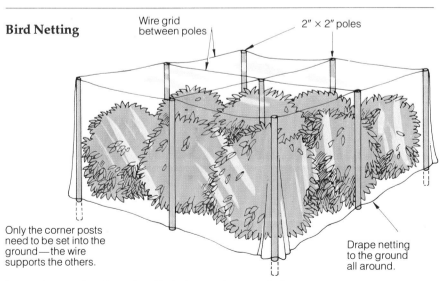

Wire grid between poles

2″ × 2″ poles

Only the corner posts need to be set into the ground—the wire supports the others.

Drape netting to the ground all around.

Lay netting over the wire grid and let it drape to the ground all around. Overlap netting about 6 inches where pieces join. Sewing or twist-tying the overlap will prevent openings.

Top: Gooseberries
Above: Currants

ing habit. High-quality berries are aromatic but tart until ripe, and resist cracking and premature fruit drop.

Currants and Gooseberries

Put a few plants of currants and gooseberries in the shrub border for attractiveness as well as for jams and jellies.

Plant care. For maximum quality and yields, fertilize consistently—every spring when growth starts. If growth lags, make a second application after harvest.

Pruning. Prune currants and gooseberries to keep them from developing too many canes. Plan for a plant of 12 to 15 canes, which should include 3 or 4 each of 1-, 2-, and 3-year-old canes, plus 1 or 2 of the stronger 4-year-old canes.

Currant varieties. 'Perfection'. Large, bright crimson berries grow on a fairly productive, somewhat spreading bush.

'Red Lake'. Large clusters of large, light red berries grow on a big, upright bush.

In addition, the New York State Fruit Testing Association at Geneva recommends 'Minnesota 71' and 'White Imperial'.

Gooseberry varieties. 'Fredonia'. Very large, attractive, dark red berries are good in quality.

'Pixwell'. This vigorous, productive, mildew-resistant bush has few thorns. The pink-colored berries are easy to pick.

'Poorman'. Brilliant red, medium to large good-quality berries are sweet enough to eat off the bush. The plants are large and very productive.

Caution: In some areas, it is illegal to plant varieties of currants and gooseberries that might be hosts to blister rust, a disease of the Five-Needle Pines. Check with your county agent for information regarding your area.

Raspberries

The raspberry is a highly perishable, delicate fruit that tastes best when picked before breakfast.

If you plant only 12 raspberry plants (and care for them well), they will produce from 10 to 15 quarts a year for ten years or more. By selecting both early- and late-bearing varieties, you can harvest berries over a two- to three-month period, depending on the length of your growing season. Varieties are red, purple, black, and amber.

The performance of varieties changes according to local soil conditions. Check with your county extension agent.

Planting and care. Since raspberries will live in your garden for years, give them a trellis, setting them 2½ to 3 feet apart. When planting, cut back the cane to about 6 inches. The first year, three to five strong canes will shoot up. These will produce fruits the next year; cut them to the ground after they have fruited. In the second year, canes will shoot up very abundantly. Thin out all but 8 to 18 canes near the crown of the mother plant. Tie the canes to the top wire (see illustration).

Red raspberries. 'Amber'. Named for its color. Excellent dessert quality.

'Hilton'. Late. Largest of all red raspberries. Very attractive and of excellent quality. Vigorous, productive, and hardy.

'Newburgh'. Mid to late. The large berries are of good quality. Very productive. Hardy.

'Taylor'. Mid to late. Attractive, firm, red berries of excellent quality. Vigorous and hardy.

Everbearing raspberries. 'Fallgold'. Golden-yellow berries.

Red raspberry pruning
Remove weakest canes and suckers. Leave only five to seven strongest canes.

Red raspberry training
Arch half the canes from each plant over each wire and lock them under the canes of the next plant.

Black raspberry puning
Top canes at about 24". Cut laterals so two to six buds are left on each.

Black raspberry training
Cut canes at top of 2-1/2' to 3' stake and tie in two or three places. Strong canes topped at 2' don't need support.

'Fallred'. Large berries, ideal for canning and freezing.

'Indian Summer'. Large, good-quality fruit is a good yielder. The fall crop is late and subject to frost in short-season areas. Good as a summer crop.

'September'. Vigorous. Hardy. Medium to large berries. One of the best fall-bearing varieties.

Purple raspberries. Purple raspberries, a cross between hardy red and black varieties, are prized for canning and preserves.

'Clyde'. Early. Large, firm, dark purple berries are of excellent quality. Vigorous. It is replacing 'Sodus' in popularity.

'Sodus'. Midseason. This large, firm fruit is of good quality but tastes quite tart. Productive.

Black raspberries (blackcaps). 'Allen'. The fruit is large and attractive. The plants are vigorous and productive.

'Black Hawk'. Late season. Large black berries have good flavor and a large yield. Plants do not sucker.

'Bristol'. Midseason. Good size and flavor. Excellent for canning and freezing.

'Cumberland'. This old-timer produces large, firm berries of good quality.

'Huron'. Large, glossy-black berries are of good quality. Vigorous, productive, and hardy.

'Morrison'. Midseason. Large berries, but the total crop is smaller than that of 'Bristol'.

Strawberries

Strawberries will grow in a garden, but they will also do well in boxes, planters, and hanging baskets. So if you're longing for home-grown strawberries, you have no excuse not to grow them.

However, their flavor and yield are not predictable from year to year, depending on spring growing conditions. And what's considered the "best" variety in one location may be only "fair" in another, so check with your county extension agent before choosing varieties.

Planting and care. There are two ways to grow strawberries—using the "matted row" or the "hill" system.

There are two types of matted rows: in one, all the runners are allowed to grow; in the other, only the early-formed runners are allowed to grow, spaced about 8 inches apart. The spaced-runner system offers the advantages of larger berries, easier picking, and larger total yield (see illustration).

In the hill system, plants are set 12 inches apart, and all runners are removed. Plant in rows of 12 to 15 inches apart in groups of 2 to 3 rows 30 inches apart. For poor runner producers and everbearers, use the hill system.

To encourage vigorous growth of regular varieties, remove all blossoms that appear the first year the plants are grown. For everbearers, remove all

Top: Red raspberries
Above: Blackcap raspberries

Planting Strawberries

Plant strawberries with roots spread in fan shape. Barely cover the crown.

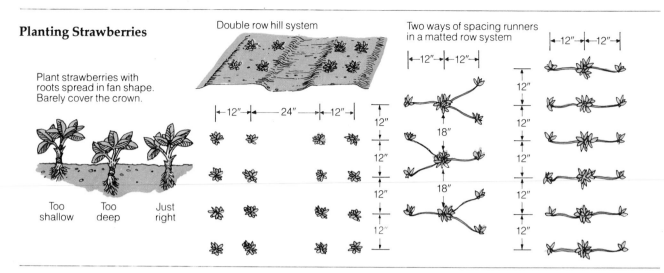

Double row hill system

Two ways of spacing runners in a matted row system

Too shallow   Too deep   Just right

Plastic mulch helps retain water and warms soil around strawberry plants.

blossoms the year the plants are put in until about the middle of July. The blossoms that form later will produce a late-summer and fall crop.

Plant in well-draining soils. Do not set plants too deep or too shallow—the bud should be level with the surface of the soil (see illustration).

If you grow strawberries in containers in a disease-free soil mix, you won't have to worry about verticillium wilt and red stele (root rot), both of which are caused by soil-borne fungi. But whether your strawberries will grow in containers or in garden soil, start with plants that are certified to be disease free.

Mulching. Strawberries need winter protection where alternate freezing and thawing of the soil may cause the plants to heave and break the roots. Low temperatures also injure the crowns of the plants. Straw is one of the best mulch materials.

Place a 3- or 4-inch-deep layer over the plants before the soil is frozen hard. Remove most of the mulch in the spring, when the centers of the plants are yellowish-green. Leave an inch of loose straw over the plants. They will grow up through it, and the straw will keep the berries clean.

Varieties for the South. 'Albritton'. North Carolina introduction. Berries are large, uniform in size, and excellent for eating fresh or freezing. Develops a good flavor in North Carolina.

'Blakemore'. Early. Maryland introduction. The small, firm berries have a high acid and pectin content and fair flavor. Excellent for preserving. Plants are vigorous, with good runner production. Highly tolerant of virus diseases. Very resistant to verticillium wilt. Adapted to a wide range of soil types in the region from Virginia to Georgia, and westward to Oklahoma and southern Missouri.

'Daybreak'. Early. Louisiana introduction. Large, medium-red berries are very attractive, with good flavor and preserving quality. Very productive.

'Earlibelle'. This widely adapted variety produces large, very firm fruit. Good for canning and freezing. An early-maturing variety with medium-sized plants, but good runner production. Resistant to leaf spot and leaf scorch.

'Florida 90'. Early. Florida introduction. Berries are very large early in the season, with very good flavor and quality. Productive. A heavy producer of runner plants.

'Headline'. Midseason. Louisiana introduction. Large, medium-red berries are of good quality. Plants are vigorous and productive, and grow runners freely. Resistant to leaf spot.

'Sunrise'. Early. Maryland introduction. The berries are medium-sized, very symmetrical, and firm, with very good flavor (although they do not freeze well). Vigorous grower. Resistant to red stele. The leaves are resistant to leaf scorch and mildew.

'Suwanee'. Early. Medium to large, tender berries have very good quality, fresh or frozen.

'Tennessee Beauty'. Late. Berries are medium-sized, attractive, glossy-red, and firm, with good flavor. Productive. Good freezing quality. Good runner production. Resistant to leaf spot and leaf scorch. Tolerates virus diseases.

Varieties for the Midwest and North. 'Catskill'. Midseason. Large berries of good dessert quality are excellent for freezing. Will grow over a wide range of soil types, from New England and New Jersey to southern Minnesota.

'Earlidawn'. Early. A fresh and freezing variety. The large berries are of good dessert quality. Moderately resistant to leaf spot and leaf scorch. Adapted to Maryland, north to New England.

'Fairfax'. Medium early. Maryland introduction. Attractive, medium-sized berries are bright red outside, deep red inside. Excellent flavor. Plants are especially productive when late-season runners are picked off. 'Fairfax' is grown from southern New England to Maryland.

'Fletcher'. Midseason. New York introduction. Berries are medium-sized, with a medium-red, glossy, tender skin. Excellent flavor quality. Very good for freezing. Well adapted to New York and New England.

'Howard 17' ('Premier'). Early. Massachusetts introduction. Medium-sized berries are of good quality. Productive. Resistant to leaf diseases and highly tolerant of virus diseases.

'Jerseybelle'. Late. New Jersey introduction. Its large, showy fruits have a mild flavor but will not freeze well. Very susceptible to diseases.

'Midland'. Very early. Maryland introduction. Large, glossy berries have deep-red flesh. Eating quality is good to excellent. Freezes well. Best grown in the hill system. Adapted from southern New England to Virginia.

'Midway'. Midseason. Maryland introduction. Berries are medium to large, glossy, rich red, and of good dessert quality. Freezes well. Susceptible to leaf spot, leaf scorch, and verticillium wilt. Productive in the Northeast, south to Maryland.

'Raritan'. Midseason. New Jersey introduction. Medium-sized plants are very productive. Large, firm berries have good flavor.

'Redstar'. Late. Maryland introduction. Large berries are of good to very good dessert quality. Plants are tolerant of virus diseases, leaf spot, and leaf scorch. Grown from southern New England south to Maryland.

'Sparkle'. Midseason. Productive plants. Bright red, attractive berries are fairly soft, have good flavor. Size is large in early picking, but small in later ones.

'Surecrop'. Early. Maryland introduction. Berries are large, round, glossy, and firm, with good dessert quality. Resistant to red stele, verticillium wilt, leaf spots, leaf scorch, and drought.

A variety that grows nearly everywhere. 'Pocahontas'. Maryland introduction. Good fresh, frozen, and in preserves. Plants are vigorous, resistant to leaf scorch. Adapted from southern New England, south to Norfolk, Virginia, and west to Missouri.

Everbearing varieties. 'Gem'. ('Superfection' and 'Brilliant' are open-pollinated seedlings of 'Gem' and are considered to be nearly identical to it.) Small, glossy, tart, red fruit is of good dessert quality.

'Geneva'. Large, vigorous plants fruit well in June and throughout the summer and early autumn. Berries are soft and very highly flavored.

'Ogallala'. Berries are dark red, soft, and medium sized.

'Ozark Beauty'. Large, sweet, good-flavored berries are bright red outside and inside. Produces on mother plants but not on runner plants during summer and fall.

Strawberries from your own garden are an unbeatable summer treat.

LAWNS AND GROUND COVERS

Lawns and ground covers bring together all the other elements of the landscape and make it a unified whole.

Nothing quite matches the look of a well-kept lawn. Its expanse of green is a treat to the eye, a newly mowed lawn is a treat to the nose, and walking barefoot in fine-textured grass is a treat to the feet. And nothing else does a better job of carpeting the soil and yet allowing water and nutrients to reach tree and shrub roots in the soil below.

But a beautiful lawn doesn't just happen—it has to be groomed. Happily, caring for a lawn isn't necessarily the tedious job it used to be. There are power mowers and trimmers, selective weed killers, and modern fungicides and insecticides to help you. There are even automatic sprinkling systems that will water your lawn when you are on vacation, or when you get too busy to keep to a schedule.

Basic Lawn Know-how

Whether you start a lawn from seeds, sod, sprigs, or plugs, or simply work with the grass that's there already, the basic steps for soil preparation are the same.

If your ground is not already reasonably level, you may have to do some leveling. If the leveling job looks difficult enough, you might consider hiring a professional with grading equipment. However the grading gets done, the important thing is to grade so that the lawn will slope (and drain) just slightly away from the house. If the lawn area has been cut up by utility lines or other trenches, fill them in with soil and soak well to settle them.

The first step is to add amendments (see pages 57–61). Use whatever is locally available—peat moss, ground bark, leaf mold, sawdust, rice hulls, or any number of other organic byproducts. Organic matter, in particular, improves soil drainage yet retains water during hot weather.

When a lawn is new, it needs special attention until the first mowing. When grass seed germinates, the primary roots reach 4 to 6 inches down into the soil. During the first weeks of growth, these roots do all the collecting of water and nutrients. The more fibrous and secondary roots start developing only 1 to 4 weeks after germination. Because this initial root system is so limited, take these precautions: apply ample water until the seedlings are 1 inch tall; don't walk on a brand-new lawn (if you must, first lay down a plank to walk on); and don't mow or kill weeds until the time recommended (usually after the grass grows about 2 inches tall and starts to curve).

In the early stages of a newly seeded lawn, watering is especially critical and slightly difficult. Once seeds sprout, they need constant moisture to continue growing. If you have to sprinkle three or more times a day in hot weather, do it—but don't overdo it: turn off the water before puddles form and runoff carries the seeds to low spots. Use sprinklers or a hose nozzle with a fine spray, particularly on sloping lawns where runoff is even more likely.

Planting and Grooming Your Lawn

1. *Piling.* Generously pile on organic matter—peat moss, compost, or whatever is available. Make a 2- or 3-inch layer. Organic matter increases the water-retention capacity of sandy soils and helps open up light clay soils.

2. *Spreading.* Spread on 5 to 10 pounds of lawn food per 1,000 square feet of lawn. This will last past the first mowing. If lime needs to be used in your area, have your soil tested (see page 55). Add lime for bluegrass if the soil has a pH below 6.0.

3. *Tilling.* Till the soil, working organic matter, food, and lime into the top 6 inches. Work in a back-and-forth direction until all ingredients are blended.

4. *Rolling.* Roll with a heavy roller to remove air pockets, and smooth lumps. Shovel high spots into low areas. First roll one way, then across. If organic matter wasn't added as the first step and if the soil lacks natural humus, do not use the heavy roller.

5. *Leveling.* First remove stones, sticks and other debris; then, using a T-board or rake for the final grade, break up clods. Scrape high spots into low ones, and make sure that the grade of the finished slope is the way you want it.

6. *Final rolling.* If much soil has been moved to fill low spots, roll again a final time. Use an empty roller and go in two directions. If you still see low spots, rake, then roll again.

7a. *Seeding.* You can broadcast seeds by hand, but for a more accurate spread use a spreader. Rake in. Just barely cover with mulch. Roll with an empty roller. Keep moist.

Planting a Lawn

1. Pile on organic matter—peat moss, sawdust, or whatever's available. Don't scrimp. Make 2- or 3-inch layer. Adding organic matter increases the water-holding capacity of sandy soils and helps open up tightly compacted clay soils.

2. Spread on 5 to 10 pounds of lawn food per 1000 square feet of lawn. This will carry lawn past first mowing. If you live where lime is commonly used, have soil tested. Add lime for bluegrass if soil has pH below 6.0.

3. Till the soil, working organic matter, food, lime into the top 6 inches of soil. Go back and forth until all are blended. If organic matter hasn't been added, go easy on power tilling and rolling (the next step)—to avoid pulverizing and packing down soil.

4. Roll. Heavy roller takes out air pockets, smooths lumps. Shovel high spots into low. Roll in one direction, then another. If organic matter wasn't added as the first step and if the soil lacks natural humus, don't use the heavy roller.

5. Level. Pick out stones, sticks, other debris. Use T-board or rake to get area to final grade. Break up clods. Scrape high

spots into low ones. Make sure finished slope conforms to grade you've planned.

7b. *Sodding.* Lay sod strips straight, staggering the ends. Press the joints together with your hands. Cut strips to fit corners. Roll lightly. Water to 8 inches.

7c. *Sprigging.* For running grasses like Bermuda, lay sprigs (pieces of stems) 3 to 6 inches apart, in rows a foot apart. Cover with soil, but leave tips exposed. Roll.

8. *Mowing.* When to do the first mowing depends on the type of grass and the season. In general, wait until the grass is about 2 inches tall and starts to curve. Then, when the grass is dry, set the mower at 1½ inches and mow.

After the second or third mowing, reduce the watering schedule to once a week (less often in cool weather). This is the time to use broadleaf weed killers and lawn fertilizer.

To weed, you can lay down a plank to kneel on and pull the weeds out by hand. But if this sounds too tedious, you can wait the weeds out, instead—after all, mowing and weed killer will control most of the weeds later on.

Watering the Lawn

Unfortunately, there is no formula for how much and how often to water. A lawn's water requirements vary by climate, soil type, season, type of grass, and other factors. Experience will teach you best and help you work out a watering schedule. Just stay flexible enough to alter it when seasonal or climatic changes demand a different schedule.

Since roots will go only where there's water, wetting just the top few inches of soil will give you shallow roots. And a shallow root system will

6. Final rolling. If you moved much soil to fill low spots during final grading and level, roll again for the last time before planting. Use an empty roller and go in two directions. If low spots still appear, rake and roll some more.

7a. Seeding. Broadcast seeds accurately with a "Whirlybird" or spreader. Rake in. Just barely cover with mulch. Roll with an empty roller.

Keep moist.

7b. Sodding. Lay strips straight with ends staggered. Press strips together so that they are firmly joined. Cut strips to fit corners. Roll lightly. Water to a depth of 8 inches.

7c. Sprigging. For running grasses like Bermuda, lay sprigs (pieces of stems) 3 to 6 inches apart, in rows a foot apart. Cover with soil, but leave tips exposed. Roll.

8. Mowing. How soon the first mowing should be done depends on the type of grass and the season. Generally wait until the grass grows about 2 inches tall and starts to curve. Then set mower at 1-1/2 inches. Mow when grass is dry.

One way to measure the amount of water applied to a lawn is to set out same-sized containers on a grid pattern in the sprinkler area. Check the amount of water in the containers at 30-minute intervals. The water needs of individual lawns vary, but the general rule is to apply 1 inch of water with each irrigation.

Above: When footprints make a lasting imprint and the grass doesn't bounce right back, it's a nearly foolproof sign that a lawn needs water. Water right away.

Below: Soil sampling tube removes a core of soil to give you a look at what's happening a foot below the surface—how deep water penetrates, how deep roots go.

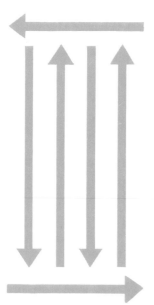

The best pattern for spreading fertilizer is to go along ends, then back and forth.

require frequent watering, which can pose a problem. Frequent watering keeps the surface wet, and a wet surface breeds weed seeds and diseases.

However, if you water deeply, the deeper roots can draw from a larger water supply, and the lawn can go much longer between waterings.

Try to water so that it sinks 6 to 12 inches into the soil. To determine how deep the water goes, use a soil-sampling test (see illustration), or poke a screwdriver into the ground—if it goes in 6 inches without much resistance, the lawn is wet enough.

In hot weather, lawns need between 1 and 2 inches of water per week. (An empty coffee can placed on the lawn makes an excellent raingauge.) If you use a sprinkler, turn it on, then off, then wait a few hours and turn it on again. Repeat until the water has run for about 2 hours total, or until the screwdriver test shows that 6 inches of the ground are wet.

After receiving that much water, the lawn can go dry for quite a while. Let the lawn dry out for about a week—this will allow air into the root zone. Then, when a poke of the screwdriver meets some resistance, water again. (For more on watering, see pages 70–73.)

Fertilizing the Lawn

For 1,000 square feet of lawn, add the following amounts of nitrogen per year: common Kentucky bluegrass and fescue—3 pounds; bent—4 pounds; improved bluegrasses—5 pounds; Bermuda—7 to 12 pounds; St. Augustine—4 to 6 pounds; carpet and centipede—3 pounds; and zoysia—5 or 6 pounds. If you choose a lawn food that is roughly $\frac{1}{5}$ nitrogen, bear in mind that 5 pounds of it will equal one pound of nitrogen.

Nitrogen is what lawns need most of—it greens up the leaves and builds up the roots. Soils tend to have little of it, and to lose what nitrogen they've got when irrigated or rained on.

The best method is to apply only as much nitrogen as a lawn can handle comfortably: about one pound per feeding.

Cool-season grasses—most of the grasses that will grow well in the Northeast—should be fed mainly in the cool (but not cold) months of spring and fall, when the grass is most active and forming the most roots. Spring feedings help lawns get a headstart on pests, weeds, and the oncoming heat. Except for bent grasses, don't feed in July or August.

The most important feeding of the year (marked red in the illustration) comes in fall. This is the one that will keep the grass green, let it grow for a longer time into cold weather, and give the lawn a chance to store food for the following spring. Since little top growth occurs in fall, a lawn can use most of its energy building up roots and growing denser.

Some of the improved bluegrasses need up to 50 percent more food than do common bluegrasses, so apply an extra feeding in spring, and again in fall.

Warm-season grasses—most of the grasses in the South—grow most in midsummer, taper off in fall, and continue until frost. They begin to get green in spring, when the soil is still cold. That's the time to use lawn food with quick-acting forms of nitrogen and phosphorus to green up the grass.

The other most important feeding time comes in late fall. This keeps grass growing and green as long into cold weather as possible, and also strengthens it to fight off cold winters.

Move the feeding dates on the accompanying chart up or back, depending on where you live. Growth starts earlier and lasts longer in mild climates, and is shortened at both ends by colder weather. The surest way to tell is to look at your lawn: start feeding when it first gets green, and stop when the green is gone.

To apply, use a lawn-food spreader that can be cranked while you walk over the lawn, or one that can be pushed along on wheels. The best application technique is shown in the diagram on page 134. Cover the ends first, then go back and forth the long way. For even and thorough coverage, walk at normal speed, and keep the spreader level. For best coverage, spread at half the rate, and go over the area twice in cross directions. Afterwards, brush or wash out the spreader; dry it thoroughly before putting it away.

Feed Your Lawn According to Its Growth Cycle

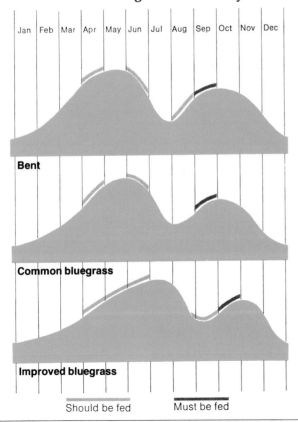

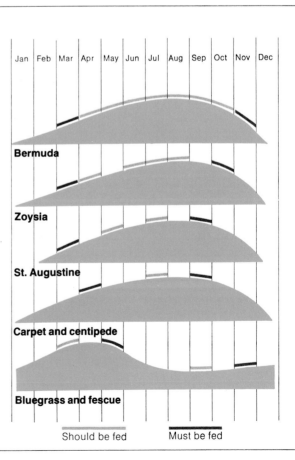

Mowing

Despite the old idea of the stereotypical suburban family wearily pushing a lawn mower around every weekend, mowing is not that much of a burden—indeed, well-kept secret though it is, mowing can actually be enjoyable. You get a bit of exercise, a chance to check out your portion of the neighborhood, and some heavenly odors, as well.

How often should you mow? This depends on the kind of grass and the time of year. As a general rule of thumb, mow when the grass grows ¼ or ⅓ taller than its proper cutting height.

However, this rule may not suit your preferred mowing habit or allow for vacations. For instance, the hybrid Bermudas and bent grass have cutting heights of less than 1 inch, but they may grow ¼ or ⅓ inch in 2 or 3 days.

But whether you like the rule or not, it pays to follow it. Otherwise, if you let the grass grow high and then cut it low, you expose stems to the sun that previously were shaded, making them susceptible to sunburn, and giving the lawn a scalded look. Also, defying the mowing rule deprives roots of food, and they may take a long time to recover from the shock.

How high should you cut? Again, that depends on what kind of grass you've got. Except for Bermuda, zoysia, and bent, which need very low mowing to prevent thatch buildup, most grasses do better with high mowing.

Low mowing is probably the greatest cause of bluegrass damage—it cuts off a big portion of the green, food-producing part, and it robs much-needed shade from the soil and base of the grass plants. Generally, the taller the grass, the deeper the roots. The higher the cut, the more soil is shaded and the cooler it stays.

One common method is to increase the height of cuts as temperatures increase in summer and in hot climates.

However, not all mowers can be adjusted to cut as high as we recommend. To determine the heights at which your mower will cut, choose a level spot and measure from the ground up to the mower's lowest blade.

Additional precautions. Don't cut wet grass. Pick up stones and sticks before mowing.

Don't leave clippings on the lawn, particularly if they're long or wet, or if the weather is hot or humid. Clippings may smother roots and cause thatch to build up.

For the final pass in a given mowing, go over twice (crosswise or diagonally, the second time).

After mowing, clean the blades to remove clippings and weed seeds.

Mowing Heights

Grass	(inches) Height
Bahiagrass	2-3
Bentgrass	¼ - 1
Bermudagrass	
Common	½ - 1½
Hybrid	½ - 1
Bluegrass	
Common	2-3
Improved (varies by variety)	¾ - 2½
Buffalograss	1-3
Carpetgrass	1-2
Centipedegrass	1-2
Dichondra	½ - 1½
Fescue	
Chewing	1-2
Red	2-3
Tall	3-4
Annual ryegrass	1½ - 2
Perennial ryegrass	1 - 2½
St. Augustinegrass	1 - 2½
Zoysiagrass	½ - 1½

Which Grass Is Best?

The ideal grass is always disease free, shade tolerant, drought tolerant, and wear resistant. Unfortunately, so far there is no such thing. The nearest equivalent is "mixtures"—four or five grasses put together by seed companies (for example, one or two improved bluegrasses, red and Chewing fescues, and perhaps the new turf-type ryes). This mix of several varieties gives you pretty good insurance against failure. If one part of the lawn area doesn't get enough direct sun for Kentucky bluegrass, the fescues will thrive. If one of the Kentucky bluegrasses succumbs to disease, the bluegrass partner will take over. Conceivably, you can begin with a mixture of five grasses and then after a few years find that three have disappeared.

There are two types of seed mixtures: for the "picture-book" display front lawn, and for the play-area lawn. Seed companies combine the fine-leafed modern Kentucky bluegrass with other fine-leafed grasses to produce (ideally) a perfect blend in color and texture.

Sod producers of "instant" lawns also want to produce a sod of mixed grasses that will broaden the adaptability of modern bluegrasses.

Play-area grasses forego the attractive appearance of the fine-leafed grasses for more practical advantages, such as lower cutting height and greater wearability. Check with your local nurseryman or county extension agent for the best grass mixtures for your climate and your type of lawn.

Cool-Season Grasses

Fescues. The fine-textured fescues have a soft appearance and a deep green color. Varieties include 'Creeping Red', 'Illahee', 'Rainier', and 'Chewings'. All these thrive in shade as well as sun. They work best where summers are cool, such as the coastal Northwest or at higher elevations.

The coarse-textured fescues grow faster, and are wear resistant and drought resistant. However, they don't look as attractive as the fine-textured fescues, and they may tend to clump over time. Varieties include 'Meadow', 'Alta', 'Kentucky 31', and 'Goars'.

Kentucky bluegrasses. These favorites have a dark, blue-green color and a fine, soft texture. They work best in moderate-summer areas. Varieties include 'Kentucky', 'Merion Kentucky', 'Newport', 'C-1', 'Windsor', 'Delta', 'Park', and *Poa trivialis*.

Ryegrasses. Medium-coarse with sparsely-set leaves, these fast-growing grasses do well as a quick cover, and adapt to a wide variety of climates. Where the common ryegrasses were once viewed as unfit companions for the lusher bluegrasses, they now appear in lawn seed mixes.

Turf-type perennial ryegrasses—for example, 'Manhattan' and 'Penn-fine'—have been bred specifically for soft fiber so that they could be mowed cleanly. When mowed, the ends don't fray—and it's the frayed ends that cause common ryegrass to have a brownish color.

In addition to their remarkable mowability, these ryegrasses have narrower leaves than the common ryegrass, and blend well with the bluegrasses.

Ryegrass is either perennial or annual. Both species work best in coastal regions where winters are mild and summers are cool.

Warm-Season Grasses

Bahiagrass. Although Bahiagrass lawns are not beautiful, they are popular—they can thrive in sandy soil, take any amount of foot traffic, and resist attacks of insects and diseases.

The varieties of Bahiagrass favored for use in lawns are 'Argentine', 'Paraguay', and 'Pensacola'. 'Argentine' is a coarse, wide-bladed grass and very deep-rooted in sandy soils. 'Paraguay' and 'Pensacola' are narrow-leaf types.

Bahiagrass grows best in moist soils but can tolerate drought fairly well. It will take part shade and some salt. It works best from the central coast of North Carolina to east Texas and is very popular in Florida.

Mow weekly from March to November, and less frequently in winter. The tough seed-heads require mowing with a sharp rotary mower.

Bermudagrass. This makes a fine-textured, golf-course-worthy, beautiful lawn, but it needs special care.

Improved Bermudagrasses such as 'Floraturf', 'Tifgreen', 'Tiflawn', and 'Everglades No. 1' establish within three months (sprigs are 3 inches apart with 6 inches between rows). They are traffic resistant and reasonably salt resistant, but not at all shade resistant. These grasses work best in the South and Southwest.

Caring for them means: mowing them two to three times a week at ½ to 1 inch high; watering at least twice a week in sandy soils (every day if the weather is dry); and making sure that they don't spread out into flower beds and shrubs.

Red fescue

Bahiagrass

Bermudagrass

"Common" Bermudagrass is less fine-textured than the "improved" varieties. Mow frequently at 1¼ to 1½ inches to maintain a 1-inch mowing height.

Carpetgrass. This is a low-maintenance, coarse-textured utility grass that does best on moist, acid soils. Carpetgrass withstands periods of flooding and will take some shade, but has no salt resistance. Mow weekly to 1½ to 2 inches in summer to prevent flower spikes. Browns in winter.

Centipedegrass. This coarse-textured grass is easy to maintain. Mow only every 10 to 14 days at a height of 1½ to 2 inches. Centipedegrass is restricted to the southern states.

St. Augustinegrass. This grass suits more soil types than other grasses, grows well in the shade, and over the years has been the most popular for southern lawns. It is basically restricted to the Gulf Coast states.

Although its texture is quite coarse, it is very rich looking. Mow every 7 to 10 days at a mowing height of 1½ to 2½ inches (never less). St. Augustinegrass covers fairly rapidly and tolerates salt spray. If well cared for, it will remain green in winter in mild areas. Water every 7 to 10 days. It is subject to brown patch, dollar spot, and gray leaf spot, and actively prone to chinch bug damage. However, the variety 'Floratam' is chinch-bug resistant.

Zoysia. 'Emerald' zoysia resembles Bermudagrass in its fine texture and color. It is shade tolerant and salt tolerant, and although it works best throughout the South, it is occasionally used in the Northeast. It covers slowly, taking as much as two years to become established from plugs or stolons. Mow this tough grass to a height of ½ to 1 inch. Water frequently—about every five days. Zoysia stays green in warm-winter areas. Watch for sod webworms, brown patch, dollar spot, and invasions of common Bermudagrass.

Ground Covers

Ground covers are low-growing plants that spread to form a permanent part of the garden floor. They can be used to solve many landscape problems.

For example, instead of grass, use a ground cover on a bank or slope where it would be hard to mow and water. Plant it where shade or shallow-rooted trees would kill a lawn. Try a low, dense ground cover between stepping stones, over mounds, or around large rocks. Plant a moisture-loving ground cover around a faucet or under a hose bib.

Use the plants to subtly direct foot traffic by guiding visitors to a path or entry. Add a border or background planting to the lawn for interest and contrast.

Although it's true that ground covers require less care than lawns, they still have maintenance requirements. Mowing, however, isn't one of them.

Prepare the soil as thoroughly as you would for a lawn; the growing roots should be able to penetrate easily and should have adequate air, moisture, and nutrients.

When planted, ground cover plants are spaced rather sparsely, to leave them room to fill in as they grow. Until the young plants grow in, however, weeds will be a problem. Hand weeding will do for a fast-growing plant, but the best technique for a slower-growing plant is to cover bare patches with about an inch of mulch. Weeds won't sprout as easily, and those that do you can remove quickly.

Junipers and some other woody plants need special attention to stay neat and weed-free. Before planting, cover the entire planting area with black plastic. Plant through the plastic, and cover the exposed surface with a mulch of ground bark chips, or even gravel or rock. This double mulch will be weed proof and attractive for many years, and will save you from

A planting of low-maintenance caladium with mondo grass can replace annuals in flower beds or cover a corner lot.

Ground Cover Chart

Name	Height	Exposure			Space	Uses						Comment
		S*	PS	FS		Under Trees	Bank	Stepping Stones	Special Site	Large Area	Small Area	
AARON'S BEARD (Hypericum calycinum)	12"		●	●	18"	●	●			●	●	Stems sprout from underground runners. Fast growth. Yellow flowers. Cut down in spring. Use an underground barrier to confine invasive runners near lawns and beds.
BIG BLUE LILY TURF (Liriope muscari)	12-18"	●	●		12"				●		●	Grasslike mounds form a shaggy mat. Growth is moderate. Flowers form in violet clusters. Protect from heat. Big Blue forms clumps; Creeping Lily Turf (L. spicata) spreads by runners. Trim dead leaves. South only.
CARPET BUGLE (Ajuga reptans)	3-9"	●	●	●	6-12"	●	●	●		●	●	A dense, low mat spread by runners. Grows quickly. Tolerates some traffic. Blue flowers. 'Atropurpurea' is purple-bronze. Bigleaf 'Giant' and 'Jungle' are either green or bronze.
COTONEASTER (Cotoneaster species)	12-36"	●	●		36-48"		●				●	Tiny, green to gray leaves grow thickly on woody branches. Slow to moderate growth. Flowers are white, berries are red. Prune or pin erect growth. Forms: C. adpressus (12" by 6'); C. dammeri (6" by 10', stems root); C. horizontalis (mounds to 3' by 15'; open growth permits weeds). Northeast only.
ENGLISH IVY (Hedera helix)	6-12"	●	●	●	12-18"	●	●			●		Vines root along the stem. Slow starter. Cut woody growth to the ground in spring. 'Baltica' is very hardy; 'Hahn's' is small-leafed; 'Glacier' is a variegated form. Cut back from trees and shrubs.
HALL'S HONEY-SUCKLE (Lonicera japonica 'Halliana')	18-24"	●	●		24"		●			●		Arching stems, deep green foliage. Grows quickly, but cut back to ground each spring. White flowers turn yellow. Very fragrant. Close-up, this plant is disorderly. Northeast only.
JAPANESE SPURGE (Pachysandra terminalis)	10"		●	●	6-12"	●				●	●	Dense, erect stems, dark green leaves. Fast growth. Takes dense shade. Fragrant white flowers, white berries. 'Silver Edge' has variegated leaves.
JUNIPER (Juniperus species)	12" (spread of 4-10')	●			48-60"		●		●	●	●	Forms a dense cover, but grows slowly. Lowest forms: Juniperus conferta 'Sargentii' (gray-green); shore juniper (bright green); 'Bar Harbor' (purple in cold weather); 'Waukegan' (bluish); 'Dwarf Japanese' (bluish). Plant widths are from 4' to 10'.
MONDO GRASS (Ophiopogon japonicus)	8-12"	●	●		3-6"	●			●	●	●	Slow, spreading grassy clumps. Lavender flowers, blue berries. Cut back ragged, old growth, or cut clumps apart and replant. South only.
MOSS PINK (Phlox subulata)	6"	●	●		12-18"		●		●		●	Finely cut, mounding foliage. Fast growth. Flowers bloom freely in white, rose, pink, and lavender. Shear old stems after bloom period.
MYRTLE PERIWINKLE (Vinca minor)	6-12"		●	●	18-24"	●	●			●	●	Shiny oval leaves on vinelike stems. Fast, dense cover. White or blue bloom. Shear to keep low. Tall form (V. major) is best in a natural, woodsy setting.
STAR JASMINE (Trachelospermum jasminoides)	18-24"	●	●		18-36"	●	●		●	●	●	Woody vine with very glossy leaves. Growth is moderate. Pin down or cut erect shoots. White flowers bloom heavily. Very fragrant at night. South only.
STONECROP (Sedum species)	6-8"	●			10-12"		●	●	●		●	Fat, succulent leaves grow on brittle stems. Sedum grows fast but may die in patches. Some leaves are reddish. There are many kinds, some tender. S. acre (yellow bloom), and S. spurium (red) are good in colder areas.
WINTER CREEPER (Euonymus fortunei)	2-6"	●	●	●	24"		●		●	●	●	Tough, woody plant. Slow growth. Prune to prevent mounding. 'Colorata' turns reddish in cold; 'Gracilis' is less vigorous, good for small areas; 'Kewensis' is fine textured with dense, small leaves.

*S = sun; PS = partial shade; FS = full shade

Right: Ivy covers banks and rolling hills too steep to mow.

Opposite page: Entryway to the Haskell garden nursery, New Bedford, Massachusetts, features a low hedge of Japanese barberry (*Berberis thunbergii* 'Crimson Pygmy') and a bright green carpet of kinnikinnick (*Arctostaphylos uva-ursi*). The full moon maple (*Acer japonicum* 'Aureum') in the background picks up the color of the barberry.

having to fight back weedy grasses and plants. However, don't use plastic if your ground cover normally roots along the stem or spreads by underground runners.

Once a ground cover is established, maintain it regularly. Shear flowering plants such as ajuga after they bloom. Cut back plants such as ivy, hypericum, and honeysuckle severely before spring growth begins, or else they will build up many tough, old stems. And prune or pin down plants such as cotoneaster to keep them low and even. Expect to do some kind of maintenance once or twice a year for most plants.

The chart on page 139 includes those ground covers that are most common and that can be used in a wide range of landscaping situations. Ajuga forms a tight, flat mat, will take some foot traffic, and does well in shady places. Winter creeper or hypericum both are fine soil-holders on a bank, and either one can be used instead of a lawn. Pachysandra is good in really dense shade.

For further recommendations, check with your nursery and your county agent. A few good but uncommon plants include Irish moss or chamomile around stepping stones or over mounds and rock gardens; strawberrylike *Potentilla verna* or *Duchesnea indica* next to paving or over uneven ground; snow-in-summer, with its grey leaves and contrasting white flowers; or perhaps violets or baby's tears in a large container or a moist spot in deep shade.

Above: Juniper hides fallen leaves from deciduous birch trees.

Right: A carpet of *Carpobrotus*, an ice plant, is offset by a large rock and low shrubs.

Index

Page numbers in italics indicate illustrations.